Survey Research Practice

Gerald Hoinville, Roger Jowell
and associates

Survey Research Practice

Gerald Hoinville and Roger Jowell
in association with

Colin Airey, Lindsay Brook, Gillian Courtenay,
Barry Hedges, Graham Kalton, Jean Morton-Williams,
David Walker, Douglas Wood

Heinemann Educational Books · London

LONDON EDINBURGH MELBOURNE AUCKLAND TORONTO
HONG KONG SINGAPORE KUALA LUMPUR NEW DELHI
NAIROBI JOHANNESBURG LUSAKA IBADAN KINGSTON

ISBN 0 435 82418 X
Paperback ISBN 0 435 82419 8
©SCPR 1977
First published 1978

Published by Heinemann Educational Books Ltd.
48 Charles Street, London W1X 8AH
Printed and bound in Great Britain by Biddles Ltd.
Guildford, Surrey

Foreword

by Sir Claus Moser

Survey methods are now widely accepted as a means of getting information for decisions and for research. Governments the world over use surveys on a big scale; and in the Government Social Survey (part of the Office of Population Censuses and Surveys) this country can boast one of the best survey organizations in the world. Surveys are a crucial part of the apparatus of market and opinion research and are used extensively in social and economic research.

But if surveys as such no longer need advocacy, the need for high professional standards in carrying them out does. Too many people think that anyone with reasonable common sense can carry out a good survey. Common sense is an important ingredient. But the competent practitioner must also have an understanding of statistical theory (certainly if sampling is involved), familiarity with sociological and psychological methods, and enough knowledge of computing techniques to plan for handling large quantities of data. The pitfalls are many, and the world is littered with poor surveys, carried out at considerable cost to the sponsor and unnecessary inconvenience to the respondents. To avoid them requires both training and practical experience in the social sciences.

It is one of the merits of this book that it points to so many of the problems likely to arise. Intended as an introduction to the subject, it is deliberately practical in its focus, confining its attention to the methods and procedures by which survey theory should be applied. Drawing on their considerable experience of survey work at Social and Community Planning Research, the authors take the reader carefully through the various organizational routines that achieve economy and reliability in the conduct of surveys; and in doing so, they guide the newcomer past the possible pitfalls along the route. It is apparent throughout that the book has been written by people who have themselves been through the survey process many times, and have learned the lessons.

In restricting its compass to practical aspects of survey design and execution, the book complements others. We learn, for example, about the methods by which interviewers are recruited, how postal surveys are organized to induce high response rates, how editing and coding can be administered to best effect, and so on. In combination, the various chapters reveal a range of conventions and practices that distinguish good surveys from indifferent ones, and show how careful the practitioner has to be over minute points to produce good survey results.

I have no doubt that the book will help students of survey research, not to mention the growing number of people in the academic and business world who may want to carry out surveys. Most important, perhaps, by exposing and explaining the routines and organizational practices inherent in surveys, the book should improve communication between those who commission or use surveys and those who conduct them.

I said earlier that the conduct of surveys requires both training in the social sciences and practical experience. Perhaps it is because the authors have had both that they have produced such a valuable and well focused book.

Contents

Authorship and Acknowledgements

This book is the product of a collaborative effort by ten contributors. The principal authors, Gerald Hoinville and Roger Jowell, are responsible for the structure, presentation and final drafting of the book and have also contributed heavily to most chapters. Graham Kalton has contributed technical and editorial material to all chapters. The other authors are responsible mainly for the individual chapters that bear their names.

All the authors are on the staff of *Social and Community Planning Research (SCPR)*—an independent institute for social survey research registered as a charitable trust. SCPR carries out and advises on research into aspects of social policy both through its own grants and on behalf of government departments, local authorities, universities and other institutions. One of SCPR's primary aims is the improvement of survey methodology through its programme of work and publications.

Gerald Hoinville and Roger Jowell are SCPR's co-founders and co-directors; Colin Airey and Barry Hedges are its deputy directors; Jean Morton-Williams is a research director and, with the other four directors, a member of SCPR's executive committee; Graham Kalton is a visiting research fellow at SCPR while holding the Leverhulme Chair of Social Statistics at the University of Southampton; Lindsay Brook, Gillian Courtenay, David Walker and Douglas Wood are all senior members of SCPR's research or technical teams.

A great deal is owed to the indulgence of all members of SCPR's staff during the lengthy gestation period that the book required. In particular, the authors wish to express thanks to Vikki Gladwell, Christine Russo, Rosemary Peddar, Sheila Brennan and Hemali Seneviratne for their skill and patience in the typing and retyping of endless manuscripts; to Isobel Campbell for her editorial advice and criticism both before and after her period on SCPR's staff; and to the forty or so other members of staff on whose advice and experience all the authors have relied so heavily.

Chapter 1. Introduction

The tendency for societies to collect data about themselves—their characteristics, their behaviour patterns and their attitudes—has grown dramatically during this century. Decision-makers in government and industry have increasingly sought feedback from the public about their policies and performance; they use survey research to describe aspects of society and to monitor changes so that they can respond to them. Surveys are also contributing increasingly to academic theory and scholarship.

The growth in survey research activity has meant that many more people than in the past now come into contact with surveys, albeit temporarily. They may have to assist in the design of a survey as part of their work or education, to commission and supervise a survey, to evaluate the methods used, or to interpret and apply survey results. Although none of these tasks can properly be carried out without a working knowledge of survey methods, most people who are only temporarily involved will have neither the time nor the inclination to undertake a detailed study of the considerable body of literature on sample surveys, which draws its techniques from a very wide range of disciplines, including statistics, psychology, sociology, anthropology, economics and computer science. It is to these people that we hope this introductory volume, which focuses on the basic principles of survey research and their application, will be particularly useful. In selecting this focus we occasionally include what may seem to be minutiae. We have chosen to err on this side, however, in order to produce a detailed practical guide that can be used, where necessary, in conjunction with the more theoretical treatments already available.

The idea for a survey can arise in many different ways: a survey may be required to provide the solution to a problem of public policy, or to produce data needed for business management, or to update a continuing series of trend measurements, or to test hypotheses developed by social scientists. Sometimes the general outline of the survey design, if not its detail, follows directly from the statement of the problem; on other occasions it is very difficult to transform the initial problem statement into a viable survey design, and the process may extend over several months of discussion, desk research, definition and redefinition.

Probably the commonest type of population survey, and the one on which this volume concentrates most of its attention, is the household survey. It usually involves interviewing a sample of adults in their own homes for about forty-five minutes on a subject such as housing, shopping, recreation, purchasing behaviour or television viewing. Other surveys involve interviews with employers or employees at their work, with users of a bus or train service interviewed in transit, with students in schools and colleges, with cyclists or pedestrians using a particular route, with shoppers at particular stores, with patients in hospitals. Some of these surveys necessitate a long, detailed interview; others require the respondent to complete a simple postcard. They may involve one interview with each respondent or a series of interviews, perhaps employing diary records maintained by a panel of people. Some surveys involve parallel enquiries with, say, a sample of schoolchildren and their teachers and parents. Some involve researchers working alongside other professionals such as engineers who take noise measurements of the traffic outside each home, or doctors who undertake a medical examination of each respondent.

Whatever form a survey takes, however, its design and structure cannot be determined until three factors have been clarified: the purpose of the enquiry, the population on which it should focus and the resources that are available. We discuss each of these briefly in turn.

Establishing the survey purpose can be a lengthy process, usually involving three overlapping phases. The first phase is to translate the survey's general purpose into a reasonably specific central aim. It would be impossible to design a survey that had such a vague aim as, say, 'the measurement of people's travel patterns'. The purpose behind the measurement must be established, since each of the following purposes would produce a different design and structure from any other:

—to obtain a detailed description of local transport usage
—to develop or test a theory of public transport demand
—to develop a predictive model of travel behaviour
—to assess the likely impact of changes in transport policy
—to discover the mobility patterns of disadvantaged minorities

—to increase understanding of modal choice

—to examine attitudes and preferences in relation to local transport

—to link travel behaviour to other aspects of behaviour, such as recreational patterns.

Having established the central purpose of the survey, the second phase is to itemise subsidiary topics that relate to that purpose. If the purpose was to assess the likely impact of changes in transport policy, for instance, the range of subsidiary topics might be:

—current roles of public and private transport

—likely growth in car ownership

—factors that influence or inhibit public transport usage

—safety considerations

—environmental considerations

—public attitudes to pedestrian precincts, parking restraint, road building, etc.

—the extent and nature of travelling difficulties

—viability of alternative forms of transport services: dial-a-ride, minibuses, etc.

From these subsidiary topics, the third phase is to formulate specific information requirements relating to those topics. To identify the current roles of public and private transport, for example, some detailed behavioural information would be needed, probably in the form of a record of journeys made by various types of transport for different purposes by each member of the family; respondents' perceptions of the suitability of public and private transport for different types of journeys would also have to be discovered. Thus, the process would be to move from the main topic areas to subsidiary topics and, finally, to specific information requirements—more detailed checklists being developed at each stage.

As the detail unfolds, consideration must be given to the appropriate data collection methods for different items of information: perhaps a self-completion diary for the journey information, traffic counts or physical noise measurements to assess the environmental impact of traffic. There might be merit in combining postal and interview methods or in introducing a self-completion supplement after the interview.

For some subjects, particularly when a survey is required to monitor the effects of a new facility (such as a new bus service), the design may need to incorporate 'before' and 'after' measurements to examine changes in behaviour or attitude arising from the introduction of the facility. Occasionally the opportunity arises to employ survey methods as part of a controlled experiment, where respondents are randomly allocated to one of two experimental groups: one group may be offered, say, free bus and train travei passes, while the other group (the control) is not. The effect of the free travel pass can then be assessed by comparing changes in behaviour patterns of the experimental group with those of the control group. Or a more elaborate panel (or longitudinal) study may be necessary, in which information is collected regularly from the same sample of people at monthly or longer intervals. This would have the advantage of enabling information to be linked to particular changes in circumstances—a process that often cannot be performed satisfactorily from cross-sectional surveys.

The second task in determining the design and structure of a survey is to decide which groups of people are relevant to the study—a subject dealt with more fully in Chapter 4. Some members of the population are difficult to include—very young children, some people in institutions. Others may be ruled out on budgetary grounds: in a study of smoking habits, for instance, a lower age cut-off, perhaps 12 or 13, might be employed to make the most effective use of the resources available. In some cases the decision to restrict the coverage required for the survey is immediately clear: a researcher who wishes to study the reactions of people who live in a particular tower block will have little difficulty in deciding the population to be sampled. In other cases care must be taken not to restrict the coverage inappropriately: in a survey to examine the market for a new public swimming-pool it would be important to include those who do not visit existing pools as well as those who do. The reasons for not going to pools would be as relevant to an understanding of the market as the collection of information from existing swimmers. Similarly, in a survey to discover why some people were leaving a profession or moving away from an area there would be little point in confining the coverage to those who remained.

The third key factor influencing the design and structure of a survey is the budget. Sample surveys are labour-intensive. It is wrong to think of surveys as consisting essentially of fieldwork with only a modest amount of office work. Although fieldwork is the largest single task in most surveys, it usually accounts for well under half of the total cost; almost as many person-hours may be spent, for instance, in organizing, training, administering and supervising interviewers as are spent by the interviewers themselves in the field. As a rough guide, the following framework illustrates the time taken to complete the various stages of a survey of about 3,000 interviews:

> *Unstructured design work* may take a minimum of six to eight weeks, during which time the *sample design and selection* are also carried out.
>
> *Questionnaire construction* (including *pilot work* and the

design and printing of the final questionnaire) may take at least another six to eight weeks.

Briefing the interviewers, followed by a *fieldwork phase* for seventy-five interviewers, each covering forty respondents, may take about five to six weeks.

Editing and coding will run concurrently with fieldwork, but (to allow for postage and the sorting out of queries) will end about four to five weeks later.

Card punching, computer editing and card correction take a minimum of three to four weeks more.

In total, some six to eight months—and well over a hundred people working on different aspects of the survey—will be needed to bring this survey to a 'clean computer file', the stage at which analysis and interpretation can begin. When there are complicated scheduling problems, when a survey is competing for the same labour resources as other surveys, or when school holidays, bad weather, sickness, industrial disputes, machine failures and so on intervene, an even longer period will be needed.

Up to a point, a good research design and its efficient execution can save time and costs. But undue savings will affect the quality of the data. When resources are limited it is tempting to cut short the preliminary design work, to omit the briefing of interviewers, to relax quality control checks, to dispense with supervision, or to fudge inconsistencies in the data by programming the computer to suppress them. Any of these courses of action is likely to increase the number of errors contained in the data. And since some errors are an inherent feature of all surveys, it is risky indeed to introduce new ones.

Survey errors vary greatly in their cause, nature and importance. They can arise, for instance, because surveys collect information from only a selection of the total population. However careful the sampling scheme may be, the laws of chance determine that a sample will rarely represent a total population perfectly. There might, by chance, be slightly too few men or too few young people; or a particular occupational group might be over-represented. But rigorous application of the principles of sampling will ensure that errors deriving from chance (or probability) will be small and, more important perhaps, their approximate size is calculable.

Errors can arise also because the list (or sampling frame) used as the basis for selection is deficient. It might not, for example, contain immigrants in their true proportions, in which case they will have an incorrect chance of appearing in the sample. These deficiencies can often be overcome or reduced but it is usually costly to do so.

Even when the sampling frame is accurate, errors will occur through non-response, because an achieved sample will almost always fall short of the selected one: some members of the sample will be away from home, some will refuse to participate, some will be too ill. Survey response rates of above 85 per cent are rare; more commonly in interview surveys they range from about 75 per cent to 80 per cent, although in inner city areas they may well be lower by some 10 per cent or so. Postal surveys produce greater variation but they should commonly yield response levels of between 60 per cent and 80 per cent. Maintaining high response rates is more difficult in panel studies where the same people are asked questions on several occasions. The effects of geographical mobility, non-contacts, refusals and sickness are cumulative so that a 10 per cent loss at the second and third rounds of the survey would result in an effective response rate of only 65 per cent at the end of the third round. Unless the characteristics of non-respondents are identical to those of respondents, the achieved sample will contain bias. And the bias will be serious when the characteristics of non-respondents are related to the subject under study.

The way in which questions have been designed, administered and answered can also produce errors. Respondents may misunderstand a question, interviewers may make recording errors, answers may not be truthful: an obviously middle-class, middle-aged interviewer, for instance, may cause some respondents to express views they do not hold; a rather severe interviewer may intimidate a nervous respondent and cause him to give incorrect answers; the respondent may want to create a certain impression of himself to the interviewer; he may feel that certain answers are expected of him. Respondents also have a disconcerting habit of answering questions they do not understand, about subjects in which they have little or no interest, in a manner that confidently disguises their confusion or indifference. Errors are therefore difficult to identify.

Coders may make errors as well by misclassifying a response; punchers may mistakenly hit the wrong key when transferring the survey responses onto punched cards for analysis. Most of these errors can be identified by detailed subsequent clerical or computer editing checks; a few will escape unnoticed.

It can be seen, therefore, that surveys can produce only approximations, never precise measurements. Throughout the various phases of a survey, human errors can and will be made. These phases—covered in subsequent chapters—are:

Qualitative work—an exploratory phase to help in the design of the questionnaire content and its construction.

Questionnaire construction—deciding on the questions to be asked, the precise wording, the sequence of questions and the layout.

Sampling—the task of determining those to be interviewed,

deciding how many, where the interviews should be located and the method of selecting respondents.

Interviewing or postal methods—the two main alternative (or complementary) means of data collection and the core of a sample survey.

Fieldwork organization—a task that demands unusual management skills in recruiting, training and controlling an interviewing team.

Data preparation—transforming the raw data recorded on questionnaires into a form appropriate for analysis.

Classification—defining and selecting the analysis categories that will assist interpretation.

The final phase of the survey process—analysis—is not covered in this book, although brief reference to interpretation of data is made in the concluding chapter. There is, however, a substantial body of literature already available on data analysis methods at both an introductory and advanced level, much of which is appropriate to the particular problems of analysing survey data. We choose here to confine our attention to the considerable problems of survey design and data collection.

Notes on Further Reading

1. There are several general books on survey research, for instance, Babbie (1973), Backstrom and Hursh (1963), Lansing and Morgan (1971), Moser and Kalton (1971), Parten (1950), Warwick and Lininger (1975) and Young (1966). In addition survey techniques are usually covered in books on social research in general: among these books, those by Festinger and Katz (1953) and Selltiz *et al.* (1959) are particularly recommended.

2. The uses of survey research in the fields of sociology, political science, psychology, economics, anthropology, education, social work and public health are considered in the book edited by Glock (1967). Raj (1972) contains chapters on methodology for surveys in agriculture, demography, consumer expenditure, employment, health, industry, trade and transport. The relationship between survey research and sociological theory is examined in the book edited by Leggatt (1974). The special problems of longitudinal surveys are covered in a paper by Goldstein (1968).

3. Belson and Thompson (1973) and US Bureau of the Census (1974) provide bibliographies of survey methodology.

4. There is a large literature on errors in surveys; a selection of references is provided in the notes appended to later chapters. The paper by Deming (1944) provides a list of sources of error,

and Zarkovich (1966) discusses all sources of non-sampling error. Sudman and Bradburn (1974) provide a recent review of the literature on response errors, and include an extensive bibliography. The careful studies of the ways in which response errors arose in the National Readership Surveys (Belson, 1962) and in the 1966 Sample Census of England and Wales (Gray and Gee, 1972) are well worth consulting.

Chapter 2. Unstructured Design Work

Principal contributor: Jean Morton-Williams

In large-scale survey work, questionnaires need to be structured: respondents must be asked the same questions in the same way and their answers must be recorded and coded uniformly so that they can be aggregated across the sample. The soundest basis for developing structured questionnaires is preliminary small-scale qualitative work to identify ranges of behaviour, attitudes and issues; this avoids forcing respondents' views into a false or irrelevant structure.

A Qualitative Approach

The essence of qualitative research is an unstructured and flexible approach to interviewing that allows the widest possible exploration of views and behaviour patterns. The two main methods are individual depth interviews (which may be unstructured or semi-structured) and group discussions. In depth interviews, respondents are interviewed on their own by specially trained interviewers. Instead of a questionnaire containing individual questions to be asked, interviewers have only a list of topics for discussion: it is up to them to word the questions and to encourage respondents to talk freely on and around the topics, guiding the conversation onto new topics from time to time. In group discussions, the researcher, or a trained group leader, guides the conversation among a small group of respondents. Again, a list of topics takes the place of a formal questionnaire. Both methods allow respondents to talk at length in their own words and at their own level of understanding. Discussion can range freely to include topics that emerge spontaneously and may not have been foreseen as relevant. Interviewers and group leaders also have the opportunity to seek clarification or amplification where necessary.

At the earliest stage of qualitative work, a researcher can start with one or two almost totally unstructured discussions and a handful of interviews, using a very broad topic guide, with as few direct questions as possible, that will encourage respondents to do the talking. From this basis, he can formulate clearer ideas about the content of a more detailed guide for further qualitative work that can be used to identify, for example, the main behavioural groups in the sample, how they should be defined', the phraseology and concepts used by respondents, the variety of opinion on particular topics, the relevant dimensions of attitudes, and tentative hypotheses about motivations underlying behaviour and attitudes. In short, the researcher uses the qualitative data to stimulate his ideas and to devise a viable, soundly based framework for the study. As Glaser and Strauss (1967) argue, qualitative research has a unique* and valuable contribution to make by generating a better conceptual framework for research than would otherwise be possible.

Data collected from qualitative research differ from large-scale survey data in fitting no rigid structure: each interview or discussion covers the same topics, but the ways in which they are covered and the sorts of information obtained may vary considerably. The researcher's task is to educe a structure which he can then apply to the questionnaire for the main survey. It must take account both of the different types of information collected and of the study's overall aims. This procedure demands from the researcher a blend of receptiveness, objectivity and creativity.

A first step in the structuring may be to identify distinct behavioural groups so that at the subsequent quantification stage the characteristics and attitudes of these groups can be compared. Sometimes a large number of groups will emerge; in a study of people's money-saving habits, for example, three broad behavioural groups were identified in the preliminary qualitative research: currently active savers, past savers who had money put away, people with no current savings. Within these groups, among savers there were those who put all their money into one savings medium and those who invested more widely, those who saved for future commitments (household bills or summer holidays), those who saved for a rainy day or their old age, those who saved all their surplus income, and so on. In the design of the main questionnaire a series of interrelated questions had to be formulated to distinguish members of each group.

A second step towards structuring is to use the qualitative data to formulate hypotheses as to why people fall into one or other behavioural group, for instance:

> *Characteristics and circumstances:* Are variables such as age, socio-economic group, household size and composition, car ownership, type of house, likely to be important?

Way of life and habits: Has a particular way of behaving developed through custom or habit?

Experience: To what extent is current behaviour the outcome of past behaviour that has failed to achieve its objects or been unsatisfactory in some other way?

The social context: Does the behaviour being studied take place in a social context? If so, who is involved and how does the behaviour link them?

After these factors have been considered the researcher would go on to examine the roles that *attitudes, values* and *beliefs* play in leading people to behave as they do. These attitudes are likely to have been moulded by a variety of factors including fashion, the prevailing culture, individual life-style and upbringing, circumstances and habits, exposure to external influences, and so on. In deciding the attitudinal content of his proposed questionnaire, the researcher has to look for themes emerging from the qualitative material. If, for example, in a qualitative interview about savings, one respondent says, 'I should feel terribly ashamed if I had to ask someone for financial help' and another says, 'It's a matter of pride, I suppose, but I'd have to be very desperate before I'd go to the Social Security', the two statements have a common element: the importance of financial solvency to self-esteem. The hypothesis may then be formed (on the basis of similar statements by other respondents) that this attitude motivates people to be savers. The researcher would also look for evidence that people attach different degrees of importance to a subject or hold opposing views on the same theme. For instance, someone may say, 'I don't see why I should save; if I lose my job, I've paid my stamps and it's the State's duty to pay me adequate unemployment pay,' indicating that he has no feelings of shame about financial insolvency. Clearly a dimension of attitude to loss of financial independence has emerged—from the 'very ashamed' of the first two statements to the 'not at all ashamed' of the third—along which people will have different positions. In stages, therefore, the appropriate attitudinal content and structure of a questionnaire will begin to emerge.

The examination of attitudes in qualitative work often provides a depth of understanding that is of considerable value in itself, quite apart from its contribution to the design of a large structured survey. Indeed, some qualitative research is mounted with no subsequent quantitative phase in mind. A small-scale qualitative study of 50 women who had just had abortions, for instance, gave useful insight into the ignorance of and antagonism towards certain contraception methods (Morton-Williams and Hindell, 1972). The interviews covered a sensitive subject in considerable depth and exemplified the extent to which qualitative research can help when the aim is simply to acquire knowledge about the factors that may influence a particular form of behaviour. Subsequent quantification of the incidence of such factors may be additionally useful, but it does not diminish the initial value of qualitative research in identifying the range of factors involved.

The Communication Process

In qualitative research, two principles should be remembered in attempting to obtain information from respondents: first that questioning should be as open-ended as possible to encourage respondents to talk spontaneously about their behaviour and opinions; second that the questioning techniques should encourage respondents to communicate their underlying attitudes, beliefs and values.

Frank discussion can be impeded in four main ways:

By attempts at rationalization: Respondents will often try to put forward only logical reasons for their behaviour, ignoring their emotional feelings and evaluations based on attitudes and beliefs.

By lack of awareness: Most respondents are not accustomed to putting their feelings into words—they may never have conceptualized them, even to themselves, and may be unable to describe them objectively.

By fear of being shown up: Respondents will often avoid describing aspects of their own behaviour or attitudes that are inconsistent with their self-image; obtaining information about personal hygiene can be difficult, for instance, because people tend to say what they think they ought to do rather than what they actually do.

By overpoliteness: Respondents may be shy or overanxious to impress the interviewer; they may feel that particular views are expected or desired and tailor their answers accordingly.

To break down these barriers the interviewer or group leader must be able to put respondents at ease and make them feel that all views and all types of behaviour are acceptable and interesting. A relaxed and unselfconscious interviewer who is not obviously from either extreme of the socio-economic scale is most likely to succeed in establishing the necessary rapport. Training can ensure that depth interviewers and group leaders are neither condescending nor deferential, that they look at respondents often enough to convey interest without appearing dominating or intrusive, and that they are tactful in their attempts to get at the meaning of vague or evasive statements.

Encouraging people to talk

As we have mentioned, an aim of interviewing in qualitative work is to ensure that respondents feel able to talk freely and at length about themselves and their lives, at a level that means something to them. In interviews about a proposed new motorway, for example, people were encouraged to talk about specific problems—how they would then get to their local shops or get across the area to visit friends, how they feel about their children using the subways after dark— rather than to discuss motorway severance in the abstract. As a rule, even if the discussion is eventually steered towards more abstract concepts, it should start with simple, concrete, everyday topics.

Personalizing the discussion is important in establishing underlying attitudes. At this level the respondent may reveal his own thoughts unselfconsciously rather than offer what he thinks is the right thing to say. So instead of merely asking people what they think about a policy, say immigration, in the abstract, it is helpful to encourage them to talk about their own experiences of immigrants, at work and in their neighbourhood, in order to assess the origins of particular views and to gain insight into the nuances of opinion.

Even when the conversation has gathered impetus, the interviewer has to continue encouraging the free expression of attitudes. The interjection of a simple 'mmm' or 'uh-huh' will indicate understanding and interest. A more direct 'that's very interesting; I'd like to hear a bit more about that' will usually obtain amplification of specific points. A short pause and an expectant look will often lead the respondent to expand his remarks. While these simple tactics are always useful, more specific *probes* are sometimes required. To get people to reveal attitudes in depth and to establish the emotional significance to them of the behaviour, experiences or beliefs being discussed, the interviewer may, for example, ask: 'What were your *feelings* when you first heard about the redevelopment plan?' 'How did you feel when you heard there was no place for your child in the nursery school?' Another useful technique is to repeat an expression of emotion made by the respondent—'You said you felt furious with your landlord. . . ?' and pause expectantly.

The interviewer should also try to establish the *range* of attitudes and reactions by prompting respondents to look at different sides of an issue: 'You've told me how much you like this district; is there anything you dislike about it?'; or by getting respondents to make comparisons: 'How does this district compare with the one you lived in before?'

Questioning techniques
The general approach to asking questions is to make them as direct and as straightforward as possible. There are, however, certain techniques that can prove useful in special cases. When attitudes to a number of items need to be investigated and compared, for

instance, the *repertory grid* is helpful. This method has been adapted from clinical psychology, where it is used to identify and evaluate a patient's relationship with his family (Kelly, 1955; Bannister, 1962). It consists of presenting three stimuli to the respondent (for example, noise from aircraft, noise from traffic and noise from children) and asking him to say which two are most alike, and in what ways, and how they differ from the third. The questioning procedure is then repeated with other triads. The method helps respondents pinpoint the similarities and differences they perceive between concepts. Dimensions of opinion can then be identified by the researcher. If, for example, several respondents give the view that noise from aircraft and children occurs only occasionally while traffic noise happens all the time, 'continuity of noise' would emerge as one dimension or variable for use in a structured questionnaire. Other respondents may say that traffic and aircraft noise occur through the day and night, while noise from children occurs only in the daytime. Time of day would form a second variable, and so on.

Projective techniques are a range of methods designed to encourage respondents to express their views indirectly. For example:

Sentence completion: The respondent is asked to finish a sentence, e.g. 'The noise from the motorway . . .' or 'Joining the Common Market has meant that . . .'. Several such sentences should be used rather than a single one to obtain a range of opinions.

Indirect questioning: 'How do you think other young people feel about the change to decimal currency?' People seem to be more ready to reveal negative feelings if they can attribute them to other people. Since they probably have little concrete information about other people's feelings, they are likely to arrive at an answer mainly from their own attitudes.

Personalization of objects: Various games can be played in which emotion is attributed to inanimate objects. For example, people may be asked 'If your house were a person, how would it feel about the redevelopment plans?' or 'If your car could talk, what would it say about using the motorways?' This technique, particularly valuable in interviews or discussions with children, has also proved surprisingly useful with adults. Obviously it should not be used indiscriminately and interviewers must introduce questions of this type very carefully.

Picture techniques: Clinical psychologists have found it revealing to ask their patients to say what they think is happening in an ambiguous picture, or to say what characters in a picture are saying, or to insert captions in balloons above the characters' heads. The technique is appropriate to some studies but it needs skilled handling, is time-consuming and is therefore rarely used in social research.

Group or individual interviews?

The two main methods of qualitative data collection are depth interviews (semi-structured or unstructured) and group discussions. Each has advantages and disadvantages. Group discussions are quicker and cheaper to organize than individual interviews with the same number of respondents. They can provide a good deal of general information about behaviour and attitudes which individual interviews cannot give, allowing the researcher to see how people interact on a topic and, specifically, how they react to disagreement with their views. But a group discussion with eight people lasting between one and two hours will not produce nearly as much detailed information as eight separate interviews; in particular, it will not provide detailed information about an individual's characteristics and background that can be related to his behaviour and attitudes.

Although some issues are difficult to handle in a group discussion or in any public context, it seems nevertheless that people will often admit to things in a group that they would not admit to in private. Their embarrassment is reduced when they can identify with others in the group and hear them being open and frank. In a group of young mothers discussing the problems they had in bringing up their children, for example, one said, 'I'm so relieved to hear that others have the same problem; I felt a complete failure as a mother and was terribly ashamed about it.' This exemplifies a particular strength of group discussions in that they help to identify attitudes and behaviour patterns that are not considered to be socially acceptable.

A disadvantage of group discussions is that not everyone invited will agree to come along; certain types of people—for instance the very old, disabled people and senior businessmen are difficult to bring together. Respondents tend, therefore, to be more self-selected than for depth interviews which obtain high levels of co-operation.

Depth interviews are a more suitable approach when the object is to develop hypotheses about individual motivations, when the psychology and circumstances of respondents need to be interrelated. Moreover, the interviewer can probe in much greater detail into particular attitudes and the explanations for them. The disadvantages of depth interviews are the time and cost involved in conducting them and in absorbing and analysing the transcripts.

Using group discussions and depth interviews in tandem may often have advantages. A few exploratory group discussions can be followed by a series of individual interviews; alternatively, people from those sections of the population which tend to be most willing to take part in group discussions (such as housewives with school-age children) may be approached by this method while individual interviews are taken with those who are difficult to recruit for a group discussion.

In some projects, a researcher may want to obtain both qualitative and quantitative data from his interviews by using a semi-structured questionnaire. This is laid out like a structured questionnaire with questions asked in precise terms and in a specified order, but most are open-ended rather than pre-coded. The interviewer records answers verbatim, and, where instructed, probes for as much information as possible. Plenty of room, sometimes as much as a whole page for a single question, is provided for writing in the answers. The data provided by semi-structured interviews are, to some extent, quantifiable since all respondents are asked the same questions in the same order.

The questionnaire will usually be coded and punched so that the basic analysis can be carried out by computer. In addition some questions will be content-analysed to give a fuller picture and to provide verbatim quotations. The researcher may also read through a selection of the interviews to get broad ideas about the interrelationships of data. Semi-structured interviews are cheaper to carry out than depth interviews, since they need not be transcribed and do not have to be done by people with special depth-interviewing skills. Normally they can be carried out by experienced interviewers who have had some additional training in open-ended probing.

A semi-structured questionnaire is most appropriate when attitudinal information is required from a population that is difficult and too expensive to cover on a large scale, and where the sample size is between about 100 and 200 people. These numbers would allow for broad quantification across the sample but not for any detailed analysis of subgroups. The drawbacks of semi-structured interviews are the limitations of small sample sizes and the time required to construct code lists and carry out content analysis of the answers. They may, however, provide the researcher with the opportunity to study the issues in greater depth than is usually possible with a larger, more structured study. The semi-structured questionnaire may itself be based on a small-scale unstructured study using depth interviews or group discussions.

Sampling and Recruitment

One aim of qualitative research is to discover the range of behaviour and attitudes on a subject. It is thus important that the sample should cover a wide spectrum of people. Another aim is to develop hypotheses about the relationships between attitudes, behaviour, circumstances and other characteristics, and an important part of the analytical procedures required for this purpose is the comparison of subgroups. Sample sizes for qualitative work are necessarily small, but it is essential that there are enough people within each subgroup to provide the researcher with a basis for comparisons.

The selection method
Wide coverage of the population by probability sampling methods cannot usually be justified within the budget for qualitative work. Samples are normally therefore designed to provide specified numbers in each of the subgroups to be examined, by the use of purposive selection rather than random sampling. Because of the difficulties of analysing and absorbing qualitative information, it is rare for more than about 50 depth interviews or 12 group discussions to be undertaken.

A sampling scheme that exemplified the use of both depth interviews and group discussions was employed in the qualitative phase of a study in an inner city area (Morton-Williams and Stowell, 1974). The objectives of the study were to examine residents' attitudes to aspects of life in their area, some parts of which were being demolished or rebuilt, others renovated; it had a high proportion of recent immigrants; 'problem families' had been moved into one part; vandalism was said to be rife and young people were suspected of being responsible for it. To study both the area and the characteristics of its residents, six group discussions, each comprising about eight people, and twenty depth interviews were carried out. Two groups of men and two of housewives were recruited, one of each from the two main sections of the area, with one of the male groups including some immigrants; the fifth group consisted solely of immigrants and the sixth of teenagers. The depth interviews covered people difficult to recruit to groups, such as mothers of very young children and members of 'problem' families.

In general, the sample for qualitative work must be broadly enough based to allow for comparisons not foreseen as important at the planning stage. In a study of attitudes to traffic noise, for instance, the main consideration in the sample design might be to ensure that the sample includes people experiencing different traffic conditions outside their houses. But people's attitudes to traffic noise may also be affected by the time they spend at home or by the noise they are used to at work; they may vary by age, sex, socio-economic group, and so on. To take account of these factors in a depth interview study, streets with varying traffic conditions could be selected as the first stage of the sample; within streets, recruitment controls may then be set to ensure that the sample includes, say, men and women, people of different ages and in different socio-economic groups. The interviewer may call at every fifth house and follow a random procedure for selecting an individual within the household. This type of carefully controlled selection scheme is normally practical only for depth interviews; it is generally inappropriate for group discussions because of the difficulties of persuading certain types of people to attend.

Where little is known in advance about the subject of research or where the object is to develop theoretical concepts, a rather different sampling approach is required. The qualitative study may then take place over a period, starting with a small number of broadly based depth interviews and/or group discussions. Preliminary hypotheses may suggest that some subgroups of the population ought to be interviewed in more depth. A second phase may then have to be undertaken, the analysis of which may give rise to a third phase of interviews with other subgroups, and so on. Glaser and Strauss (1967) call this approach 'theoretical sampling' because the emerging theory determines the subgroups to be sampled at each stage. In this type of study, the ultimate sample size may be larger than the samples earlier suggested as practicable for qualitative research.

Recruiting a discussion group
There are no firm rules about the ideal number for a group discussion. Generally, about eight is desirable: with more than ten participants the group becomes difficult to control and tends to split into subgroups. With fewer than about five people, it may be difficult to get a discussion going at all. However, with highly articulate and informed people, a smallish group may be preferable since it gives everyone ample opportunity to talk.

If possible, discussions are generally held in a private house so that the atmosphere is relaxed and informal. Interviewers often recruit people from an area within easy access of their home and hold the discussion there. Otherwise, a respondent may be paid a small fee for holding the group in his home. If a private house is not available, a room in a nearby pub, hotel, or community centre may be hired so that people do not have far to travel. The venue should not be so grand, however, as to inhibit participants from holding a relaxed, informal discussion.

To ensure that the group is of the required composition for the study (for example, non-working housewives, half under 40 and half 40 or over), the recruiter is given the characteristics of the people to be invited. Since some will not turn up, ten or eleven people are generally invited in the hope that about eight will arrive.

Precautions can be taken against the risk that only a handful of the people who accept the invitation will appear. For example, recruiting is best carried out about three days before the discussion—if it is done earlier, people tend to forget and make other arrangements; if later, people may already have other commitments. Friday and Saturday evenings, when many people want to be with their families, are best avoided, as are obviously awkward times such as the two weeks before Christmas. Evenings on which major television attractions such as Royal Command Performances or international football matches are shown should be avoided. A brief reminder note sent by the recruiter by first-class mail the day before the discussion also helps to ensure a good attendance.

If the respondents are elderly or have to travel some distance, transport may be offered from their homes to the discussion venue. As a rule, payment (given at the discussion) is offered for attendance; about £1.50 is the usual figure at 1977 prices.

When the invitation is issued care should be taken to make the subject of discussion sound interesting to respondents, and to explain why the discussion is being held. A letter explaining the purpose of the study may be left with the people invited, along with a card giving the time and place of the discussion, instructions on how to get there, and the recruiter's name and telephone number. Potential participants are generally told that the group will be informal, with about eight people 'like yourself' discussing an interesting topic, and that they will not need any special knowledge. It is explained that someone is coming specially to lead the group and the importance of turning up is stressed. Potential respondents are encouraged to let the interviewer know if they cannot come, in enough time for someone else to be recruited.

The time of the discussion is arranged to suit the respondents being recruited—for instance, to suit mothers who have to meet their children from school, or to allow people time to have their evening meal (taking into consideration such factors as that commuters, for instance, eat later than people who live near their work).

It is usually advisable for the respondents in each discussion group to be of similar age, socio-economic group and so on, to prevent group members being inhibited about expressing their views. Sometimes, however, there may be a virtue in juxtaposing the views of, say, young and old, men and women, drivers and non-drivers. Participants in group discussions should obviously be able to speak reasonable English (if the discussion is to be in English) and should not be hard of hearing.

Diffident or shy people (as some very young or very old people or recent immigrants tend to be) may prefer to be asked to attend in pairs, although the spread of opinion may then be reduced since friends tend to think alike and follow one another's leads. Friends who come along uninvited are, where possible, turned away on the grounds that the numbers and types of people asked have been carefully planned; or if they are allowed to remain they are asked not to participate.

Members of the public who have a special interest in or knowledge of the survey subject, for instance those with a professional connection, may sometimes have to be excluded from a discussion. People who have attended a discussion before, particularly within the previous six months, are best excluded on the grounds of 'overexposure'.

Data Collection

Both the depth interview guide and the discussion guide should list the topics to be discussed in an order the researcher thinks appropriate. The guide will usually suggest that the interview or discussion starts with generalities about behaviour and attitudes, picking topics that will be interesting and reassuring to respondents who may not yet be at ease, then proceed to specific topics, deeper levels of probing, and indirect questioning. If the guide has evolved from preliminary fieldwork this will usually work well. Interviewers and discussion leaders are generally made aware, however, that they need not follow the order indicated if discussion of topics flows more easily and naturally in a different order.

Conducting a depth interview

Depth interviewers should have had some experience in survey research interviewing or in a profession that relies on extensive verbal skills; they should be able to communicate easily and perceptively with a wide range of people, and be unprejudiced and able to conceal strong personal beliefs and attitudes. Usually the researcher in charge of the study is not the ideal depth interviewer (even though he may find it very helpful to undertake one or two of the early interviews) as he may already have formulated hypotheses and opinions that could constrain the interviews. He is unlikely, in any case, to have had the necessary specialist depth-interviewing training—in the use of a guide, in probing and in general communication techniques.

Interviewers should be thoroughly briefed on the background and objectives of any project which they are to work on. Care should be taken, however, not to give them preconceptions about what they will find. Unless the subject involves interviewing specialists on their own subject, a useful briefing technique is to get the interviewers to express their own views and to indicate points that demand additional probing.

Since depth interviewers will not have the background knowledge that the researcher has, they will need a detailed guide. The layout of a depth interview guide is shown in the Appendix. The broad topic areas are indicated by the capital letter headings; subsidiary topics are indented.

In the guide, questions about the respondent are addressed to interviewers to remind them that their job is to find the answers. But the topics are presented in a way that enables comprehensible questions to be framed by interviewers. Care must always be taken to bridge the gap between the research concepts and the level at which most respondents put their thoughts and feelings into words.

In depth interviews, as in survey interviews generally, there are various methods of promoting co-operation from respondents. Interviewers have to identify themselves and be able to show authority cards of some kind. They have to describe the subject of the interview and its purpose in a way that captures the interest of the potential respondent, highlighting the relevance of the study topic to them and making it sound specific and concrete: if the subject is presented in abstract terms, respondents may feel that the interview is going to be both difficult and dull. Interviewers have to be able to assure respondents, particularly when tape recordings are to be made, that all information will be treated in confidence.

Depth interviews are usually conducted in the respondent's home and, where possible, with the respondent alone, since the advantage of the depth interview is the opportunity it offers to explore attitudes and experiences openly. A respondent's willingness to talk freely about himself can evaporate in the presence of a familiar person.

All depth interviewers, however experienced, should ideally get feedback from the researcher on the first few interviews on a project so that they know whether they are covering the ground adequately and can be told, if necessary, how to improve their performance.

Leading a group discussion

Group discussions are usually led by the researcher who is going to interpret the information and write the report. If more than four or five discussions are being carried out, however, someone else may need to lead some of them. This has the advantage of introducing a second viewpoint but it means that the project leader will have more difficulty in obtaining an overall view of the emerging pattern of responses. The skills of leading group discussions are fairly easy to learn, and the group leader does not necessarily have to have had any specialist training. If the study is concerned with complex problems and sophisticated concepts, however, it is a good idea to have as leader an experienced researcher who is practised in keeping the research objectives in mind while playing a creative role in the discussion. Others may stick rather unimaginatively to the brief so that one of the advantages of group discussions is lost. Learning is usually a mixture of listening to discussions led by experienced group leaders and allowing them to criticize one's own. The errors a beginner is most likely to make are lack of control—allowing everyone to talk at once, or letting the dominant participant steal the show—failure to follow up relevant leads, overdirection, and keeping too tight a rein on the discussion by allowing participants to talk only to the leader rather than to one another.

The leader has to ensure that every member of the group speaks early on in the discussion. Anyone who remains silent for the first half hour will find it more and more difficult to pluck up the courage to take part. If necessary, the less talkative members of the group can be asked direct questions from time to time: 'Some people have said ... others have said ... What's *your* view?' 'I'd like to ask some of the younger/older members of the group who haven't said much yet what they think about this.' If possible the question is phrased so that it demands a sentence in answer, rather than a simple 'yes' or 'no'.

Efforts should be made to prevent one participant from dominating the discussion. This can be difficult, since the technique of the dominator is to go on talking until he or she can be stopped only by ruthless interruption. One method is to seize upon a point made by the dominator and break in saying 'Can I interrupt you there; I was interested in what you said about ... and would like to ask other people in the group what they think.'

As long as the discussion keeps to the topic, the leader should interfere as little as possible, now and then summing up the views expressed on a particular subject and feeding them back to the group to stimulate discussion and possible disagreement. Pointing out inconsistencies can encourage participants to take a wider view of the subject in an effort to justify their views. It is often useful, too, to stimulate people's courage to disagree by countering views put forward with 'In another group several people disagreed with that; do any of you here disagree?' The leader has also to be aware of the value of keeping silent, thus leaving the onus to continue the discussion on the participants.

A group discussion guide will be much shorter than an individual interview guide—no more than a couple of pages, so that the leader can review the range of topics rapidly during the discussion to make sure that nothing has been missed. Some rearrangement of topics may have to take place before he can draw the group out on a subject. Part of the skill of leading a group discussion is remembering which topics have not been fully explored and reintroducing them subtly. If the researcher concerned with the whole study is leading the discussion, he will have the overall research objectives firmly in mind to help him interpret the guide.

People should be told at the beginning that the discussion is being tape-recorded so that what they say can be remembered accurately, and that this means that only one person should talk at a time. They should be reminded of this during the discussion, if necessary.

On a practical note, tea and biscuits or drinks before the discussion help people to relax. People should be seated in a semicircle in front of the leader so that all can easily see and be seen by the leader, who should have a seating plan that enables him to refer to respondents by name. People sitting in corners or almost beside the leader tend to get overlooked and to resort to expressing their views to the person next to them. As well as being distracting for the leader, their muttering spoils the recording.

Recording, Transcription and Analysis

Tape-recording a group discussion allows the leader to concentrate on listening to and controlling the group and probing people's views where necessary. Relying on one's memory of what people have said can lead to distortions.

The recording must be of high quality, however, especially if people other than the leader have to listen to the tapes. A good-sized tape-recorder and, in particular, a high-quality microphone are therefore necessary. If the tape-recorder is small, two or more microphones may be needed to ensure that all participants are audible. A tape that is very old or damaged may affect the recordings, as will a microphone placed on top of the recorder. All equipment should be checked, both before the discussion and in location.

Factors in the location itself that might affect the recording should be taken into account. Large rooms with very little furniture may echo and make the recording difficult to decipher. Sources of outside noise such as traffic, aircraft or children's playgrounds should be avoided if possible.

Tape-recording is also frequently used for depth interviews; alternatively the interviewer may take extensive notes or make a verbatim record in longhand or shorthand. Obtaining a full record of the interview in the respondent's words is important because the researcher needs to receive the material verbatim, not in paraphrase. Taking notes is probably the least desirable method of recording, since the respondent's own words tend to be lost. Recording in longhand is also undesirable because it involves slowing the respondent down and may interrupt both spontaneity and flow.

Whatever the main method of recording, some depth interviews (preferably including some from each interviewer) should be tape-recorded for the benefit of the researcher and to provide a basis for quality control of the interviewing. Ideally, taped interviews should be transcribed in full, but this is sometimes too time-consuming and wasteful since digressions get transcribed along with the other material. Depth interviewers therefore normally write up their own interviews using as much verbatim material as possible. It should be remembered in the budgeting of a study that writing up may take twice as long as interviewing.

The transcript of a taped interview is usually laid out with wide margins so that question numbers or guide topic numbers can be inserted and space allowed for notes and comments during analysis. But it should be written up so that someone who was not at the interview can understand it without constant reference to the original guide. Since the questions may not have been used precisely as stated in the guide, giving a question number and the verbatim answer is not enough; the question either has to be specified precisely or edited in to the answer. For example, the exchange:

Q. 'When did you last move house?'
A. 'In 1965.'

could become 'I last moved house in 1965' so that the interview reads as a monologue rather than as a dialogue.

By whatever means the interview was recorded, the record should be examined as soon as possible afterwards. If it is written in longhand, the interviewer has to examine its legibility; if in note form, or shorthand, it has to be amplified; if on tape its audibility must be checked. None of these tasks can be left too long if errors or omissions are to be rectified.

The major part of the analysis consists of reading the write-ups of the interviews and listening to tape-recordings of the discussions. To obtain some preliminary ideas, the researcher may listen first to a small selection of interviews and discussions, organize the interviews into broad groups, and make comparisons both between and within groups to acquire indications of the differences.

The researcher will usually first read the interviews as a whole to gain an overall view of their contents, then select specific topic areas and read only sections of interviews. During the analysis he will make notes under headings (possibly on separate cards) suggested by the theoretical framework and the objectives of the study, as discussed in the early part of this chapter, subsequently revising and extending them as necessary. As he delves further into the material he may need to devise a method of categorizing respondents on a number of dimensions.

This largely impressionistic analysis may be backed up by a more systematic content analysis of sections of the interview. The value of systematic content analysis is that it allows the researcher to gain an impression of the range of opinion on a particular topic and also facilitates the development of hypotheses about differences between subgroups. The objective is to organize all the data on one topic for easy review; the process is more common for depth interviews than for group discussions because of the greater wealth of detail in the former.

Since response is rarely sufficiently uniform to be aggregated simply, the process is laborious, but it can often be done by people without special skills. Generally, it involves giving each respondent an identification number; large sheets of paper are used with identification numbers at the head of fairly wide columns. The topics to be analysed are written down the side, with plenty of space left between them. Each respondent's answers are then entered in the appropriate columns. For ease of comparison between subgroups it is convenient if respondents whose answers are grouped on a single page are members of the same subgroup. The subgroup may be defined by more than one characteristic—for example, sex and age.

Where possible, the responses on the analysis sheets will be given in the respondent's own words. If a section of an interview is particularly long, however, a brief summary may have to be made.

Reports on qualitative research have to be largely impressionistic, since they are based on small samples and unstructured data; for this reason reference to numbers or percentages should be avoided, and expressions such as 'most' or 'a few' must be used cautiously. It is important to stress that hypotheses based on comparisons between sample subgroups (for example those in manual versus professional occupations, young versus old) can only be tentative. Nevertheless, the depth of coverage at an individual level provided by reports on qualitative studies provides a useful complement to the quantitative studies that succeed them.

Notes on Further Reading
1. Glaser and Strauss (1967) provide a very good exposition of the use of qualitative work in the development of theory in the social sciences. Selltiz *et al.* (1959) and Argyle (1967) also describe its application in the broad field of academic social research.
2. Sampson (1967), MacFarlane-Smith (1972), Smith (1954) and Henry (1963) describe the use of qualitative research primarily in the context of market research.
3. McKennell (1974) and Oppenheim (1966) put unstructured studies into the broader context of questionnaire design and attitude scaling. Morton-Williams (1971) gives a case history that illustrates the use of qualitative research as a first phase in a large-scale attitude study.

The techniques of interviewing and group discussion leading are described in MacFarlane-Smith (1972), Richardson *et al.* (1965) and Goldman (1962). Lindzey and Aronson (1968, Vol. 2) have chapters on various practical aspects of qualitative research including one on content analysis.

Chapter 3. Questionnaire Construction

Principal contributor: Gillian Courtenay

Questionnaires come in many shapes and sizes, from postcards to be filled in by respondents to multi-page documents to be filled in by interviewers. Broadly, however, the same design rules apply to all of them. A good questionnaire has to be designed specifically to suit the study's aims and the nature of its respondents. It needs to have some of the same properties as a good law: to be clear, unambiguous and uniformly workable. Its design must minimize potential errors from respondents, interviewers and coders. And, since people's participation in surveys is voluntary, a questionnaire has to help in engaging their interest, encouraging their co-operation, and eliciting answers as close as possible to the truth.

This chapter focuses on the types of questionnaires used in structured interviews, where each question is precisely specified and, for the most part, the range of possible answers is printed on the questionnaire as 'precodes'. Chapter 7 discusses the additional design requirements for self-completion questionnaires; most of the information in this chapter, however, applies broadly to questionnaires of all types.

The Construction Process

The starting point of questionnaire construction is reached after the preliminary design work—to identify the coverage and general content—has been concluded. The researcher now has to move from a general framework of information needs (outlined in Chapter 1) to a more specific structure that embodies questioning approaches relevant to each item of information required. Flow charts can help to identify the structure of various sections of the questionnaire, as follows:

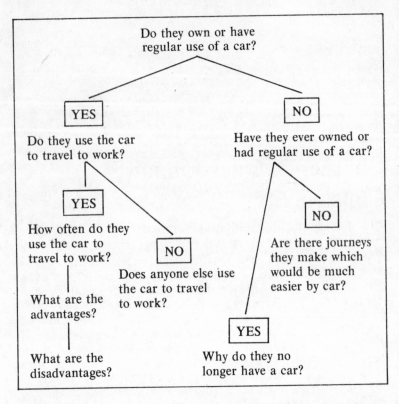

The detailed design work can now start—formulating precise questions, ordering the questions and sections, listing possible categories of answers, adding instructions and signposts for interviewers, and inserting data processing requirements. At the drafting stage pilot work, discussed at the end of this chapter, is essential to test the questionnaire in the field. The researcher has to keep four main design considerations in mind.

First the questions must be designed so that they are easy for respondents to understand and to answer accurately and clearly. The vocabulary used therefore has to be comprehensible to all respondents (not just to the majority). An unfamiliar or ambiguous word, even if it is not a key word in the question, may make it difficult for the respondent to understand the rest of the question.

Next, the questionnaire must be easy for interviewers to administer. It must be clear, for example, what is to be read out to respondents and what is instruction for the interviewer. Signposts for filter questions (that is, instructions that restrict certain questions to some respondents) must be easy to identify. It must be easy for interviewers to record all answers, including those that do not fit the predetermined framework.

Third, the questionnaire should be constructed so that the recorded answers can easily be edited, coded and transferred onto a computer file for statistical analysis. For this purpose, respondents' answers have to be given code numbers. The normal procedure is to adopt a layout that facilitates the direct transfer of responses from the questionnaires to punched cards or tape. For most questions interviewers circle a code number (corresponding to the answer) that is to be punched:

	Code
'Are you . . . . . *(READ OUT)* . . . . married,	1
. . . . . . single,	②
. . . . widowed,	3
. . . . separated or divorced?'	4

But response categories (i.e. the code list) cannot always be determined in advance. Some questions have to be left 'open' for interviewers to record verbatim answers for coding in the office later. There must be space on the questionnaire for these answers to be recorded in full, and provision made in the layout for code numbers to be added afterwards. The probing of open-ended questions and the method of compiling coding frames from responses to them are discussed in Chapters 5 and 8.

Finally, the flow, structure and length of the questionnaire should encourage and keep the respondent's interest. The subject of the survey and the approach to the respondent will be primary factors in securing co-operation, but the format of the questionnaire can help to maintain it. The first few questions set the tone: they should be interesting and easy to answer. If there is a series of repetitive attitude scales they should be staggered to avoid tedium and fatigue; topics should flow easily.

If all these requirements are met, respondents' interest can usually be maintained for at least forty minutes on most subjects. Brevity is not always essential for maintaining co-operation. When an interview is long, as many interviews tend to be, what is possible depends mainly on the respondent's interest in the subject: he may be happy to talk for two hours about the education of his children, but may be bored and unco-operative after half an hour on subjects that he feels have little relevance to his life.

Quantifying Attitudes and Behaviour

In the past, attitudinal research had the image of being rather 'soft' and woolly in comparison with behavioural research—which enjoyed the image of being 'hard', rigorous and precise. But the stereotypes were wrong: in the first place, the categories are not discrete as the labelling suggests; in the second place, the validity of both types of research depends on careful design and interpretation that takes into account their respective strengths and weaknesses. Some of these general issues are covered here, before we go on to discuss particular types of questions to avoid.

Problems of memory

Measurements of behaviour depend on the ability of respondents to remember and describe their activities accurately and to the level of detail required. In practice, however, though most people are able to recall important or unusual events in their lives—for instance, holidays, car or house purchases—they are usually unable to recall such minor details as the time it took to get to the resort or how many cars they looked at before they made their choice. Moreover, most events are much less significant than these, and people have no need to store minor details of their everyday lives—their purchases, their travelling, their recreation, and so on. They forget or distort the details, particularly small deviations from their usual behaviour. The rule to use is that only special events in people's lives are memorable to the degree of accuracy that most questionnaires demand. The remainder are forgotten, or remembered so hazily that detailed questioning is futile.

It cannot be assumed that even infrequent and important events will continue to have the same special significance later. One survey, for instance, asked middle-aged men and women to complete details of the subjects in which their eldest child had gained 'O' level examination passes, and what class of pass had been achieved in each subject. No allowance was made for looking up the information, nor any recognition given to the possibility that such detailed information will often be forgotten, particularly when similar events have intervened to blur the accuracy of memory (in this case, second and third children attaining 'O' levels in different subjects and with different success rates).

The same general rule applies to attitude measurements. It is not possible, for example, to obtain accurate answers retrospectively about the attitudes that middle-aged respondents held when they left school and their aspirations at the time. Their subsequent work experience and the passage of time will mean that the answers are unlikely to be accurate.

Faulty memory is also a problem with questions about the timing or frequency of events. The time between events often tends to contract in people's memories; if it is important to pinpoint events, special steps to aid recall can be taken, perhaps by reference to major events that took place at the same time as the events under investigation; or by reference to documents: to establish the particular television programmes people watched, for instance, they can be taken through copies of the *TV Times* and *Radio Times*. In collecting certain types of behavioural data, however, it may be necessary to go further than aided recall and ask respondents to complete some sort of diary. In travel surveys that cover more than one day's journeys, for example, a diary, or at least an *aide-mémoire*, is generally used. Otherwise respondents might forget or confuse details of journey times, fares, origins, destinations and purposes. Diaries are also used in surveys of personal expenditure and in surveys concerned with how people spend their time (time budget studies).

When conventional questioning is used instead of a diary, account must be taken of the tendency for respondents to blur the distinction between usual and recent behaviour. The two must be differentiated, or the answers will generally understate minor departures from, or recent changes in, habitual behaviour. To encourage respondents to distinguish between the general and the particular they can be asked about both, starting with the general question:

'What time do you normally leave home on your journey to work?'

followed by:

'At what time did you leave home yesterday on your journey to work?'

Problems of sensitivity

Some questions touch on sensitive subjects, but respondents are generally less embarrassed about answering such questions than researchers are about asking them. Researchers should certainly avoid the use of complex, diffident or apologetic wording in order to soften the blow. It can confuse the issue and make a straightforward question seem sensitive: a classic example is the question 'Would you mind telling me whether you and your husband sleep in single beds or a double bed?' to which the deserved answer is 'Yes'. Particularly sensitive areas do, however, need special techniques to obtain frank answers.

An elegant summary of four established techniques for eliciting sensitive information was given in a paper by Barton (1958). He takes as his example the delicate issue of whether a respondent has murdered his wife.

First, he says, there is the *casual approach:*
'Do you happen to have murdered your wife?'
Then there is the *numbered card approach:*
'Will you please read off the number of this card which

corresponds to what became of your wife?'
Third comes the *everybody approach:*
'As you know, many people have been killing their wives these
days. Do you happen to have killed yours?'
Finally, there is the *other people approach:*
'Do you know any people who have murdered their wives?'
PAUSE FOR REPLY. AND THEN:
'How about yourself?'

In general, Barton's principle is a serious one: in appropriate
circumstances, if a question cannot be asked directly, these methods
of indirect questioning can ease the situation.

On some subjects, particularly those concerned with criminal or
deviant behaviour, further steps need to be taken to put respondents
at ease and to allow them to answer honestly without fear of
recrimination. Belson (1975) for example, went to elaborate lengths
to protect his respondents when interviewing juveniles about crimes
they had committed, conducting the interview almost as if in a
confessional. Another approach, suitable for isolated questions that
are highly sensitive, is the randomized response technique, of which
there are several variations. A simple version is one in which each
respondent chooses (at random) one card from a pack of cards. Each
card contains only one of two questions. One of the questions is the
sensitive one (e.g. 'Have you ever stolen money?'); the other is
innocuous (e.g. 'Were you born in the month of January?'). The
interviewer does not know which question has been answered. But
since the researcher knows the probability of a respondent
answering the sensitive question (determined by the proportion of
the pack of cards containing that question) and the proportion of
yes/no answers he would expect from his innocuous question, he can
estimate statistically the proportion of yes and no answers given to
the sensitive question.

Indirect questioning
It is all too easy for researchers to 'create' attitudes by putting ideas
into respondents' minds or words into their mouths. It would be a
mistake, for example, to ask people about their attitudes towards,
say, National Savings Certificates before finding out if they knew
what they were or had even heard of them. To ask people about the
disturbance from traffic outside their home, before gauging whether
they had even noticed it, would be a similar error.

To avoid the error, the questioning often needs to approach a
subject gradually, starting, for instance, with general questions
about how respondents feel about their area and street and what, if
anything, they dislike about them, then moving on to traffic

disturbance as a specific issue. Respondents may have to be taken through a series of questions that relate to an issue before being asked about the issue itself.

In some cases it may be best never to tackle the issue directly: in a study of racial prejudice, for example, it would be counter-productive, to say the least, to begin by asking respondents whether they considered themselves racially prejudiced. We know from experience that certain verbs ('to be prejudiced' is one) seem to have no first person singular. So we need to derive measures that will correlate broadly with racial hostility rather than to tackle the subject directly.

Open-ended questioning
Respondents are not always able to supply answers that are readily codeable into a series of precodes. For example:
'What are the main problems you encounter in your job?'

Poor pay	1
Poor conditions	2
Poor management	3
Long hours	4
Too few fringe benefits	5
Too many strikes	6

The leading character of the question is not the point at issue here. Even if the precodes were not read out to respondents, and even if the categories of answers were comprehensive, interviewers could not accurately code the long and complicated answers that would undoubtedly emerge into the preprinted categories as the respondent gives them.

Infinitely more time and attention is required to analyse and classify the answers than is available during the course of an interview. Coding of this kind requires a preliminary study of responses from a reasonably large and representative subsample of questionnaires, as discussed in Chapter 8.

These kinds of questions have to retain an 'open' format even though they occur in a structured questionnaire. For these questions, and others—for which the potential range of answers may be too uncertain to be specified in advance—space is left for a verbatim record of the answer instead of inserting a precoded range of possible answers which would produce distortion.

Formulating attitude scales
Many attitude questions seek to position respondents on some sort of rating scale. At its simplest the scale may have only two possible answers—Yes/No or Agree/Disagree. More commonly, a four-point

or five-point scale is used, which may take several forms. For example:

'Membership of the Common Market weakens Britain's ties with Commonwealth countries.'

Strongly agree 1
Agree 2
Neither agree nor disagree 3
Disagree 4
Strongly disagree 5

An alternative to the verbal scale is the spatial or diagrammatic scale, which measures respondents' leanings to either side of a neutral point. Respondents might be asked, for example, to rate different attributes of a bus service—reliability, cleanliness, safety and so on—on a diagrammatic scale, as follows:

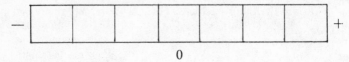

Osgood's semantic differential scale (Osgood *et al*, 1957) combines the verbal and diagrammatic techniques by inserting adjectives at either end of the diagram and listing a series of items in a self-completion questionnaire. It is an easy scale for respondents to use and can be applied rapidly to a large number of items or dimensions. The task set for respondents varies: they may be required to rate several different items (bus services, train services, the underground) on the same set of rating scales, or to rate one item (the bus service) on a number of different dimensions. For example, the bus service could be rated on the following dimensions:

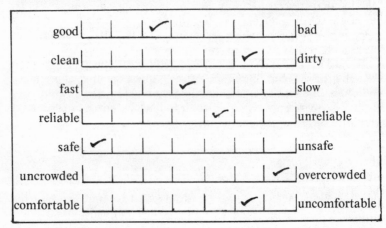

An alternative to verbal and diagrammatic scales are numerical scales where respondents are asked to assign scores or marks (for example from 0 to 5 or 7 or 10) to indicate the level of satisfaction with a particular aspect of a service or product. Some researchers favour asking for marks out of ten, since it is an easy and familiar task to most respondents, but no uniform view has emerged on the best number of points to include in scales. For bipolar scales odd numbers have the advantage of offering a mid-point between the two poles, and some researchers prefer seven-point scales to five-point scales on the grounds that they offer more scale positions (and therefore discriminate more finely). In practice, however, five-point scales are probably the most frequently used, the easiest to understand and generally sufficient for most purposes.

The extensive literature on scaling techniques draws attention to the advantages and defects of the various methods. However, since a rating scale is not an absolute measure of attitude but a way of placing people in relative positions on a dimension, there is no particular way of presenting scales that is intrinsically better than others. The object should be to find the way that discriminates most effectively between respondents.

A feature of applying a series of rating scales on the same subject is that there is usually a good deal of correlation between the answers: the ratings that a group of people gives to the reliability of a bus service are likely to be correlated (but not perfectly) with the ratings they give to the speed of the service; the ratings given to comfort and overcrowding are likely to be negatively correlated. In designing a questionnaire the researcher should be aware of these correlations and reduce the number of scale items to be included in the survey accordingly. Pilot-testing can be useful here. If, for example, responses to two scales are perfectly correlated there is little point in including both.

Even where preliminary sifting and reduction has been carried out, however, the responses to a series of rating scales are still likely to be correlated. To some extent these correlations can be observed and understood by conventional cross-analysis. Alternatively, techniques of multivariate analysis, such as factor analysis, can help to sort responses into identifiable patterns, the aim being to determine the broad dimensions underlying the particular attitudes expressed.

A correlation analysis might indicate, for example, that people who give the local bus service a negative rating for, say, overcrowding, tend to give a negative rating to various other items such as cleanliness and availability of seats. A factor analysis might take this further and indicate three broad dimensions of people's attitudes to the local bus service—the first relating to timing (speed, reliability, the amount of time spent waiting, etc.), the second to cost (the fare, value for money, etc.), the third to comfort (overcrowding, cleanliness, safety, seating, etc.). In some circumstances it is possible to build a sort of hierarchy of attitudes. Within the 'comfort' dimension, for instance, it may be possible to distinguish two subcategories, the first relating to psychological aspects of comfort (such as safety) and the second to physical aspects (such as seating).

A problem associated with factor analysis is that, when it fails to produce a clear and coherent grouping of attitudes, the researcher may be tempted to squeeze or push attitudes into spurious groups to which he can attach equally spurious names. Another problem is that factors can be formulated only in relation to those items covered by the rating scales. If, for example, questions on aspects of comfort had not been included in the questionnaire a different pattern of components or factors would have emerged from the analysis. To some extent, therefore, the factors are an artefact of the choice of items. This underlines the importance of preliminary qualitative work to identify the attitude dimensions likely to be important.

In contrast to the multivariate approach to scaling, which attempts to combine ratings in order to expose a range of attitude components, much of the early work on scaling sought to produce unidimensional scales, based on a combination of separate ratings, to provide an overall assessment of a single attitude dimension, for example racial prejudice or noise disturbance.

At its simplest, a combined scale can be devised by looking at the answers to a series of questions about an issue or topic, linked in some kind of logical or natural progression. One of the first celebrated scales of this type—the social distance scale (Bogardus, 1933)—was concerned with racial attitudes, and it marked the beginning of attempts to produce combined, hierarchical scales. To sort respondents according to their degree of acceptance of members of another race they were asked to indicate, on a seven-point scale from high to low, what level of intimacy they would accept:

1. To close kinship by marriage
2. To my club as personal chums
3. To my street as neighbours
4. To employment in my occupation in my country
5. To citizenship in my country
6. As visitors only to my country
7. Would exclude from my country

Guttman scales (Guttman, 1944) are also based on the premise that, on certain subjects, a set of ordered items can be constructed to measure an attitude dimension. Items are ordered so that, for most people, acceptance of one item in the scale implies acceptance of all those that precede it. The scale is formed by examining responses to a range of rating scales to establish the extent to which a hierarchical pattern is present. The process requires painstaking development work and, in practice, the opportunities for developing hierarchical scales according to the Guttman model have been rare.

Thurstone and Likert are the two other pioneers of unidimensional scales. Although their approaches differed, their aim was to produce a list of opinion statements, the responses to which could be used to form an overall index of, say, racial prejudice for each respondent. To arrive at a list of the most relevant statements a much longer list is used during a development stage. Thurstone made use of a panel of about 200 'judges' to sort all the statements into eleven groups so that each group was equally spaced along the attitude continuum to be studied. Statements that varied widely in the group to which they were allocated by different judges were discarded and a selection of twenty or so statements was then chosen from the remainder to form Thurstone's 'equal interval' scale (Thurstone and Chave, 1929).

Likert's method, the basis of much modern scaling work, is less laborious than Thurstone's. It also involves reducing a large number of statements to form a final scale. At the development stage, a sample of people respond to a large number of attitude statements; they give their own responses rather than attempt to arbitrate as judges. Five-point scales are presented for each statement, scored from 1 to 5 or 5 to 1—depending on whether they are positively or negatively phrased. By adding the respondents' scores, a 'summated' score is derived as the basis for a first approximation of the scale position for each statement. Subgroups with the most extreme views (say the top and bottom 10 per cent) can be identified on the basis of responses to all the statements. The statements found to discriminate most clearly between these two extreme groups are the ones that form the final Likert scale of 'summated ratings' (Likert, 1932).

Complex preference questioning
Some attitude questions attempt to achieve the deceptively easy task of discovering whether people prefer A to B, or vice versa. Where A and B differ clearly and in a very limited respect the task may indeed be easy. Moreover, in simple product tests, respondents can be asked to test alternative products before indicating their preference. On the other hand, where the object is to establish preferences between, say, traffic-free and conventional shopping centres, asking respondents to state their preferences between A and B is simplistic, and practical experiments are rarely feasible.

It might seem safer to deduce preferences from the choices that people have already made—for example, a person's home should, in theory, reflect his preferences for different features of a home—but his choice can, at best, provide only a broad indication of his preferences. In the first place, people make many choices without explicitly taking into account all the points in favour of and against each side. Other choices involve implicit compromises in which major priorities override minor preferences. In choosing a house or an area in which to live, people make their decision on the basis of a wide range of criteria, including the size of house, style of kitchen, heating, size of garden. In some of the items they will be able to achieve their ideal; in others, reality will fall short of the ideal. Any attempt to deduce housing preferences solely from housing behaviour would fail to take these factors into account.

Nor can we gain much by asking people, in the abstract, whether they would prefer one type of house to another, unless we can include all factors within our description, including intangible factors such as 'atmosphere' or 'brightness'. So the starting point of questioning about preferences must be to identify the components of a particular choice and to question people in detail about each component. Having established, say, that bedroom sizes are one of the important considerations in choosing a house, style of kitchen another, and size of garden a third, we can question respondents about their ideal requirements in respect of each of these attributes. They can then place the attributes in order of importance to them so that an overall ranking can be derived. Ranking of all items is useful, but where there are too many items to rank easily, paired comparisons of certain items may be better: respondents are asked to indicate a preference betwen A and B, C and D, and so on; although each respondent may be asked to make only a few comparisons of this kind, different respondents can be asked about different pairs; hence the full range of preferences can be determined in aggregate from a statistical analysis. Even a full examination of the preferences for individual components does not, however, convey the process by which respondents balance these preferences.

An extension of conventional preference questioning is the technique of identifying trade-offs as discussed by Hoinville (1971). Using housing to illustrate this approach, respondents are asked first to describe their existing house or flat in terms of room sizes, garage facilities, method of heating and so on. They are then asked to indicate whether and to what extent they would make sacrifices in the standard of some of these aspects in order to achieve improvements in others—in other words, how they would trade off one attribute against another. For this exercise, respondents are usually presented with a series of scales, one for each attribute. For example:

Size of main living room	Heating	Parking facilities
Very large (30′ × 15′)	Full central heating	Double garage
Large (20′ × 12′)	Partial central heating	Single garage
Medium (15′ × 10′)	Central heating in main living rooms only	Covered parking space
Small (12′ × 8′)	No central heating	Open parking space

Each scale position is 'priced' in the sense that it requires a certain number of points (roughly corresponding to the relative cost of providing the facility) to acquire that level for that attribute. Respondents are asked to indicate the position on each scale that is closest to their present situation, thus giving them a finite number of points to allocate. They are then asked to reallocate those points to achieve their optimum position on each of the three scales taken together. Some respondents choose to make sacrifices in one attribute (parking perhaps) to attain improvement in another (e.g. size of main living room). Others prefer to stay as they are. As a second stage respondents can also be asked to allocate fewer points than their present total in order to see how they would distribute an overall reduction from their present position. It can then be seen which attributes they would sacrifice first, and so on. Similarly they can be offered additional points to allocate.

In many respects preference questioning on social issues is the counterpart of product tests in commercial research. But the preferences being asked about are sometimes related not to the short term but to strategic planning issues including the allocation of resources. Surveys are increasingly being used by local authorities, for instance, as a form of public involvement, to examine residents' preferences in relation to different policies and plans. The advantage of a survey is that it can be designed to be representative of the total population, including those people who would not normally attend exhibitions or public meetings and who are not active in local associations. It can be used to explore attitudes towards many of the factors that have a bearing on policy options (Jowell, 1975).

The basic problem of using surveys in this way is that the implications of alternative policies are often very difficult to convey to respondents. The public seldom has much detailed understanding or experience of the various alternatives within strategic plans. And attempts to provide such knowledge for respondents in the context of a survey do not generally work. It is no solution, for instance, to inundate respondents with leaflets or brochures before the interview, or to ask interviewers to impart background information in any depth. The capacity for absorbing, or wanting to absorb, such information will vary dramatically between respondents. Where it is desirable that respondents should have advance information about, say, the likely effects of turning their shopping centre into a traffic-free area, a structured attitude survey should ideally be preceded by smaller qualitative studies. In these, small groups of people can be given information by videotape or in discussion or by invitations to special exhibitions. They can then be questioned about their views with more likelihood of considered answers. The answers would provide an indication of the overall preferences of small numbers of people and the factors underlying those preferences.

A follow-up quantification study would adopt a different approach. The questionnaire would probably identify all the relevant components of the policy (e.g. parking, walking to the shops, safety for shoppers, more attractive shopping area) and seek to obtain respondents' attitudes to each; respondents need not necessarily be asked to state a preference for or against the policy. The answers on different aspects of the policy can then be used by planners to help them evaluate their options instead of relying on the alternative, quasi-referendum approach of asking for a straight choice between the two broad options. If respondents were to be asked to indicate their overall preference, this would best be done towards the end of an interview that had dwelt on each of the many aspects in turn. In this way respondents would have been encouraged to consider the various implications of the policy and be in a better position to make a balanced choice. It would, however, be necessary to relate respondents' overall preferences to their prior levels of knowledge and experience of traffic-free shopping areas in order to distinguish between choices of those with different levels of knowledge and experience.

Questions that are Difficult to Ask

Catch-all questions

In an attempt to save time, some questionnaires employ what in another context would be called economy measures. In these cases interviewers might reword questions, with a consequent risk of bias. For example:

'Can you tell me the type, coverage and terms of your current house insurance policy?'

There are at least four questions in this catch-all, the first of which should be:

'Do you have an insurance policy on this house?'

Expanded separate versions of the next three questions would then follow for those answering 'yes' to the first question.

Another, slightly different, example of a catch-all or double-barrelled question is one that seeks a single response to two (or more) different subjects:

'Do you feel you have enough space in your kitchen and bathroom?'

Attempts at economy by combining questions are almost always counterproductive; in the end the questions will be more tortuous and certainly more confusing than if a series of questions had been devised.

Long questions and tongue-twisters
Long questions have the disadvantage that one part may get lost and responses will relate only to the beginning or end. For example:
> 'Do you think there are enough job opportunities for a person like you in this district, or do you think there are better jobs elsewhere for a person like you?'

This particularly bad question has two faults: first the alternatives offered are too cumbersome; second, they are not really alternatives. The two parts of the question could be answered independently (and should have been asked independently). As it stands the question will generate some answers to the first part only and some to the second part only.

Where definitions or qualifications are essential, they should be printed on a show card and handed to the respondent for him to consider as he answers. Some questions are long because researchers try to squeeze in too many of the qualifying points of definition:
> 'Do you use a car regularly to get to your place of work—by car I mean 3-wheeled cars, 4-wheeled cars and estate cars; by regularly, I mean 4 days out of 5; by place of work I mean the one you go to most often as part of your work?'

The pedantic researcher may well be satisfied with that question in that there is little room for ambiguity. But there is equally little chance of an accurate answer. The qualifying definitions create obscurity rather than clarity. Interviewers would inevitably reword the question to make it manageable.

Whatever instructions are given to interviewers about using the exact words printed on the questionnaire, they will also generally be ignored when a question turns out to be a tongue-twister. Moreover, there are no excuses for including questions that cannot be read aloud without stumbling: a simple pre-test, consisting of no more than half a dozen trials, will be sufficient to identify the tongue-twisters so that they can be removed.

Over-use of show cards
The practice of using show cards and other visual aids with questionnaires has been increasing over the years. It is generally a valuable practice, making the questionnaire more interesting and easier to understand. Too many show cards, however, are likely to be counterproductive. An interviewer cannot be expected to produce a string of show cards in quick succession, followed by a second string

and often a third string without fumbling, creating confusion and irritation. In these circumstances even the most diligent interviewer may end up leaving out some cards. Limiting the use of show cards is therefore essential if the flow of the interview is to be maintained and the impact of the visual aid is to be maximized. Moreover, show cards that are untidy or difficult to read are a burden rather than an aid. The cards should be produced in a form that will not mark or deteriorate rapidly with use.

Questions that are Difficult to Answer
Unfamiliar words and phrases
Terms such as 'management', 'workers', 'modern youth', 'mugging' do not have a uniform meaning to all respondents. Questions that incorporate them may get answers, but the answers will be impossible to interpret accurately. As a rule, words that are either pejorative or complimentary—depending on your point of view rather than on near-universal norms—have no place in questionnaires.

But it is not only in-phrases that should be avoided. It is equally important to ensure that the vocabulary used is not beyond the comprehension of the sample members. Most questionnaire designers or researchers have had some higher education, while most respondents have had rather less formal education. A barrier to successful questionnaire design is that researchers will take a great deal for granted about their respondents' knowledge and vocabulary. An effective way of avoiding this hazard is to conduct some qualitative work before the questionnaire is designed; otherwise thorough piloting is the minimum requirement. The interview is an exercise in communication and the means of communication must be appropriate.

In qualitative work the researcher will be able to get respondents to use their own words and phrases to describe their feelings and experiences, so that an appropriate vocabulary can emerge. Phrases such as:

Taking all factors into consideration. . . .
How frequently, if at all, would you be inclined to. . . .
How much . . . do you consume. . . .
What was the proportion of. . . .
Do you hold a contrary view. . . .
Does this represent your feelings. . . .
On the assumption that. . . .
How well acquainted are you with. . . .

would never find their way into questionnaires if more care were taken in preliminary design and piloting.

Generalizations and abstractions

Since even an hour-long interview is hardly long enough for an exhaustive treatment of a subject, most surveys have to restrict themselves to a fairly general treatment of the subject. But operating at a general level is not the same as demanding sweeping generalizations in response to a single question, such as 'How would you rate the overall performance of your car?' 'Performance' is a difficult word in the first place; the addition of 'overall' makes it even more difficult, since it involves employing a unidimensional scale for a multi-dimensional concept. How does a rational respondent answer when he owns a car that has poor acceleration, good petrol consumption, average braking power and good road holding?

Similarly, abstractions can cause difficulties in questionnaire design. Researchers often need to develop the questionnaire from abstract concepts. For example, planners and researchers may find it easy to think of motorways as causes of 'severance' or 'visual intrusion'. But they cannot hope to get sensible responses to direct questions about these concepts: they have to be broken down into a series of questions. Concepts such as 'regions' and 'neighbourhood' mean little to most people, and what they mean differs widely in ways that cannot be deciphered, still less measured.

Negatives

Questions that use negatives, particularly when respondents are being asked to agree or disagree, are virtually impossible to understand at the first hearing. Imagine, for example, the mental feat required to understand what disagreement with the following statement means:

Children who steal should not be punished.

This problem arises because it is often desirable to mix positive and negative statements in attitude scales. But the researcher should seek, where possible, to find positive ways of expressing negatives, e.g.

Children who steal should be let off with a caution.

Hypothetical questions

In attitudinal research, hypothetical questions cannot always be avoided, but they are difficult to administer and often give rise to unreliable results. Some people become confused or even alarmed when asked to respond to a hypothetical situation. The question: 'If you were buying a house, what features would you most want it to have?' would produce a range of responses based on different assumptions: some respondents would answer in terms of their ideal; others would be more cautious and answer in terms of what they thought they might achieve. Answers would also reflect experience and levels of expectation. There would be many unsolicited responses about the desirability or otherwise of ownership as against renting, and—from many respondents—an absolute inability or refusal to hypothesize about a situation that they know will never occur.

Questions that Invite Distortion
Leading questions
There are several familiar types of leading question, and the ordering of questions itself can in some cases be leading. The simplest variety is one that assumes the respondent holds a particular point of view and therefore fails to provide for the contrary view: 'What is it that makes you like your job?' rather than starting with 'Do you like or dislike your job?' Then there is the variety that gives only selective alternatives: 'Do you have any complaints about your job—things like pay, hours, supervision?' Or even more extreme: 'Do you agree your hours of work are unsatisfactory?' There are countless other examples—sometimes more subtle, sometimes more blatant—to be found in contemporary surveys.

Probably the most subtle variety of a leading question is the type that suggests to respondents that there is only one socially acceptable answer to a given question. The subjects of these questions usually relate to feelings of fairness, justice or duty:

'Do you think that punishment for stealing should be:
.... more severe than it is now
.... less severe than now
.... or should the punishment fit the crime?'
'Do you think that old age pensioners should:
.... be forbidden to work
.... or be allowed to work if they wish to?'

Use of certain words or phrases in questions can create bias: respondents may agree with 'not allowing' old age pensioners to work, while disagreeing with 'forbidding' them.

Reference to government in a question can also lead respondents to give one type of answer rather than another. Before the 1975 referendum on British membership of the EEC, experiments were carried out to show the likely effects of different forms of questions that might be asked (National Opinion Polls, 1975). The conclusion was that questions that included an explicit reference to the government's position produced a notably higher endorsement of that position than when it was only implicit or absent. The same tendency is likely to exist when local authorities are seeking residents' opinions. If they make their own policy clear in a questionnaire, they are likely to produce more agreement with it than would otherwise exist. In some cases, of course, where residents are highly critical of a local authority, the reverse might be true. Either way a distorted picture is likely to emerge.

Secondary questions
For reasons of economy, in many household surveys only one member of the household is interviewed even when information is required about all household members. The assumption is then made that the respondent can give accurate replies on behalf of someone else. This is often mistaken. Many wives, for example, do not know their husbands' precise incomes or job descriptions; even more husbands are unaware of details of their wives' jobs. In any event, ethical considerations have to be borne in mind in asking for information about others: people may object, for example, to details of their income being disclosed without their permission. So caution has to be exercised both in deciding what information to seek from one member of a household about the rest, and in interpreting the information that has been collected. When precise or detailed data are required about each household member, either all should be interviewed or self-completion questionnaires should be left for those not present.

Principles of Layout
The architecture of a questionnaire has to fulfil three independent aims: to promote fluent questioning by interviewers, to facilitate accurate and comprehensive recording of answers; to assist economical transfer of data into a machine-readable form for computer analysis. A good layout will minimize the risk of error at all three stages.

Promoting fluent questioning
Interviewers need to be relaxed and fluent; they need to be able to find their way around questionnaires comfortably and confidently; they need to be able to identify instructions quickly and interpret them accurately. While good training can help interviewers to become familiar with the questionnaire, the layout of a questionnaire is probably the key factor in achieving these aims.

Obsessive saving on space in questionnaire layout is usually a false economy. A crowded questionnaire is difficult to negotiate and likely to generate faltering questioning and faulty recording.

Space is one criterion of good layout; consistency is another. In a long questionnaire, standard conventions of lettering (or typefaces), underlining, bracketing and numbering are helpful. One such convention is to print all interviewer instructions in upper case letters and all questions and precodes in lower case; interviewers quickly get used to the rule that only lower case words are to be read out aloud.

In a structured questionnaire, the range of possible answers to most questions is precoded and preprinted. The convention is to have all questions on the left of the page and all precodes on the right, directly opposite the question; where appropriate, an 'other answer' category is also provided with space for recording responses outside the precoded range. Alongside each precoded answer is a code number. Any deviation from this layout (or from any other standard layout adopted) needs to be particularly clear.

Whenever precodes are used, two points of guidance should be provided for the interviewer: first, whether the precodes are to be used as running prompts, that is, to be read out as part of the question; second, whether one, or more than one, code may be ringed for the question. The examples below contain the kind of guidance necessary for a fluent interview:

Example 1

During rush hour, is this
street usually......(*READ OUT*)...........very noisy, 1
.... fairly noisy, 2
RING ONE CODE .... or not noisy? 3
Don't know 4

Example 2

Which of these statements describe your street
and which do not?

(*READ OUT IN TURN*)	Describes street	Does not describe street	Don't know
RING ONE	It's fairly quiet except at	1	2	3
CODE FOR	rush hour			
EACH	It's lorries that cause			
STATEMENT	most noise in this street	1	2	3
	Traffic noise in this street			
	is not very noticeable	1	2	3

Example 3

On which of the past seven days have you left
home for work before 8 a.m.?

Monday 1
Tuesday 2
MORE THAN ONE CODE Wednesday 3
MAY BE RINGED Thursday 4
Friday 5
Saturday 6
Sunday 7
Never in past 7 days 8
Can't remember/Don't know 9

Although space and consistency are probably the two most important criteria for promoting fluency, another very important consideration is the way in which filtering is handled. Sometimes whole blocks of questions are to be asked only of subgroups of respondents. If, for instance, the questionnaire is concerned with different types of journeys to work, car commuters may be asked one series of questions, rail commuters another, and so on. Where the questionnaire divides in this way it is helpful to use different coloured pages for the different sections. Interviewers can then see at a glance which sections of questionnaire are to be asked of which groups. It makes for easier administration of the interview and for easier checking by both the interviewers and the office coders.

In most cases, however, the filtering will apply only to individual questions scattered throughout the questionnaire. A convention then needs to be devised as in the example below:

			SKIP TO
(a) During rush hour, is this street usually.... (*READ OUT*)...very noisy,		1	
.... fairly noisy,		2	(c)
or, not noisy?		3	(c)
Don't know		4	(c)

IF 'VERY NOISY' (CODE 1)

(b) What types of noise are there in this street?

(PROBE AND RECORD FULLY) _____

_____

_____

_____

_____

_____

ASK ALL

(c) Which of these statements describe your street and which do not?

Three features of this example contribute to a smooth flow. First, the column on the extreme right of each page of the questionnaire signals a filter as soon as the interviewer has recorded an answer. As the code 2, 3 or 4 is ringed, the interviewer will see that question (b) should be skipped and that question (c) is the next question for that respondent. When there is no skip instruction (as for code 1) the interviewer proceeds with the next question—(b) in this case. Second, to make doubly sure that the filter question is seen to be reserved for only some respondents, it is indented and clearly labelled as applicable only to a specific group. Filter questions like these should fall on the same page as their master questions since an indentation at the top of the page would be missed. Third, as soon as the filter questioning has been completed, the question numbers/ letters return to the margin and the instruction *ASK ALL* is inserted.

Without the aid of good layout and consistent procedures, conscientious interviewers would have to devise their own systems of checks, which might be more subject to error. There are few greater irritations for interviewers than inadequate filter instructions, since they drastically interrupt the smooth flow of an interview.

A common mistake in questionnaire design arises from the desire to keep the questionnaire short. For example, a question on ownership *and use* of household vehicles might be followed by an instruction such as: *if owns car, skip to Q.42*. The instruction does not make it clear whether ownership implies registration of the vehicle in the respondent's name or only regular access to the car. The respondent is kept waiting while the conscientious interviewer refers to the project instructions for clarification. Wherever possible, the filter instruction should employ identical words to those employed in the question and its precodes, so as to leave no room for ambiguity.

Facilitating accurate recording
Factors that improve fluency, such as space and consistency, also enhance accuracy on the part of interviewers. If verbatim answers are required to open-ended questions, adequate space must be left for them; if there are 'other answer' categories, it is very frustrating for interviewers to have too little space to write out the answers. In layout, as in question wording, the questionnaire designer must make generous allowance for the fact that respondents are not all alike, that idiosyncratic minorities need to be catered for and have their answers recorded, and must ensure that structuring a question- naire does not have the effect of a straitjacket. It is clearly impractical always to allow precodes for very rare responses. But it is essential that space is allowed for these rare answers to be recorded. An important principle of questionnaire design is that the temptation to ignore the tail of a distribution of answers must be firmly resisted: an 'other answer' category is a minimum requirement.

Some obvious rules for layout help reduce the chance of interviewer error: ensuring that all the precodes for a question appear on the same page as the question; ensuring that questions that apply only to some respondents follow as closely as possible on the question that creates the filter rather than relying on the interviewer to remember (or to turn back to find out) who answered what; ensuring that questions and answers are aligned so that interviewers can concentrate on the respondent rather than on discovering where to record the answers.

There are also some less obvious rules. The fact that a question has been asked needs to be recorded in some way by the interviewer, regardless of the answer given. To return to the example given earlier:

On which of the past seven days have you left
home for work before 8 a.m.?

	Monday 1
	Tuesday 2
MORE THAN ONE CODE	Wednesday 3
MAY BE RINGED	Thursday 4
	Friday 5
	Saturday 6
	Sunday 7
	Never in past 7 days 8
	Can't remember/Don't know 9

The last two precodes are as crucial to this question as the other seven. Although non-workers would have been filtered out at an earlier question, those who did not work during the previous week and late risers need to be catered for; otherwise there would be no indication of whether that question has been missed out. Occasionally, particularly in long questionnaires, questions or parts of questions will be overlooked by interviewers; sometimes, because of poor layout, the same question may be missed consistently by one interviewer or, exceptionally, by all interviewers. Unless there are obvious ways of discovering these errors the data may be distorted. An even safer way of asking and precoding the question under discussion would have been as follows:

On which of the past seven days have you left
home for work before 8 a.m.?

		Yes	*No*	*Don't know/ Can't remember*
	Monday	1	2	3
RING ONE CODE	Tuesday	1	2	3
FOR EACH OF	Wednesday	1	2	3
7 DAYS	Thursday	1	2	3
	Friday	1	2	3
	Saturday	1	2	3
	Sunday	1	2	3

With this layout, it is immediately apparent whether the interviewer obtained answers for all days of the week. Seven codes have to be ringed since the coding frame now explicitly demands seven answers.

The same principle applies to all other aspects of layout. Conventions that may seem to be pedantic and expansive often add substantially to clarity. It is as important for the researcher to ensure that the layout minimizes ambiguity and distortion as it is to ensure that the wording is precise and neutral.

Assisting economical transfer

Up to now, the questionnaire has been considered mainly as a means of communication between interviewer and respondent. Its other role is as a working document for coders and punch operators, as a medium for the transfer of data to computer disk or tape. Chapter 8 contains details of the procedures involved in data preparation. In this section some of the layout conventions that make the procedures easier to operate are described.

A questionnaire designed solely with interviewers in mind would not meet the requirements of card punchers. In the past, therefore, many surveys employed an intermediate transfer sheet on which all coded responses from the questionnaire were entered onto a new form for punchers. This practice has now quite properly been generally abandoned as wasteful and prone to error. Questionnaires are now designed to meet the different needs of those who use them without having to compromise on clarity.

Punch operators work in much the same way as typists do and at similarly high speeds. Any feature of a layout that reduces those speeds can be expensive, since the costs of punching are directly related to time. Moreover, like typists, punch operators develop a momentum and rhythm of working. They need to be able to cast their eyes down a column or along a row without having to search all over the page. So the layout should be as internally consistent as possible.

The punch operator is concerned only with codes, not with written or printed words, or with interpretation. If possible, therefore, the codes should be positioned consistently in the same column on the questionnaire, spaced so that codes for one question are easily identifiable from those for another. A common convention is to distinguish codes for one question from codes for the next by printing an unbroken line across the column between them. It is helpful to print on the questionnaires the column numbers on which the data are to be punched. This can be done only when the researcher and technical team are certain that no changes will be made to the layout. Care must be taken to allow enough columns for each open-ended response and for all the administrative codes such as questionnaire identity numbers, interviewer number and the project identity number.

These brief points of guidance are included not as a comprehensive set of rules for the questionnaire designer, but as an introduction to the range of separate items that have to be taken into account in questionnaire layout. Poor layout in any of these respects can lead to expense or errors or, more frequently, both. Moreover, guidelines for layout are more difficult to specify than those for question wording. Good layout depends on the researcher being able to imagine himself in the role of the interviewer, coder and punch operator. The more perceptive he is about the likely problems, the more successful he will be in solving them.

Pilot Work

It is fortunate, perhaps, that the creation of good questionnaires does not have to rely solely on perceptive researchers. At some stage in the design process the questionnaire should be subjected to a field test. Such pilot work is extremely useful in refining the wording, ordering, layout, filtering, and so on, and in helping to prune the questionnaire to a manageable length. Where time permits it may be useful to have a series of field tests, starting with a handful of interviews for early drafts and following up with larger-scale and more rigorous pilots of subsequent drafts. Like other exploratory work, piloting takes time and resources. But it should not be confused with the qualitative work described in Chapter 2. That work provides a basis for designing a questionnaire; the pilot work helps to refine points of detail. Its contribution to determining the questionnaire coverage is sometimes marginal, although it often identifies redundant or ambiguous questions and obvious gaps.

For most purposes a pilot survey of between thirty and a hundred interviews is adequate. But the exact size will depend on the aims of the particular test: two or three interviewers doing five to ten interviews each will often be able to reveal wording and layout problems. Where the pilot is to assist in establishing precodes, the number of respondents answering each open question must be fairly large, probably between fifty and a hundred, to cover the necessary range of verbatim answers. An even larger pilot survey (perhaps as many as 300 interviews) will be required if the pilot is to be used to decide on the items for inclusion in attitude scales. In some instances a factor analysis will be carried out on pilot survey results to develop scales and to form the basis of selection of items for the main questionnaire.

The interviewers who carry out the pilot need to be briefed by the researcher; it is also extremely helpful if they are debriefed at the end of the pilot. The debriefing can range over all the questions;

interviewers can comment on the ordering of questions, identify questions that caused respondents difficulty, discuss the method of introducing the survey, and so on. This will provide a much fuller picture than completed questionnaires alone can give.

A useful device in pilot work is to tape-record some interviews. The recordings can illuminate ambiguities and tongue-twisters more readily than other methods. Researchers can hear for themselves how questions come across and what problems they present to respondents. If possible, however, the researcher should also conduct some interviews himself or accompany an interviewer to observe the questionnaire being administered.

Interviewers need to play a much more creative role in pilot work than they need to do in the main survey. If, for example, they have doubts about whether a respondent has understood a question or given accurate information they should probe the subject, perhaps inserting an additional question 'Please tell me what you understood by this question?' or 'Please tell me how you arrived at that answer?', questions that are rarely, if ever, required of them in the final survey. At key questions, interviewers may be specifically instructed to probe in this way with all their respondents. And they are always asked to note certain points such as whether:

  they had to repeat or amplify a question before it was understood;

  they had any difficulty in recording the answers or finding their way through the questionnaire;

  the respondent seemed not to understand a question or found it difficult or ambiguous;

  there were any questions for which visual aids should have been provided or where aids already provided were inadequate or unnecessary;

  there were points at which interest flagged or co-operation seemed strained;

  the questionnaire flowed naturally from one question to the next;

  the precodes fitted the range of answers being given;

  the questionnaire seemed too long or too detailed in some places (it is helpful for interviewers to record details not only of the duration of each interview, but of the duration of each section).

Pilot work is a relatively inexpensive way of avoiding obvious mistakes in questionnaires and improving question wording and order. There are no rigid rules for designing questionnaires: the wording and ordering of most questions are seldom obviously right or obviously wrong; more important, they can frequently be adapted and refined. Rather than impose a precise format too early, the researcher is always well advised to base his final decisions about questionnaire construction on a series of tests.

For a wide range of topics much of this work will already have been done by others who have undertaken related surveys. Although these surveys may have been undertaken for different purposes from the proposed study they will usually contain a number of questions that overlap. Even seemingly unrelated surveys can guide the researcher in approaching some of his measurements. A great deal is known, for example, about questioning techniques for obtaining data on expenditure patterns, mobility, readership and other subjects. The danger of borrowing questions, however, is that errors and weaknesses in the questions will be repeated. The fact that a series of questions has been used before does not guarantee that they were based on extensive pretesting or that they proved successful. But at least they provide a starting point and, if approached critically, can save a great deal of time and carry the benefit of comparability that would otherwise be lost.

Notes on Further Reading
1. Questionnaire design is discussed in the texts on interviewing by Kahn and Cannell (1957), Richardson *et al.* (1965), and Gorden (1975) and in the chapter by Cannell and Kahn in Lindzey and Aronson (1968), Vol. 2. The book on questionnaire design and attitude measurement by Oppenheim (1966) is a useful basic text. The topic is also treated in some detail in the general textbooks mentioned at the end of Chapter 1.
2. Memory and time effects have received considerable attention, and a chapter of Sudman and Bradburn (1974) is devoted to this subject. Zarkovich (1966) also gives a detailed treatment. The studies by Neter and Waksberg (1965), Gray (1955), Cartwright (1963) and Sudman and Bradburn (1973) are worth consulting.
3. Since the randomized response technique was introduced by Warner (1966) there have been many articles developing variants of the technique and determining their statistical properties: a number of these articles are to be found in the *Journal of the American Statistical Association*, and there is a collection of papers on the topic in the *International Statistical Review*, 1976, Vol. 44, 181-230.
4. The subject of attitude scaling is a large one, and there is an enormous literature on it. The texts by Oppenheim (1966), Lemon (1973) and Dawes (1972) provide good introductions to the subject. Fishbein (1967), Summers (1970) and Jahoda and Warren (1966) have edited useful collections of papers on attitudes and their measurement. The research monograph by McKennell (1974) is worth consulting: it also gives a useful list

of references for further reading on the theory and techniques of attitude measurement.

5. The literature on preference measurement and trade-offs is wide. A standard text on welfare economics is contained in Pigou (1932) and a more specialized treatment of trade-off measurements in survey research is given by Hoinville and Courtenay (1977).

6. There has been a good deal of research on the effects of question wording, much of it reported in journals such as *Public Opinion Quarterly* and the *International Journal of Opinion and Attitude Research* in the 1940s and 1950s. From the earlier work the books by Payne (1951) and Cantril (1944) are particularly worth consulting. Among more recent references are those of Noelle Neumann (1970), Laurent (1972), Schuman and Duncan in Costner (1974), and Presser and Schuman (1975). Belson and Duncan (1962) compare open and pre-coded questions. Belson (1968) and Speak (1967) discuss respondents' understanding of survey questions. Cannell and Robinson in Lansing *et al.* (1971) present the results of an analysis of questions according to the problems they create for interviewer and respondent, based on a study of tape-recorded interviews.

Chapter 4. Sampling
Principal contributor: Barry Hedges

The preceding chapters have illustrated the way in which the researcher moves from a general statement of the survey's purpose to a structured questionnaire, piloted and ready for use in an interview or postal survey. The object then is to apply that questionnaire to a representative group of people. But representative of whom? The first step in the sampling process is to define the survey population, which might be the entire population of the United Kingdom, but it is more likely to be a sub-set of that population: a large sub-set, such as all adults, or a small sub-set, such as university students, or something in between.

Identifying the Survey Population
At an early stage of planning the survey, only an approximate definition of the survey population is needed. Even this may not be easy to achieve, because the purpose of the survey may not make it immediately obvious what part of the population should be studied. If, for example, a survey is to be mounted to study the way in which people maintain or change their patterns of participation in sport as they pass from school into adult life and onwards towards middle age, it seems obvious that there should be an upper age limit, but far less obvious what that limit should be.

That is an example of the kind of problem in defining a survey population that can be resolved early on by discussions about the survey's purpose. In other cases there may be a more serious difficulty. In studying, for example, people likely to be affected by a new road development—as residents, motorists or pedestrians— there is probably no entirely satisfactory way of defining a suitable population, although workable solutions can be found. As so often happens, the difficulty is the conceptual one of deciding to whom a new road is or is not relevant rather than the technical one of finding a suitable sampling method.

As the survey design progresses the definition of the survey population must be given precision. It is not enough to talk about 'adults'. What age defines an adult? Do we mean all adults present in the country, or only those who are resident? (And how do we define resident?) Do we want to include that part of the population that lives in institutions, or should we confine our attention to private households? These details need to be settled before the sample selection process begins.

Survey populations do not necessarily consist of people. It is possible, and not at all unusual, to survey dwellings, industrial establishments, vehicles, bus journeys and a variety of other populations whose different characteristics pose varied problems for the researcher.

It is usual, when the survey population consists of people, to obtain information directly from the sampled individuals. But this is not always so: for example, in a survey of young children information would be sought from their parents. In a survey of industrial establishments, an appropriate person would have to be chosen to provide information about each establishment.

In sampling households, which constitute one of the most commonly surveyed populations, there is a particular problem regarding whom to interview. Within a household, different members may be best placed to answer different questions. They cannot usually all be interviewed, either collectively or separately, and it would not solve the problem if they could since, in the event of disagreement, aggregation to the household level would present a major difficulty. Usually one person is interviewed. In some surveys a person designated as the head of household (see Chapter 9) is interviewed, in others the housewife. There is usually no entirely satisfactory solution, because most surveys contain some questions appropriate to the traditional role of the head and others to that of the housewife, and some include questions that would be more appropriate to a population of individuals than of households. The borderline between the concerns of the person as a member of a group (the household) and his concerns as an individual is far from clearly drawn: but the survey has to be designed on the basis of a definite view about what is required.

The Principles of Sampling

Thus far, in what may be thought of as a pre-sampling phase rather than as part of the process of sample design, little or no statistical or specialized sampling skill is required. It has been emphasized that a decision about the survey population stems more from the purpose of the survey than from sampling considerations, though these may influence it.

But now, as we move from defining the survey population to sampling it, we will need to draw upon a variety of theoretical concepts. Sample design requires both a knowledge of sampling theory and a practical knowledge of what is possible and economic. In this chapter we have tried to concentrate on the practical issues but we have nevertheless felt it necessary to provide at the outset a brief account of the main theoretical concepts. In a short space we cannot hope to do them justice, but the outline provided will be a useful background to the subsequent sections which deal with sampling practice.

In condensing so broad a subject into one chapter, we have decided to concentrate on probability sampling methods. Other less rigorous sampling methods such as quota or random route sampling are only briefly touched on in the final section.

A sample is a small-scale representation—a kind of miniature model—of the population from which it was selected. Because it includes merely a part, not all, of the parent population, it can never be an exact replica of that population. But in many respects it will resemble it closely, and it is this resemblance that makes sampling so useful in the study of populations too large to survey in their entirety: the proportions, ratios, averages and other similar measures computed from the sample are likely to correspond to those of the parent population.

How close the resemblance is depends on several factors, in particular the size of the sample and the way in which it was selected. The securest basis for sample selection is chance, although in most practical sample designs certain constraints must be placed on its operation. There is plenty of empirical evidence to show that when selections are made by non-probability methods results are liable to distortions that may be serious. That is why in this chapter we deal mainly with probability methods.

Estimating population values

In probability sampling the differences between sample estimates and population values constitute *sampling error*, of which the central ideas are explained in the following paragraphs.

Suppose a sample survey estimates the mean height of adult men as 68.2″. Would another sample survey give an identical result? Probably not; it might, let us say, provide an estimate of 67.9″. If we continued selecting fresh samples and obtaining fresh estimates of the population mean, after a time we would observe a definite pattern emerging.

This can be illustrated by imagining that we plot the mean height from each fresh survey as a square on graph paper (Figure 1). As more results come to hand their frequency distribution (or sampling

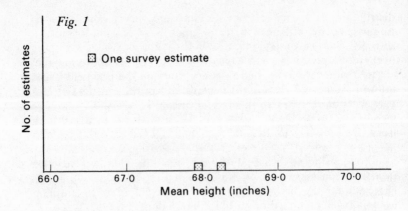

Fig. 1

☒ One survey estimate

No. of estimates

Mean height (inches)

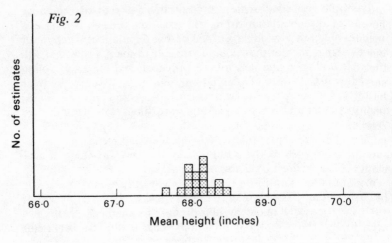

Fig. 2

No. of estimates

Mean height (inches)

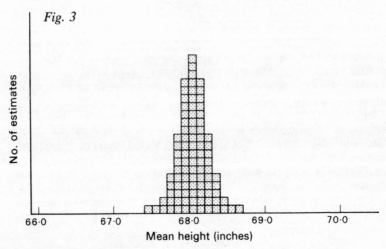

Fig. 3

No. of estimates

Mean height (inches)

distribution) begins to take on a definite pattern (Figures 2, 3), which is seen to approximate to a bell-shaped curve—the *normal distribution*. The mean of that normal distribution will correspond to the population mean.

The normal distribution has certain fixed properties that are very useful to us. There is a widely used statistical measure of dispersion, known as the *standard deviation*, and in a normal distribution about 95 per cent of the observations lie within two standard deviations of its mean. It follows that there are 95 chances out of 100 that the mean of any particular sample, chosen at random, will be within two 'standard deviations' of the true population mean. It also follows that if we have selected only one sample, the population value is likely to lie within two standard deviations of our sample estimate. If we knew the standard deviation of the sampling distribution (a quantity usually referred to as the 'standard error'), we could tell how near our single sample's result was likely to be to the population mean. In practice we do not know this, but we can estimate it from our single sample. We do not need to repeat our survey time after time to build up the pattern shown in Figure 3; by carrying out our survey only once—which is of course the real situation—we have the basic elements we need: an estimate from our sample of the population mean, and a statement of how likely it is that this sample estimate will be within any distance we choose to nominate of the population mean. We do not know exactly where our particular sample lies in relation to the population mean but we know how close it is likely to be.

For example, if our sample estimates the average height of men at 68.2″, and the standard deviation of the sampling distribution at 1.0″, we can say that we are 95 per cent confident that the true average height of men is between 66.2″ and 70.2″ (the observed value plus or minus twice the standard deviation). But we could equally well say that we are 90 per cent confident that the true average height is between 66.5″ and 69.9″ (1⅝ times the standard deviation). Or that we are roughly 99 per cent confident that it is between 65.6″ and 70.8″ (2½ times the standard deviation).

The intervals in these statements are known as *confidence intervals* and the different probabilities—95 per cent, 90 per cent, 99 per cent—as *confidence levels*. The researcher can choose to run very little risk that the interval will fail to cover the population value by opting for, say, a 99 per cent confidence level (which gives him a wide interval), or he can choose a lower confidence level in order to narrow the confidence interval. The 95 per cent confidence level is the most commonly used.

Bias and precision

The foregoing discussion can now be used to explain two basic ideas. We have said that if we carry out repeated sampling to produce a sampling distribution, then the mean of that distribution will coincide with the true population mean. But if there is *selection bias* in drawing members of the sample, repeated sampling will produce results that would centre on some value other than the true mean. If, for example, some feature of the sampling method means that tall men have a greater chance of being sampled than short men, the average of the means produced by repeated sampling would be higher than the population mean. Estimates from samples with this biased selection procedure will thus generally tend to be too high (although it is still possible that some of these samples may produce estimates exactly corresponding to the population mean).

The other essential idea is that of *precision*. The narrower the sampling distribution (the more tightly the estimates are bunched together), the narrower the confidence intervals, the greater the precision of the estimate, and the smaller the sampling error.

Sampling error and bias are not connected. A sampling method which involves a selection bias may nevertheless yield results of high precision. Another sampling method may be unbiased but yield results of such low precision that sampling error is too large for the results to have any practical value.

Sampling error depends on three factors. First, the variability of the characteristic under study in the population in question: the more varied the population is with respect to that characteristic, the larger the potential sampling error will be. Second, the size of the sample selected: the larger the sample the smaller the sampling error. People sometimes think that the proportion of the population sampled (*the sampling fraction*) determines the amount of sampling error, but unless this fraction is fairly large—more than 1 in 10— its effect on sampling error is negligible. Where large populations are being sampled, it is rare to reach a 1 in 10 fraction, and even with smaller populations such a fraction seldom occurs. The important factor is thus the sample size rather than the sampling fraction. The third factor influencing the amount of the sampling error is the sample design. The aim of the sampler is to construct a sample design that minimizes sampling error and bias within the available resources.

Sample size

For a given sample design and survey population, the likely amount of sampling error, and hence the width of the confidence interval for a specified confidence level, depends on the sample size: the larger the sample, the smaller the amount of sampling error to be expected, and the narrower the confidence interval.

Deciding what sample size to use is almost always a matter more of judgement than of calculation. Textbook methods demand that the survey designer should start from information about the distribution of the variable to be measured and about the precision (width of confidence interval) required by those who are to use the results. In most surveys, the first condition is difficult to apply because surveys have more than one purpose, with many variables to be studied, each of them having a different distribution. The second usually cannot be applied, because research users are rarely able to specify the degree of precision they require.

In practice, the main determinant of sample size is almost always the need to look separately at the results of different subgroups of the total sample (separate age groups, socio-economic groups, and so on). The total sample size is usually governed by the sample size required for the smallest subgroup: as a rough guide, the smallest subgroup will need to have between fifty and a hundred members.

In most surveys, therefore, samples of fewer than 1,000 people are of limited use for exploring variations within the total population. But samples do not often need to comprise more than 5,000 people; among the exceptions are transportation studies, where analyses of a great many geographical subdivisions are usually required, and general purpose population descriptions such as the General Household Survey conducted by the Office of Population Censuses and Surveys.

Sampling error decreases as sample size increases, but not in direct proportion. The decrease is proportionate to the square root of the relative increase in sample size. The additional cost that an increase in sample size entails is more nearly proportionate, although the increase usually brings some economies of scale.

Systematic sampling
The method of sampling in which selections are made by chance alone is called *simple random sampling*. To draw a simple random sample of, say, 100 people from a list of 2,500, every person in the list would be numbered and then 100 numbers would be chosen at random; in this way every member of the population would have an equal chance of being selected into the sample. A table of random numbers, such as that provided by Fisher and Yates (1963), would probably be used for this purpose. It is a laborious procedure, little used in practice. The alternative method of *systematic sampling* is more commonly used. With this method the first sample member is selected from the list by a random number and subsequent members are selected according to a fixed *sampling interval*. This interval is

calculated by dividing the total number of names on the list by the required sample size. The random starting number must lie within the sampling interval. To select 100 people from 2,500 the sampling interval would be 25, and a random starting number would be chosen between 1 and 25. If this were 14 then the people selected would be those numbered 14, 39, 64 . . . and so on. Like simple random sampling, systematic sampling gives every member of the population the same chance of being selected.

Care needs to be taken in the application of systematic sampling. If, for example, on a list of married couples the husband's name always precedes the wife's, and the interval is an even number, the sample will be all men or all women, depending on the random starting number. But lists are usually arranged in alphabetical or other orders in which this type of regular pattern rarely occurs: systematic sampling is then satisfactory. Sometimes the order of a list can help rather than hinder the survey designer. For instance, if all the men are listed in the first half of the list and all the women in the second half, systematic sampling ensures that the sexes are represented in their correct proportions. This is an example of *stratification*.

Proportionate stratification

Stratification is the process of dividing the population to be sampled into distinct groups or strata and selecting a separate sample from each stratum. If we choose the separate sample sizes so that they are proportionate to the population of each stratum, the procedure is known as *proportionate stratification*, which is discussed in the next few paragraphs. Disproportionate stratification is considered in the next section.

By using proportionate stratification we ensure that we have selected the correct proportions from each stratum, and thereby reduce the sampling error for survey variables to which the grouping is related. The more closely related the stratification factors—the characteristics that determine the composition of the strata—are to the main variables being studied by the survey, the more effective they will be. In a housing study, for example, rateable value would be a good stratification factor, since it is related to many housing characteristics. In the unlikely event that the stratification factors in a proportionate scheme are entirely unrelated to the survey variables they will achieve nothing (neither will they do any harm, apart from possibly wasting effort or preventing more useful factors being employed).

If the information on which the stratification is based is inaccurate (perhaps out-of-date) it loses some of its effect. For example, we may want to stratify by current income, but have only a list of individuals' incomes compiled several years ago. The passage of time may have altered relative incomes so that some of the individuals who formerly made up, say, the top 10 per cent no longer belong there. But though the stratifying effect will be weakened (assuming it is *current* income to which the variables being studied are related), it will not be destroyed.

As noted at the end of the preceding section, systematic sampling can be used to give stratification of a kind often referred to as implicit (as opposed to the explicit procedure of dividing the population into entirely separate groups). If, for example, a fixed sampling interval is used throughout a list of individuals that is ordered by income, the different income levels will automatically be reflected in the sample in approximately their correct proportions.

Several stratification factors can be employed simultaneously. If our list of individuals included their income and age, we could stratify by both. To do this we would reconstruct the list into a matrix based on the income and age data (both variables being grouped as appropriate). There might be very few people in some cells of the matrix (for example in both the top income group and the bottom age category). If so, these could be combined with adjacent groups in the matrix.

It is not uncommon to construct a number of explicit strata in this way and then list the population elements within strata in order of some other relevant variable so as to achieve a final stage of implicit stratification by the use of systematic sampling.

In taking samples of the general population, the main use of stratification is not in sampling individual people, about whom the most common sampling frame, the electoral register, gives little information, but in selecting areas in which interviewing will be carried out. Areas can be stratified by several factors including those discussed in Chapter 9.

Although the electoral register lacks useful information for stratifying individuals, other frames that may be used for sampling special populations often afford the opportunity for stratification.

Disproportionate stratification
In the foregoing discussion of stratification we have assumed that the sampling fraction is to be uniform—that the same proportion of the population elements within each stratum is to be selected, so that the distribution of the sample across strata corresponds to that of the population.

This is not always so. If the sample designer wants to study a small stratum on its own he may need to depart from a proportionate allocation of the sample, because such an allocation would yield too small a sample in that stratum for separate analysis. He may therefore decide to over-represent it by employing a larger sampling fraction than in the other strata. *Variable sampling fractions* are used so that more selections are made in that stratum than would be the case with proportionate stratification; and a large enough sample for separate analysis is thus obtained from it.

Whenever variable sampling fractions are used, adjustments are needed before the different samples representing each stratum can be added together. The overall sample will be distorted and the balance needs to be restored at the analysis stage by attaching differential *weights* to the sampled units to adjust for their differing selection probabilities.

Variable sampling fractions and weighting must be used with great care. The weights complicate the analysis and usually increase sampling errors for statistics relating to the total sample. In particular, large weights should normally be avoided because they can seriously impair the sample's overall efficiency. Kish (1965) gives methods for computing the loss of efficiency due to weighting: this should be estimated in advance whenever alternative designs are being considered.

It should be noted that the use of variable sampling fractions gives different individuals different chances of selection. This does not contravene the basic requirements of probability sampling. While the simplest case is one where each member has an equal chance of selection, their chances of selection may be unequal provided they are known (and non-zero). Knowledge of unequal selection probabilities permits correction at the analysis stage by weighting.

Although the most usual reason for using variable sampling fractions is to over-represent a small stratum, they can also be introduced to improve the overall efficiency of a sample design where interviewing costs or the variability of responses are known or expected to differ between strata. See, for instance, the discussion of optimum allocation in the survey sampling textbooks mentioned in the Notes on Further Reading at the end of this chapter.

Clustering
In a national interview survey it would be highly uneconomic for the sample to be scattered over the country at random. A way of *clustering* it usually has to be found so that each interviewer has a substantial batch of interviews in a single area. Working there for, say, between two and three weeks will give the interviewer time to call back in a systematic way on people out at the first or second visit.

The size of the area that an interviewer can work will vary according to circumstances such as population density and the sampling fraction. Wards are usually suitable; in urban districts it may be possible to cover a larger area, possibly up to the size of a parliamentary constituency. However, increasing the size of the area over which a given number of interviews is distributed tends to push up costs, and may lead to a less efficient system of calling back and to lower response rates.

The disadvantage of clustering is that it reduces the precision of the sample. The sampling error for a given sample size will usually be larger when clustering is used, because people in the same area will tend to be similar in respect of the survey variables. If the area is small they may all live in the same type of housing, or be mostly in the same socio-economic group. The greater the similarity of people within the clusters, the more a clustering scheme will increase the sampling error relative to that of a simple random sample of the same size.

But clustering has the advantage of allowing a larger sample to be interviewed for a given cost, which in turn reduces the sampling error. The choice is thus between a clustered design with a larger sample and an unclustered design with a smaller sample. The choice between them depends on how much precision is lost in one case by clustering and in the other by reducing the sample size. Kish (1965) discusses ways of computing losses of precision due to clustering.

While the most common form of clustering is clustering by area, other forms may meet particular needs—for instance, a sample of nurses may be clustered within hospitals and a sample of visitors to an exhibition may be clustered by time of visit.

In postal surveys clustering is not needed to save travelling costs, but it may be necessary for sampling purposes. To save costs and time when a sampling frame has to be compiled, a sample of areas may be chosen as a first stage and the frame compiled only within the selected areas.

Excessive clustering must be avoided; there must be enough sampled clusters to allow for variation between people in different localities. But the sample selected in each cluster must be large enough to allow a reasonable workload for an interviewer. For national household surveys this would generally mean clusters of about 25 addresses in each selected cluster; a sample of, say, 1,250 addresses would thus involve 50 clusters.

Clustered designs of this type are examples of *multi-stage sampling*. In a two-stage sample the areas have first to be selected; these are termed *primary sampling units* (PSUs). Then within each area the individual elements have to be selected. It may, however, be necessary to achieve further clustering, for instance by drawing a sample of subareas within each selected area and then taking interviews only in the selected subareas; this would be a three-stage sample. Other stages can be added if necessary.

Sampling with probability proportionate to size

The technique of sampling with probability proportionate to size *(PPS)* is generally employed with multi-stage sampling. If in a two-stage sample—of districts and then of individuals—districts are selected with probability exactly proportionate to their survey populations, a constant number of individuals drawn from each district at the second stage will yield a sample that, overall, gives an equal chance of selection to every member of the population under study. An individual in a district with a large population has a greater than average chance that his district will be selected, but this is compensated for because his chance of being selected within the district will be proportionate to the reciprocal of its population. The PPS method has the advantage that all interviewers have assignments of the same size. If, instead, districts are selected with equal probabilities, a constant sampling fraction will be needed for sampling people within each district to ensure equal chances of selection. If the districts vary greatly in population, some interviewers will have a large number of interviews in their clusters, others only a few.

The extension of the PPS method beyond two stages of sampling can be achieved by selecting units with probability proportionate to size at every stage except the last. If the measures of size used are correct, and a fixed number of individuals is selected (with equal probability) at the final stage, overall every member of the population has an equal chance of selection. A three-stage PPS sample of electors could thus be designed as follows:

(i) selection of constituencies with probability proportionate to size of electorate;

(ii) selection of two wards within each constituency, with probability proportionate to size of electorate;

(iii) selection of individual electors with equal probability, taking the same number of electors from each selected ward.

The selection of the same number in each area at the final stage of a PPS selection gives an overall equal chance of selection only when the measures used for the PPS selections are the exact survey population sizes for the units or are a constant multiple of these sizes. To obtain a sample of teenagers, for example, by selecting constituencies with probability proportionate to the total electorate and then taking a fixed number of teenagers from each constituency would not give all teenagers the same chance of appearing in the sample. An appropriate procedure would be to sample constituencies with probability proportionate to numbers of teenagers. If these numbers are not known a suitable proxy (perhaps total electorate) has to be used. But the number of teenagers selected must then be allowed to vary between constituencies; if it remains fixed, overall selection probabilities will not be equal.

Systematic sampling can be used to select samples using PPS. The first-stage sampling units (PSUs) are listed with their population sizes cumulated. The sampling interval is calculated by dividing the total population by the number of PSUs to be selected. A random number (smaller than the sampling interval) is drawn: the first PSU selected is the one whose population interval includes the starting random number; subsequent PSUs are selected by successive additions of the sampling interval.

Suppose, for example, four areas are to be selected from the ten below, whose aggregated population is 104,000. The sampling interval will be $104,000 \div 4 = 26,000$. A random number—say 11,500—is then drawn. The first PSU selected will be B, since 11,500 is within B's interval of 9,001-12,000. The next PSU is selected by adding 26,000 to 11,500, and so on. Thus the selected PSUs are B, E, F and J.

	Population	Cumulated population
A	9,000	9,000
B	3,000	12,000
C	20,000	32,000
D	5,000	37,000
E	18,000	55,000
F	22,000	77,000
G	7,000	84,000
H	1,000	85,000
J	5,000	90,000
K	14,000	104,000
	104,000	

Sampling interval: 26,000

Random start: 11,500

Sampling error estimation

When simple random sampling is used, the estimation of sampling error for percentages or arithmetic means is not difficult. For a simple random sample of size n from a large population, the standard error of a sample percentage p is estimated by the well-known formula $\sqrt{pq/n}$, where $q = 100 - p$. For reasonably large samples the 95 per cent confidence interval for the population percentage is then given by $p \pm 1.96\sqrt{pq/n}$ or approximately $p \pm 2\sqrt{pq/n}$. The quantity $2\sqrt{pq/n}$ can be simply tabulated for various values of p and n, as illustrated in the upper half of the table on page 69. This table can then be used to read off, for instance, that the range of error for a sample value of 30.0 per cent based on a simple random sample of 2,000 is 2.0 per cent; in other words, the 95 per cent confidence interval for the population percentage is

30.0±2.0, or between 28.0 and 32.0 per cent. Detailed tables for the standard errors of percentages and of the differences between two percentages for simple random samples are provided by Stuart (1963).

In stratified, multi-stage sample designs, both stratification and clustering affect the sampling error, usually the first by reducing it and the second by increasing it. The latter effect is nearly always the more powerful, with the result that the sampling error is larger than that derived from the formulae for simple random sampling.

The estimation of sampling errors for stratified multi-stage designs is more complex than that for simple random samples. There are two major reasons for this. First, much lengthier computations are involved. Second, the sampling error of a percentage based on a multi-stage design depends not only on the magnitude of the percentage and the size of the sample, but also on how the variable in question is distributed among the clusters; the more patchily the variable is distributed the larger the sampling error. Since different variables have different distributions over the clusters, no single table of range of error applicable to any percentage can be produced. For these reasons, when multi-stage designs are used, estimates of sampling error are calculated at best for principal statistics only.

A common method for obtaining a rough estimate of the sampling error of a statistic for a multi-stage design is to calculate the sampling error according to the simple random sampling formula and to multiply the resulting figure by a correction factor. The appropriate correction factor is the ratio of the sampling error of the statistic for the multi-stage design to that for a simple random sample of the same size; this is called the *design effect (deff)*, when the ratio is one of variances, or $\sqrt{deff}$ when it is one of standard errors. The size of the design effect depends on the statistic under study and on the sample design. In a particular case the value chosen for *deff* or $\sqrt{deff}$ is determined by examining the computed design effects for similar statistics from similar sample designs. Sampling errors for multi-stage designs should not be computed by the simple random sampling formulae without account being taken of design effects.

The limited published evidence on design effects suggests that, for percentages based on the total sample and for the common national sample designs, most *deffs* lie between 1.0 and 2.5 (or $\sqrt{deffs}$ between 1.0 and 1.6), although much larger values have occurred. The lower half of the table on page 69 illustrates the effect of including a $\sqrt{deff}$ of 1.5. Whereas the 95 per cent confidence interval for the population percentage was calculated above as 28.0 to 32.0 per cent for the sample value of 30.0 per cent based on a simple random sample of 2,000, the corresponding interval for the multi-stage design is widened to 30.0±3.1, or between 26.9 and 33.1 per cent.

RANGE OF ERROR (±)*FOR 95% CONFIDENCE LEVEL

		Percentage found by survey				
		5% or 95%	10% or 90%	20% or 80%	30% or 70%	50%
Simple random sample						
Sample size:	100	4.4	6.0	8.0	9.2	10.0
	200	3.1	4.2	5.7	6.5	7.1
	500	1.9	2.7	3.6	4.1	4.5
	1,000	1.4	1.9	2.5	2.9	3.2
	2,000	1.0	1.3	1.8	2.0	2.2
	5,000	0.6	0.8	1.1	1.3	1.4
	10,000	0.4	0.6	0.8	0.9	1.0

Stratified multi-stage sample (assumes $\sqrt{deff}$ =1.5)

		5% or 95%	10% or 90%	20% or 80%	30% or 70%	50%
Sample size:	100	6.5	9.0	12.0	13.7	15.0
	200	4.6	6.4	8.5	9.7	10.6
	500	2.9	4.0	5.4	6.2	6.7
	1,000	2.1	2.9	3.8	4.4	4.7
	2,000	1.5	2.0	2.9	3.1	3.4
	5,000	0.9	1.3	1.7	2.0	2.1
	10,000	0.7	0.9	1.2	1.4	1.5

*Range of error is twice the standard error.

Achieving Population Coverage

At the beginning of the chapter we stressed that before the sample could be designed it was necessary to have a definition of the survey population. This definition could in the early stages be broad, but subsequently needed to be given precision as a first step towards evolving a satisfactory sample design. We pick up the thread again here, beginning at the point where a precise definition of the survey population has been agreed. Our first requirement is a suitable sampling frame.

Sampling frames

A sampling frame is (usually) a list of population elements from which a sample can be drawn, and if it is to fulfil its purpose satisfactorily it must meet a number of criteria. Few frames do in fact meet all of them; sometimes the deficiency can be remedied, sometimes not. A number of primary considerations must be taken into account.

First, is the frame composed of the same kind of population elements as the survey population? Or if it is not, are its elements capable of being translated into those of the survey population? As an example of the latter, consider the use of the electoral register as a frame for sampling households: it does not list households, but it does list addresses, which can be translated to households during fieldwork.

Second, is it complete? Are any members of the target population likely to be missing? If so, why, and how many? Are there any means of bringing the missing elements into the sampling process?

Third, are any elements listed more than once? If they are, their probabilities of inclusion in the sample will be correspondingly greater, introducing a bias. It is not sufficient to look for duplicates among those actually selected for the sample; the problem must be dealt with either at the outset by eliminating duplicate entries, or by re-weighting in the analysis.

Fourth, are there elements in the frame that do not belong, or no longer belong, to the survey population? Interviewers will make wasted calls on these: they are out-of-scope, or 'deadwood'. Provided they are not numerous, the wastage will not involve heavy costs, but if they comprise the majority of elements of the frame a major 'screening' exercise will be involved in eliminating them in the field—or, better, at the sample selection stage if this is possible.

Fifth, does the information given provide an adequate means of finding the sampled units, and is it up-to-date? If addresses are no longer current, for example, it may not be possible to trace people at all—or, if it is, it may be very expensive.

Sixth, is there information on the frame that could be used for stratification? And if there is, can it be effectively used? If it is on magnetic tape, with good access, stratification will be easy to undertake, but if it is in the form of, say, an index of cards to which access for re-sorting is limited, stratification may be, if not impossible, at any rate too expensive to be worthwhile. The physical form of the frame can exercise an important influence on the sampling procedure.

Seventh, if the survey is to be conducted by personal interview rather than by post, is there any means of selecting a clustered sample that will lend itself to an efficient allocation of interviewers? Like stratification, this depends a good deal on the physical form of the list, but it is a rather more important issue since the costs of unclustered interviews can be very high indeed and the design consequently inefficient when both precision and cost are considered together. One solution, if the frame is very large, is to select an unclustered sample much smaller than the frame but considerably larger than the eventual sample. This 'subframe' may be small enough to make a clustering operation manageable, though of course the resulting clusters will be much looser than would have resulted from clustering the entire frame.

If there is no extant frame, it is sometimes a practical proposition to construct one. For example, if no complete list of hospital nurses exists, a list of hospital management committees may be found (or compiled) which permits a sample of hospitals to be selected, contacted and asked to provide lists of nurses from their records. Or school leavers may be sampled by first sampling schools and utilizing their records.

Sometimes the frame exists, but in a piecemeal form. The best list of business and industrial establishments, for example, is the Employers' Register, held locally at nearly 900 Employment Offices. Utilizing this frame gives rise to additional practical and technical problems, involving a nationally distributed team of sample selectors. The rating lists are similarly dispersed over the country.

Non-response

It is rarely possible to obtain a response from all those selected for the sample. In a typical national household interview survey, the level of response is likely to be around 80 per cent, and non-response therefore around 20 per cent. Non-response can be a source of bias, since non-respondents may well differ in their characteristics from respondents, and it is essential to reduce it to a minimum. Increasing the sample size will compensate for the numerical loss, but will do nothing to remove any bias. Achieving high response levels is largely a matter of field training and procedures, though other factors, such as questionnaire design, play their part.

Non-response must be carefully distinguished from elements being out-of-scope (deadwood). Selected sample elements that turn out not to be, or no longer to be, members of the survey population are out-of-scope: they should not have been included in the sampling frame and, when found, can simply be deleted. Selected sample elements that prove to be in the survey population but do not yield any data are non-respondents; they should have yielded data and the fact that they have not done so opens the door to bias. Every survey report should contain a clear statement of the number selected, the number that proved to be out-of-scope and the number that responded. The base for calculating the response rate is the number of in-scope elements selected (not the total number initially selected). The analysis of response should also break down non-response into its various categories—refusals and failure to make contact usually being the most prominent.

As an example, the following pattern of non-response might be found from an interview survey with a sample of heads of household:

	Number	%
Issued sample:	2,000	
Empty premises	15	
Demolished premises	3	
Business premises (no		
household resident)	7	
In-scope addresses	1,975	
Number of households at these		
addresses	1,988	100
Not interviewed because:		
Known to be away temporarily	60	3
Out after at least four calls	119	6
Refused	178	9
Interview not possible		
(sick, too old, etc.)	58	3
Total non-response	415	21
Successful interviews	1,573	79

Given that there will usually be a not inconsiderable number of non-respondents even when field procedures are near-optimal, the researcher has to consider what, if anything, he can do about the possibility of bias. First he must consider what is known, or can be ascertained, about non-respondents, either directly or by inference based on a comparison of the achieved sample with information already available about the population. To obtain direct information about non-respondents he will normally have to make special arrangements, for example, sending a follow-up postal questionnaire to them, or having a field supervisor make a special call: but these methods are themselves likely to yield a low response. Rather more productive, but also limited in scope, is the recording by interviewers of observable facts such as type of house. This seems to be rarely done, but can be useful. In a survey of the environmental effects of road traffic, for example, it was found that the non-respondents tended to live on main roads and other busy streets, a bias relevant to the survey's subject-matter.

The sampling frame itself may provide useful data about non-respondents. The electoral register does not contain much information of this kind but some other frames do. One example is the rating list, which gives rateable value and some other housing data. Another is provided by vehicle registration lists, which give cubic capacity of engine and year of first registration. When sampling from such frames it is easy to use the data for comparing respondents and non-respondents, provided that the latter can be distinguished from out-of-scope elements.

But perhaps the most common method of assessing non-respondent characteristics is to compare known population characteristics with those of the achieved sample. If this, or any of the methods mentioned above, tells the researcher that non-respondents have different characteristics from respondents, what should he do? In general, it is desirable to *re-weight* the sample to bring it into line with the known population distribution. This will usually improve the survey estimates. Suppose, for instance, that the aim of a survey is to estimate the incidence of firms with personnel departments in a population of 1,000 firms, half of them small (with under 100 employees) and half large (with 100 or more). Of the 1,000 postal questionnaires despatched to the firms, 750 come back, 500 of them from large firms. The response rate is thus 100 per cent for large firms, and 50 per cent for small. Suppose also that in the survey population 80 per cent of large firms and 40 per cent of small firms (an aggregate of 60 per cent) have personnel departments. If these proportions are reflected in the replies received from small and large firms the survey will yield the following data:

	Large firms	Small firms	Total
Number of firms replying	500	250	750
Those with personnel departments	400	100	500
Percentage with personnel departments	80%	40%	67%

Adding the two sets of responses gives an unweighted total of replies from 750 firms, 500 of which have personnel departments. The estimate of the proportion with personnel departments would thus be 67 per cent, as compared with the true population figure of 60 per cent.

However, since we know that in the population as a whole small firms are as numerous as large, we might weight the second column by a factor of 2 before totalling. This would give a weighted total of 1,000 firms, of which 600 (60 per cent) have personnel departments—an estimate that corresponds to the population figure.

Weighting for differential non-response is often advantageous, as in this case, but there is no guarantee that it will always be so. If, for instance, 30 per cent of responding small firms and 50 per cent of non-responding small firms had personnel departments, the unweighted estimate of the incidence of personnel departments among all firms would have been 63 per cent, which is closer to the true population figure than the weighted estimate of 55 per cent would have been. The probable characteristics of the non-respondents should therefore be considered before weighting is employed.

General Population Samples

This section is mainly concerned with sampling from the electoral registers, the most widely used frame for sampling the general population in the United Kingdom, whether individuals or households are required. The less frequently used rating (valuation) lists are also discussed briefly.

As we have mentioned, samples of the general population are normally stratified multi-stage samples, whichever frame is used. Most designs have either two or three stages. In a three-stage design, the first stage is the selection of primary sampling units such as constituencies; the second is the selection of some smaller geographical areas such as wards or polling districts within each selected first-stage unit; the third is the selection of individual sampling units within each selected second-stage unit.

Sampling constituencies and wards

At present there 635 parliamentary constituencies in the United Kingdom: 552 in England and Wales, 71 in Scotland and 12 in Northern Ireland. Many surveys do not cover Northern Ireland, and the four constituencies north of the Caledonian canal are commonly excluded on practical grounds (interviews in these constituencies would be unduly expensive because the population is so widely scattered).

In samples of constituencies, it is customary to classify and organize the constituencies so that a stratified selection can be made. The first stratification factor is normally geographical region; the Registrar-General's standard regions (defined in Chapter 9) usually serve as strata, but if fewer geographical strata are required combinations of standard regions may be used. Once the constituencies have been sorted into regional strata, they are usually next stratified according to density of population: this may involve a twofold classification, for instance, separating constituencies in metropolitan counties from those in other counties. Finally, within the resulting strata, the constituencies are often listed in order of their percentage Labour vote at the last election, this measure being used as an index of a constituency's social class composition. Other variables based on Census data, such as those described in Chapter 9, may be used to create stratification indices. The systematic selection of a sample of constituencies from the ordered list then provides an implicit stratification.

If the constituencies were to be selected with equal probability, the frame would now be ready for sampling. However, as the population sizes of constituencies vary considerably, sampling with probability proportionate to size is appropriate. The size of a constituency is normally measured by the number of its electors. A sample of constituencies, selected with probability proportional to size, can be obtained by cumulating the numbers down the ordered list of constituencies and selecting a systematic sample as described earlier. There are two ways of making the selection: separate systematic samples can be drawn within each stratum formed by the combination of region and population density, or the strata can themselves be ordered (e.g. within region from high to low density, then the regions ordered from north to south), the cumulative totals carried forward from one stratum to the next, and one systematic sample taken throughout the list of constituencies.

Selecting individuals or households directly from selected constituencies would result in widely dispersed interviews and a great deal of travelling time for interviewers. An intermediate clustering stage is therefore normally introduced. The two main levels of subdivision of constituencies are wards and polling districts. Both wards and polling districts vary greatly in size; sometimes a ward comprises several polling districts, sometimes only one. Since wards are the larger units, their use produces a broader spread of interviews. For this reason, sampling at ward level is often to be preferred, but the choice of unit will depend on the individual case.

In view of their variability in electoral size, the wards within a selected constituency should be selected with probability proportionate to size (PPS). The number of electors in each ward of a constituency is readily determined from the electoral registers. Electors are normally numbered from 1 upwards in each polling district; the serial number of the last elector in the polling district thus indicates the size of the district, and the number of electors in a ward is the sum of the sizes of its polling districts. Sometimes, however, serial numbers run on from one polling district into the next one in the ward; the ward electorate is then indicated by the number against the last elector in the last polling district.

When the wards in a constituency have been listed and their electorates cumulated, the required number can be selected by the systematic PPS procedure already described.

Electoral registers
The electoral registers come into force on February 16 each year, and are current until the following February 15. They cover the whole of the United Kingdom. On the basis of information collected by electoral registration officers the previous autumn, they list electors according to the address at which they were living on October 10. By the time the registers come into use, about 3 per cent of electors will have moved, and, by the end of their life, the figure will have risen to about 12 per cent. But these national averages will vary considerably from one area to another.

The registers current from February 16, 1977, for instance, should include all British subjects who are of voting age (18 or over) on or before February 15, 1978. Commonwealth citizens and citizens of the Irish Republic who are resident in Britain are included. Other non-British residents are not entitled to vote and do not appear. But the proportion of people resident in the United Kingdom and of qualifying age who are not eligible to vote is very small.

A rather larger proportion is excluded by mistake or through misunderstandings about eligibility. In a study of the 1966-67 registers, Gray and Gee (1967) estimated that about 4 per cent of eligible persons had been omitted. Unfortunately, these omissions tend to be heavily concentrated in groups such as Commonwealth citizens and people about to reach voting age. The bias they introduce may thus be significant, depending on the subject of the survey. A small proportion of eligible people (Gray and Gee give a low estimate of 0.6 per cent) appears twice, probably because some people who move house on or near October 10 are counted at both addresses.

The registers are more nearly complete as frames of addresses than of individuals, since an address will be omitted only if all the persons resident there are excluded from the register. Premises first occupied after October 10 cannot be included; if inhabitants of new dwellings are important to a survey this omission may be serious.

Unpublished SCPR work in four London polling districts in 1972 showed that between 6 per cent and 17 per cent of addresses were missing. Some of the omissions—about two-thirds in the district with the greatest deficiency—were due to new building, but there were many other causes. The districts surveyed were considerably more likely than average to have omissions, but the figures indicate that in some areas the problem can be serious.

Electoral registers are divided into constituencies, wards and polling districts. Polling districts—the smallest units in the registers—are identified by reference letters. The heading includes the constituency, the name of the ward and a polling district identification letter.

Within urban polling districts, the registers are normally arranged by streets. Within streets, addresses are in order for each side of the street. The arrangement holds even if there are no address numbers. All electors at each address are listed: there is no rule about the order in which they appear. An illustration of the layout of the registers for urban polling districts is given below.

ELECTORAL REGISTER

(1)	(2)		(3)
	Names in full		
No.	*Surnames first*		*Residence*
	SOUTHERN AVENUE		
1670	Stephenson, Harriet E.		36
1671	Stephenson, Robert H.		36
1672	Ball, Anne L.	Flat 1,	38
1673	Ball, James F.	Flat 1,	38
1674	Jones, Judith A.	Flat 2,	38
1675	Palmer, John T.		40
1676	Palmer, Kevin T.		40
1677	Palmer, Martha		40
1678	Roberts, Lynne		40
1679	Moore, Beryl		42
1680	(14/8) Moore, Frederick		42
1681	Meadows, Nancy		44
1682	Hall, Leslie		46 (a)
1683	Morrison, Muriel		46 (b)
1684	Slater, David		1
1685	Slater, Edward		1
1686	Slater, Mary		1
1687	Hardy, Fanny A.		3
1688	Hardy, Archibald F.		3
1689	Rogers, Agnes C.		5
1690	Rogers, Barry W.		5
1691	Hetherington, Janice W.		7
1692	Hetherington, Hilda		7

Note   The (14/8) before the name of elector numbered 1680 is his birthday. He was 17 when the register came into force and became 18 on August 14 of that year.

Within rural polling districts, a frequent practice is to list all electors in alphabetical order.

Selecting a sample of households

Addresses are given on the electoral registers but there is no information about *households*. So where several households live at one address, the relevant register neither records the fact nor provides a satisfactory means of distinguishing between households; surnames are not a reliable guide. For this reason, the first step in the selection of a household sample is the selection of an address sample for conversion.

The number of electors recorded on the registers varies between addresses. If a sample of electors is selected with equal probability and their addresses listed, the list will over-represent addresses with more electors in direct proportion to their number. The balance can be restored by weighting, but it is better to eliminate the problem at the selection stage. For this purpose, each address has to be given the same chance of inclusion. The most usual method of doing this—often called *firsting*—is to sample at equal intervals down the electoral lists (e.g. every 15th named elector), accepting an address for inclusion *only* if the elector is the first listed at the address. This will ensure that an address containing five electors no longer has five times the chance of being selected as an address containing one elector, since there will be only one chance in five of hitting on the first named elector at that address. Each address will have the same chance of selection (that is the chance of their first named elector being chosen) no matter how many electors there are at an address.

The calculation of the sampling interval needs to take account of the fact that this process will often light on an elector listed second or third at the address and not result in a selection. To compute the sampling interval it is necessary to divide the required sample size into the electorate and then to divide the quotient by the mean number of electors per address (which averages about 2.2).

Wastage can also arise if addresses prove on inspection to be hospitals or other institutions. If the survey is to cover private residences only, the quotient should be divided by a figure rather larger than 2.2, since it is easier to reject a surplus randomly than to make up a deficiency. A divisor of 2.5 (3 in London) provides a safety margin that allows for institutions to be excluded and for the possibility that the district has an above-average ratio of electors to addresses.

In those rural areas where electors are listed alphabetically, people at the same address may not appear next to each other on the register. The sampler therefore has to search backwards through the listings he has passed to discover whether the elector on whom the sampling interval has lighted is the first listed at the address.

Marking off the sampling interval through the ward is made easier by the fact that electors are numbered. Carrying the sampling interval over from one polling district to the next within the same ward requires a simple adjustment. If the first polling district has an electorate of 1,175 and a sampling interval of 80 is being used from a starting point of 10, the last number selected in the polling district will be 1,130, i.e. 10 + (14 × 80), leaving 45. This figure is subtracted from 80, and the result, 35, indicates the first number to be selected in the second polling district: this is followed by 115, 195 and so on.

A sample of households can be obtained from a sample of

addresses by taking every household found at each selected address: the listing of households must be done by the interviewer. A household is usually defined as a group of people living together, sharing meals and domestic arrangements (*see* Chapter 9 for a fuller definition).

Interviewing many households at one address presents practical difficulties. An upper limit of three households is therefore usually set. The choice of households to interview, where more than three occupy one address, can be made randomly in the office, if interviewers return their lists. For most surveys, however, interviewers are asked to select on the spot by some rule of thumb, since the possibility that serious bias will be introduced into the sample from this source is not great. Over the country as a whole only about 2 per cent of addresses contain more than one household.

Selecting a sample of individuals

Various methods are used for selecting samples of individuals from the electoral registers. Not all of the five discussed below are recommended.

The most obvious procedure is to use the registers at face value as a frame of individuals. But this is unsatisfactory. Although the registers are reasonably complete as a frame of addresses, they are, as we have mentioned, deficient as a frame of individuals: those under 17 are excluded entirely, and an appreciable proportion of those aged 17 or over are omitted. Interviewers will also find that many of the selected individuals have moved away from the addresses at which they were registered.

A second and better method of obtaining a sample of individuals is first to follow the process already described to select households and then to take all individuals in the selected households. However, this procedure is usually undesirable on two grounds: the probable similarities in the behaviour and attitudes of members of the same household make it statistically inefficient, and the first interview may affect responses to the later interviews.

Third, one member of each selected household can be sampled at random, subsequently weighting the response by the number of eligible persons in the household (otherwise members of large households will be under-represented and members of small households over-represented in the sample). The main objection to this is that the weighting results in an appreciable loss of efficiency. Also, the interviewer has to start by listing all eligible persons in the household before selecting the person to be interviewed. However, well-trained interviewers cope perfectly well with this task (and with the even stiffer task of listing all eligible persons in an entire multi-household address).

A fourth method is a modified version of the third and reduces the amount of weighting required. It is probably the most efficient of all the options. Addresses are sampled by systematically selecting electors' names down the register without 'firsting'; as already noted, the chance of an address being included is proportionate to the number of electors registered for it. One person is then selected from those eligible persons who reside at the address. Since the number of eligible persons is closely related to the number of names on the register at the address, the weight to be applied (the number of those eligible divided by the number listed on the register) tends to be close to one. In principle the household could be used as the intermediate unit, but it is simpler to use the entire address in spite of the extra listing work that confronts interviewers at multi-household addresses.

A fifth method, often known as the elector/non-elector method, has been devised to make good the deficiencies of the register as a sampling frame of individuals. The register is used simultaneously as a frame of individuals to sample electors resident at their recorded addresses and as a frame of addresses for sampling all other required individuals defined according to the purpose of the survey.

The first step in this procedure is to draw a sample of electors' names from the registers, usually by systematic sampling. The address of each selected elector is noted, together with the names of other electors at his address. The interviewer has to find out whether the selected elector still lives at the address and, if so, to interview him. The interviewer is also required to list all people who are now resident at the address, other than those listed for it on the electoral register, provided that they are eligible for the survey. If a new household has moved in since the register was compiled, the interviewer will need to list all its eligible members. When a listing of these people—normally referred to as 'non-electors'—has been completed, one of them is randomly selected for interview. Thus a maximum of two interviews will be carried out at any one address.

Since the selection probabilities are unequal with this procedure, weighting is needed in the analysis. A non-elector's chance of inclusion in the sample is proportionate to the number of electors' names on the register at his address. On the other hand, since only one non-elector is chosen from a given address, his chance of inclusion is inversely proportional to the number of non-electors resident there. The weighting factor for a non-elector is therefore N/E, where N is the number of non-electors and E the number of electors' names on the register for the address. The other interviews, with persons who are named on the register and resident at their recorded addresses, have a weight of 1.

The attraction of this sampling method is that it yields a straightforward sample of the majority of the population—electors living at the addresses at which they are registered—while also providing a means of sampling the minority (movers and members of the survey population not listed on the registers). It also makes the interviewer's task a little easier, since the listing of non-electors often has to be done only after the interview has been conducted with the selected elector.

Its major disadvantage is that two interviews have to be conducted in some households. Another disadvantage, though one that is common to most of these methods, is the need for weighting in the analysis. Blyth and Marchant (1973) describe a variant that removes the need for weighting, but at the cost of needing to take more than two interviews in some households (Hedges, 1973).

The method customarily uses the household rather than the address as the intermediate unit. In principle, the address could equally well be used, with advantages that might well outweigh the disadvantages of extra listing before selecting a respondent. The same consideration applies to most of these methods.

Since institutions contain only a small proportion of the population, and are largely made up of old or sick people, many of whom cannot be interviewed anyway, it is often sensible to exclude them. If it is important that they are included, however, special steps need to be taken. With the elector/non-elector method of sampling, it may be desirable to select a second non-elector at random within the institution (or even a third or fourth) to prevent the non-electors' weight of N/E taking too high a value (the ratio of non-electors to electors will tend to be high, because only the permanent staff may be on the registers). If two non-electors are interviewed, the weight becomes N/2E, if three N/3E, and so on.

Selecting an individual from a household or address
Most of the above methods require the interviewer to list certain individuals in a household or at an address and to select one of them at random. To avoid the risk of interviewers biasing the sample, a clearly defined, objective method of selection is needed. The following widely-used procedure is based on Kish (1949).

When selecting addresses, each address is systematically assigned a number, from 1 to 12. When interviewers arrive, they list all eligible people at the selected household (or the complete address), males, then females, from the oldest down, and number them 1, 2, 3 and so on. All interviewers have a copy of the grid reproduced below. In selecting an individual within a household, the interviewers read along the row corresponding to the assigned number until they reach the column giving the total number of eligible people in

the household. The number at the intersection indicates the person
to interview. The table is designed so that in almost all instances the
numbers are distributed equally between the eligible household
members (e.g. in households with three eligible members, the first
member is associated with numbers 6, 7, 8 or 12, the second with
numbers 1, 2, 10, 11 and the third with numbers 3, 4, 5 or 9). If, as
has been assumed here, the selection of an individual is done within
the household rather than within the address as a whole, when there
are two or more households selected at an address, the address
number applies to each.

Assigned number of address	Total number of eligible persons					
	1	2	3	4	5	6 or more
1 or 2	1	1	2	2	3	3
3	1	2	3	3	3	5
4 or 5	1	2	3	4	5	6
6	1	1	1	1	2	2
7 or 8	1	1	1	1	1	1
9	1	2	3	4	5	5
10 or 11	1	2	2	3	4	4
12	1	1	1	2	2	2

Rating lists
An alternative sampling frame for selecting households is the rating
(valuation) list. Local authority rating lists are not held centrally, but
are kept separately by individual authorities. Some keep the lists in
book or card index form, and some have transferred them to a
computer file.

The rating lists are in three parts. Part I, the only relevant part for
most population surveys, includes everything other than industrial,
freight and transport premises—all private residences, shops, offices
and so on. Normally an address and a very brief description are
given, sometimes with the occupier's or owner's name.

The rating lists are more nearly complete than the electoral
registers. The extra information they offer can be useful for
stratification and occasionally provides a means of sampling certain
minorities—for example, dwellings with less than a certain rateable
value. They have major disadvantages, however, for sampling. First,
they can be consulted only with the local authority's permission.
Even where this is obtainable, sampling from them is decentralized,
expensive and not easy to control, unless the sample is limited to a
few local authority areas. Second, continual amendments are made
to the original list. The original order (usually by streets and

sometimes by wards) tends to be lost and the selection of an effectively clustered sample becomes very difficult. Other problems include the rapidity with which the list gets out of date, and difficulties in reliably identifying residential accommodation.

Sometimes, however, rating lists do provide a satisfactory sampling frame—for example, for surveys on topics closely related to housing and rateable value, and for surveys by local authorities in their own areas.

Samples of Minority Populations

A great many surveys are concerned not with the population as a whole, but with small groups within it. In principle, a sample of any small group can be achieved by sampling the general population and discarding those people who do not qualify for inclusion, but this can be a wasteful procedure.

Since the electoral registers contain only names and addresses of electors (and ages for those about to reach voting age), they are not a convenient sampling frame for most surveys concerned only with minority sections of the population. Nevertheless, there is often no alternative to embarking on a large field screening exercise at addresses selected from the register.

When screening interviews are needed to identify members of a special population it may sometimes be necessary to ask a series of questions before each person contacted can be classified as eligible or ineligible for interview; in other cases eligibility can be established very quickly. Sometimes any member of the household can tell the interviewer which members of the household possess the characteristic required; in other cases each person may need to be approached directly.

If the incidence of the group is not known, calculating the initial sample size needed to achieve the desired number of interviews may be impossible at the outset. In such cases, interviewing should be carried out in two phases. The first phase will give an estimate of the group's incidence that can be used to determine the final sample size. The larger the first phase, the more accurate this estimate. To achieve 1,000 interviews with a population group whose incidence is thought to be between 10 per cent and 30 per cent, an initial sample of 3,000 could be selected to produce between 300 and 900 interviews. If it produced 600, a second phase sample of 2,000 could be decided on, bringing the total to 5,000, since the incidence would now have been established as approximately 20 per cent. Non-response needs to be allowed for in calculating how many names need to be selected to achieve a desired number of interviews in a target group.

The smaller the group to be surveyed, the less efficient the electoral register will be as a frame. Where the target group is a small minority the use of the electoral register can be prohibitively expensive, and there are also possibilities of bias. Omissions from the frame, which are not of great importance when the entire population is being studied, can be serious when a small minority is being sampled, since they may include a substantial proportion of that minority. This is true, for example, of immigrant groups. Non-response bias is also a more worrying problem with small minorities, since the level of response from the minority will not be accurately known (where no contact is made, for example, it will not be known whether the sampled household belonged to the minority group or not, and such cases, though forming only a small proportion of the initial sample, could conceal an important part of the minority group).

Geographically concentrated minorities
Some very small groups, notably immigrant groups, tend to be concentrated in particular areas of the country and in particular districts. This fact has been utilized in designing samples of such groups. The first requirement is prior information about the number of members of the group, disaggregated to small area level. The only general source for data at such a level of disaggregation is the Census, and its smallest units, enumeration districts, which average perhaps 150 households each, are very suitable for the purpose.

Even when the Census small area statistics first become available they are beginning to be out of date. With the continuing passage of time the discrepancy between the Census and the current situation will grow, and careful consideration needs to be given to its effect on the sample design. If the situation has changed too much, other methods of sampling must be considered—though one of the attractions of the method described here is that it is difficult to find viable and economic alternatives to it.

The basis of the method is that if a sufficiently large proportion of the survey population is concentrated in sufficiently few districts, it may be justifiable to confine the survey to such districts, accepting the consequent bias that arises from giving members of the survey population resident elsewhere a zero probability of inclusion. Such a bias is clearly not desirable in itself, but it may be an acceptable price to pay for converting what might otherwise be an unviable survey into a manageable one.

Within enumeration districts, it may be desirable to construct a special sampling frame of addresses. The electoral register does not have divisions corresponding to enumeration districts, and is therefore not very convenient to use for this purpose. Additionally, immigrants are particularly likely to be living at addresses not represented on the electoral register. These two circumstances make it frequently preferable to begin by compiling a list of addresses within each district. This list is then screened in the field to identify members of the survey population who can either all be taken into the sample or subsampled as appropriate. A case history exemplifying this type of sampling approach is provided by Airey *et al.* (1976).

Sampling occupational groups

Particular occupational or professional groups are often the subject of surveys. The sampling scheme for such surveys must depend on the sampling frame available. The following two examples illustrate this point.

No satisfactory national list of nurses is available, so, for a large postal survey of nurses, the sampling was done through an intermediate unit, a list of hospital management committees. A sample of committees was selected with equal probability of inclusion and each selected committee was asked for a list of the nurses in all its hospitals. Because the committees had been selected with equal probability, nurses were selected proportionally from each list compiled. The clustering of the sample in this case was to achieve economies in the sampling process; without it, it would have been necessary to ask all hospital management committees in the country to supply lists.

For a survey among people who had graduated in social science in specified years (Westoby *et al.*, 1976) no up-to-date list of names and addresses existed. Universities and colleges were therefore selected randomly and lists of all their social science graduates and their last known addresses were obtained. Since some of the addresses were long out of date, a questionnaire and a list of fellow graduates of the same year were sent to each selected address. Respondents were asked to give details of any more recent addresses they had for any of the other people listed, so that the proportion successfully contacted could be increased.

Sampling continuous flows

An important class of sampling problems involves *time*. For example, if in a survey at a public library an interviewer questions every 10th person leaving, the sample will represent not people who visit public libraries, but visits to public libraries. Each visit has an equal chance of being included, but each person does not (his chance being proportionate to the frequency of his visits). If information about library visitors as well as about visits is required, therefore, the interviewer must ask each person how often he visits the library. The reciprocal of this frequency must then be used as a weighting factor.

Interviewing must be spread out—over, say, a week—to avoid the bias that would occur if the work were done only on a Friday afternoon. The period will depend on the subject: daily and weekly cycles must nearly always be allowed for, and coverage of two or three weeks is desirable to eliminate chance factors such as unusually bad or good weather. Sometimes seasonality is so marked that several different times of the year will have to be covered.

Time can be sampled, just as places and people can. Stratification by time of day and day of week is important, and the sampling fraction can be varied as required, for example to include an over-proportion of Saturdays, or of evenings. Time units need to be chosen to allow economic working by the interviewer. Segments involving one hour on and one hour off are usually uneconomic since the interviewer would probably need to be paid for the unusable hour off.

Time sampling can be varied from site to site to spread the coverage of the whole sample as widely as possible. As an example, suppose sampling is to be done at six libraries through one week. The period 9 a.m. to 6 p.m. is to be covered, and two interviewers will be working 6-hour shifts starting at 9 a.m. and 12 midday respectively. Each library is covered by one early shift (E) and one late shift (L), and there is an early and a late shift every day of the week.

Library:	Mon.	Tues.	Wed.	Thurs.	Fri.	Sat.
A	E			L		
B		E			L	
C			E			L
D	L			E		
E		L			E	
F			L			E

Since the shifts overlap, visits between 12 noon and 3 p.m. have twice the chance of inclusion, and therefore need to be given a weight of 0.5 in the analysis. Alternatively the shifts could be shortened so that they do not overlap. The scheme with the overlap would be preferable if shortening the shifts produced a neglible saving, or if the period from 12 noon to 3 p.m. was of particular interest.

A practical problem occurs in this sort of sampling when a building has more than one exit, since all people leaving need to be sampled, not just those who leave by one door. Moreover, at busy times, interviewers may lose count of people leaving while they are conducting an interview and, even if someone else is counting, interviews may be missed. It may be necessary at such times to approach, say, every 20th person instead of every 10th, and weight up to compensate.

Similar considerations apply in studies of exhibition and museum attendance, use of sports centres, shopping, car parking and so on.

Non-probability Sampling Methods

In the methods of selecting respondents described so far the assumption has been made that the research designer will employ a probability sample as the basis for the sample design. Even though interviewers may be required to carry out the final stages of sample selection, neither they nor the respondent should exercise any choice concerning the person to be interviewed.

Many market research surveys, however, use a non-probability method of sampling households or individuals at the final selection stage within the sampling areas, though the areas themselves are normally selected by probability methods.

The most commonly used non-probability method is quota sampling. Interviewers are supplied with 'quotas' or set specifications regarding the number of people of various kinds that they must interview. Provided that the specification is fulfilled, they are free to interview whom they wish within the designated area.

The idea behind quota sampling is that much of the variability in human behaviour is accounted for if the sample is made properly representative in respect of the 'quota' variables—usually sex, age and social class. It is argued that the quota controls, which are in effect a stratifying procedure, reduce variability and that any bias that may arise in the selection of individuals within the quota groups is unlikely to be serious, provided that the interviewer operates intelligently and with an understanding of what is required. But while quota sampling has undoubtedly often produced results that are satisfactory for particular purposes, and although it offers advantages of being cheaper in the field and easier to organize, the risk of bias of perhaps a major kind must make the user of quota sampling uneasy. For this reason, probability sampling is generally to be preferred.

Another form of non-probability sampling is known as the 'random walk' or 'random route' technique. In each specified district, a starting point is randomly chosen. From this point the interviewer follows a set route (first street on the right, first left, first right, and so on) calling at addresses at fixed intervals along it. Instructions are given to interviewers not only for the route itself but also for the selection of addresses. If random walk sampling is properly conducted (including recalls at addresses where no answer has been obtained at the first visit) it is almost as expensive as probability sampling. And unless the technique is scrupulously applied, insisting on recalls at addresses at which nobody is at home on earlier calls, the final sample is likely to be heavily biased towards those sections of the population more likely to be found at home during the daytime.

Other variants of quota and random route sampling methods exist but none can guarantee that every member of the population has an equal (or at least calculable) chance of being selected. None of these methods can therefore provide the security of a properly conducted probability sample.

Notes on Further Reading

1. There are numerous introductory textbooks on statistics containing chapters on sampling theory and the principles of statistical inference. At an elementary level Blalock (1972), Anderson and Zelditch (1975) and Mueller *et al.* (1970) are particularly recommended. Kalton (1966) provides a brief elementary account of the ideas of statistical inference.

2. The best full treatments of the practical aspects of survey sampling are Kish (1965), Hansen *et al.* (1953) and Yates (1960). The relevant chapters in Moser and Kalton (1971) and Raj (1972) are also useful. Slonim (1968) gives a simple account of types of sample design, and Stuart (1976) uses a small numerical example to illustrate the basic ideas of sample design non-mathematically. Barnett (1974) provides an elementary introduction to the statistical theory of survey sampling. Sudman (1976) discusses survey sampling procedures from a practical viewpoint.

3. Non-response is fully discussed in the textbooks by Kish (1965) and Moser and Kalton (1971). Daniel (1975) reviews the problem and methods of handling it. The problem, and in particular the question of whether non-response has been increasing in recent years, has been examined by a Working Party of the Market Research Society's Research and Development Committee and its report (Market Research Society Working Party 1976), is worth consulting.

4. Evidence on design effects for stratified multi-stage sample designs is provided by Kish (1957, 1965), Corlett (1963, 1965), Kemsley (1966), Kalton and Blunden (1973), Kalton and Lewis (1975), and Kish *et al.* (1976).

5. A valuable paper on sampling from the electoral registers is by Sheila Gray (1970). The report by Gray and Gee (1967) on the completeness of the registers, and the paper by Blunden (1966) are also worth consulting, but it should be noted that certain changes have taken place in the registers since these articles were written. Moser and Kalton (1971) and Pickett (1974) discuss the use of the registers as a sampling frame.

6. The problem of sampling rare populations is discussed by Kish

(1965), Hedges (1972), Miles (1970), Marchant (1970), Krausz (1969), Sudman (1972), and Ericksen (1976).

7. The literature on quota and other non-probability sampling methods is very limited. Moser and Kalton (1971) and Stephen and McCarthy (1958) contain discussions of quota sampling. There are also articles by Moser (1952), Moser and Stuart (1953), Stuart (1968), Sudman (1966), and Clunies-Ross (1967).

Chapter 5. Interviewing

Principal contributor: Douglas Wood

In a small-scale survey a researcher may decide to carry out his own interviews. He knows better than anyone else the purpose of his questions, and may be better able than anyone else to resolve queries that arise during the interview. To this extent, he may well get more out of the interviews by doing them himself than by entrusting them to someone else.

But a good researcher may not have the skills of a good interviewer. His greater understanding of the project and its aims may be more than offset by his shortcomings in conducting an interview. He may be unable to create a relaxed atmosphere that encourages respondents to talk freely or may find it difficult to maintain an unbiased attitude in asking the questions and recording the answers. In any case, the scale of most survey projects takes them far beyond the scope of the researcher acting as interviewer.

Usually a team of trained interviewers needs to be used to carry out fieldwork. The success of the interviewing will depend as much on the performance of this team as on the design of the questionnaire. In part, their performance will depend on the organization and monitoring of fieldwork and on the researcher's success in engaging their enthusiasm and co-operation (points covered in Chapter 6). Ultimately, however, it depends on the way they set about their task. This chapter discusses how interviewers should prepare for their task and what problems they are likely to meet in dealing with respondents. In the discussion we have assumed that the interviews will be conducted with a sample of members of the public in their homes, using a structured questionnaire. But the guidelines set out here have a fairly general application.

What follows is not intended as a detailed manual on how interviewers should be trained. It is, rather, a listing of points over which problems often arise, and an account of some common solutions to these problems.

Before turning to detailed aspects of the interviewer's work, two general points need to be stressed. The first is that the interviewer is the main contact between the researcher and the public. Respondents' reactions to research will be affected by the way they are approached by interviewers and by the way interviews are carried out. The point is clearly made in the Interviewers' Manual of the University of Michigan's Survey Research Center:

> . . . respondents usually react more to their relationships with the interviewer than to the content of the questions they are asked. . . . (They) may remember more about the interviewer and about how the interview was conducted than . . . about the topics covered. Survey Research Center (1969)

Interviewers spend their days approaching strangers, asking them for answers to questions in which they may have no special interest, for a purpose they may find obscure on behalf of an organization they may not have heard of. How the interviewer does this is critical to obtaining respondents' co-operation in particular projects and to public acceptance of survey research in general.

The second general point is that interviewing, even with a structured questionnaire, is not a wholly automatic role. Interviewers have to ask questions exactly as they appear on the questionnaire, to remember complex definitions and to record answers accurately. This is not all, however. They also have to know when to add explanations, how to probe responses and how to deal with difficult or unexpected queries. Merely following the researcher's instructions, no matter how careful these are, will not equip them to deal with all the problems that will arise. For this the researcher has to depend on the interviewer's judgement, common sense, training and experience. A good questionnaire limits the degree to which interviewers need to exercise discretion, but it does not lessen the importance of their role in the interview.

Preparatory Work

The first two stages of preparation for an interview, the design of the questionnaire and the briefing of interviewers by the research team, are described in detail in Chapter 3 and Chapter 6. Here we are concerned more with the third stage, which involves the interviewer alone.

At a pre-fieldwork briefing the researcher can explain the purpose of the survey, describe the survey method and introduce the questionnaire. The written project instructions can be outlined and some practice with the questionnaire can be given around the briefing table. But the interviewer needs time to absorb this information and to become familiar with the project; revision and rehearsal—possibly on friends or relatives—is always advisable. In particular, the sampling instructions, filter instructions in the questionnaire and special definitions have to be mastered. Any faltering over these during an interview will almost certainly upset the relationship with the respondent.

Route and call planning

An important aspect of the interviewer's preparatory work is planning the interview programme to make the best use of time. The allocation of sampled addresses to interviewers by field control staff will have been designed to reduce costs and take advantage of the resources available. But maximum efficiency will be achieved only if each interviewer plans the work at a more local level. Starting at the first address on the sample issue sheet and working through the list will seldom be the most economical way of carrying out an assignment. Lists of addresses on sample issue sheets usually follow the order of addresses on the sampling frames from which they are drawn, and there is no reason to expect that this order will constitute a logical interviewing route. The interviewer has to plan the order of calls on a map of the area to minimize travelling. Ideally second and subsequent calls should be phased in with first calls at other addresses to limit the need for special trips. The interviewer's plan ought also to allow for all addresses to be visited during the first half of the fieldwork assignment period. Otherwise there may not be enough time for further calls at the end. Efficient route planning of this kind assumes particular importance for projects in which interviews in different locations have to be controlled by week or by day of week.

In working out the programme, the interviewer can save time by choosing the time of day of first calls according to the sorts of people to be interviewed. The aim is to contact the appropriate person for interview at the first call as often as possible. Where first names can be used to identify sex, for instance, it is likely to be more efficient to leave men for evening or weekend calls. Similarly, if the survey is restricted to employed persons, evening or weekend first calls are advisable. For a survey among old age pensioners, however, first calls can be spread over the day.

Locating addresses

The interviewer has to locate sampled addresses and find out whether they are occupied. This is usually a simple matter, but each assignment will raise some problems. For example, the address on the list from which the sample was drawn may be incomplete or inaccurate; the list may be an old one and some houses on it may have been demolished; there may have been a clerical error when addresses were copied out. Addresses may be correct but still difficult to find—perhaps because they are new addresses in streets not shown on the interviewer's map. Even established addresses may be difficult to trace on a map, particularly in rural areas.

Difficulties over addresses can often be resolved with help from local residents, roundsmen or shopkeepers, particularly postmen and newsagents, and reference to the field office should sort out clerical listing errors. If the address still cannot be located, help should be sought from the local police station and council offices before it is abandoned as impossible to contact.

Interviewers will come across addresses that are unoccupied. But they have to take care not to classify an address in this way without confirmation, perhaps from a neighbour. Otherwise some occupied addresses will be classified as empty, thus excluding them from the percentage base used to calculate the response rate and hiding what is in reality a form of non-response.

Neighbours of potential respondents can often be helpful to interviewers, but there are two risks to guard against. The first is that the neighbour may pass on a garbled version of the purpose of the interviewer's visit. The interviewer needs, therefore, to keep any explanation to neighbours to a minimum and should never ask neighbours to fix appointments or to pass on messages. A second danger is that potential respondents may feel that information about them is being sought surreptitiously from neighbours, and be justifiably annoyed or alarmed. Obviously interviewers should never seek personal details about a household or its members from neighbours.

If an address looks occupied but no contact can be made with the occupants at the initial call, the interviewer's subsequent visits are likely to prove more successful if they occur on a different day of the week and at a different time of the day. It is common practice for at least four suitably spaced calls to be made, including calls on weekday evenings and at the weekend, before a household is abandoned as impossible to contact. If the interviewer is able to make more than four calls without deviating too far from the planned route this is likely to increase response still further at minimal additional cost. Chapter 6 also discusses ways in which addresses abandoned at the first phase of interviewing after four or more calls can be successfully reissued at a later stage in the fieldwork period.

Giving advance notification

For some surveys and in some areas, it may be useful to notify potential respondents in advance that the survey is taking place and that they have been selected for interview. The practice may, for example, be helpful in urban areas where unannounced callers may be distrusted or kept at bay with remote control door locks and entry-phones.

The drawback of sending a letter in advance is that a letter is seldom as good as a personal visit at persuading people to take part. By the time the interviewer calls, the advance warning may already have generated a refusal that the personal contact cannot reverse. As a rule, overall response is unlikely to be much aided by sending letters in advance; it may be hampered by it.

For most surveys, the case against contacting people by telephone before a survey is even stronger than that against contacting them by letter. Refusing to co-operate with an impersonal voice over the telephone is far easier than refusing someone face to face. And if a refusal has been given on the telephone, the interviewer cannot call at the house. If the potential respondent has been written to instead, the interviewer can still make a personal call. In a survey of businessmen or professional people at their offices, however, these factors do not apply. Secretaries or receptionists tend to bar unannounced visitors, and the telephone may be the best method of attempting to make an appointment for an interview.

Notifying the local police station in advance that the survey is taking place is also part of the interviewer's preparatory work. Contact with the police should be made formally with details of the call registered in the day book. It is also useful if the police are told the registration number of the interviewer's car. Some respondents, particularly the elderly and those living alone, will be reassured by being told that the police know of the survey.

Setting up the Interview
After the preparatory work the interviewer's next task is to identify the person to be interviewed and persuade him (or her) to give the interview. Sometimes the first person contacted at the sampled address will be the one to be interviewed. If, however, the person to be interviewed is not at home, he may be influenced by what the first person contacted says about the interviewer. So the general points made here about the approach and introduction to an interview apply both to the first contact and to the potential respondent.

The approach and introduction
Despite the very large number of surveys carried out nowadays, being approached by an interviewer is still an unfamiliar experience to most people. Their first impressions of the interviewer, which will usually be based on appearance and manner, will be very important.

The interviewer's manner has to put people at ease; it must also convey confidence and competence. If the interviewer seems hesitant about seeking an interview, the potential respondent may well be hesitant about granting one. It has to be assumed that co-operation will be granted, since the opposite expectation will tend to be self-fulfilling.

Ideally, interviewers should be fairly neutral (and certainly unexceptionable) in general appearance, style of clothing, accent and so on. If the respondent feels conscious of a considerable social distance between him and the interviewer he may refuse to co-operate or fail to give full and accurate details of behaviour and attitudes, thus biasing the results.

At the start, interviewers need to explain who they are, why they are there and give the name of the organization conducting the survey. Otherwise they run the risk of being mistaken for door-to-door salesmen, official inspectors of some kind, or possibly burglars. It is best for the interviewers to introduce themselves in their own words, so long as they cover all the necessary points. A set introduction often sounds like a recitation and has a peculiarly impersonal effect. An identity card with a photograph, of the kind described in Chapter 6, is also useful.

If a first contact at an address turns out to be with a visitor to the house, or with a minor, he or she cannot reasonably be expected to disclose details about the people at that address; the interviewer will need to ask for an adult resident at the address. However, interviewers can always check with whomever they are talking to that they are at the right address. Unless they establish that fact at the start they can waste a lot of their own and other people's time.

Getting beyond the first contact

In many surveys the first contact has to be used by the interviewer to identify whom to interview. The sample selection process may require the interviewer to list all eligible occupants of the address, or eligible members of a household at the address (as in the Kish selection procedure described in Chapter 4) before one is selected for interview. Or the person may be chosen on the basis of pre-determined rules: he or she may, for example, fill a particular role in a household (most commonly the head of household or the housewife), or meet certain screening criteria (for example, unemployed and seeking work, on a pension).

The person first contacted will sometimes refuse an interview on behalf of the potential respondent perhaps with the aim of protecting an elderly, handicapped or very busy member of the household. Such protection is sometimes justified, but people are often overprotective of others, many of whom welcome the diversion of an interview and the chance to have their say. If the interviewer is faced with a protective refusal, some attempt can usually be made to talk to the selected respondent so that he can choose for himself.

Similarly, the person first contacted may offer to make an appointment on behalf of the selected person or to seek his co-operation on behalf of the interviewer. Accepting these offers is usually unwise because intermediaries between interviewers and respondents often impede rather than enhance good communication. Many people object to arrangements being made on their behalf.

Gaining co-operation

Occasionally, particularly with government or local authority sponsored surveys, an interviewer will come across people who believe that they are legally obliged to give information. This mis-apprehension should always be corrected. Seeking information from members of the public by implying that they have to participate is operating under false pretences.

A key part of the interviewer's task is, however, to obtain the co-operation of as many of those in the sample as possible. In practice, most people are happy to co-operate and only a small minority will always refuse.

More numerous and thus more important are people who decide whether or not to co-operate on the basis of how and when they are approached. One of the public's most common worries is whether the interviewer is genuine. The interviewer's identity card will have been issued by an organization about which the potential respondent probably knows nothing. Interviewers must therefore be prepared, if necessary, to give details of that organization. They will also often have to cope, from background knowledge and experience, with more general doubts about survey research itself.

Respondents may, justifiably, want reassurance on certain points before they agree to take part. Some feel that surveys are an intrusion and that their privacy is endangered; the interviewer then has to justify the intrusion on the grounds that the aim of the survey is worthwhile and explain that answers are confidential and will never be linked to named respondents. These points can also be dealt with in an explanatory letter that is best left with respondents to reinforce and amplify the oral explanations.

Interviewers may be called upon by respondents to give an account of the sampling method: how they came to be selected for interview, why substitution is not possible, how bias can arise from non-response, and so on. This need involve no more than a brief description of the source of the sample, usually the electoral register, and the technique, usually random selection.

Respondents may also query the purpose of the survey. Inter-viewers should, therefore, be able to talk sensibly about this, although avoiding saying anything that could prejudice the respondent's replies. If the interviewer appears ignorant of or uninterested in the aims of the survey, the respondent is likely to react negatively.

During the interview, interviewers may be asked why a particular question has been included. They need to be familiar enough with the research objectives to give an adequate explanation; the researcher's briefing and instructions must ensure this. If the purpose of each question is self-evident or can be convincingly explained, the interviewer will usually get straightforward, unembarrassed answers. If the researcher cannot explain the purpose of a question, the question should probably not have been asked.

People who say that they are too busy to be interviewed may be politely hiding their real reasons for refusal. Interviewers have to use their own judgement on whether to press for an interview there and then (and risk a refusal) or arrange to come back later. If at all possible, an outright refusal should be avoided, leaving interviewers the opportunity for a more successful contact later. Although in practice most respondents do not wish to stop in the middle once the interview has started, it will sometimes be obvious that an interview should not be started with a respondent who is very busy at the initial call; instead an appointment should be made, preferably a definite appointment rather than some vague time. If a busy person asks how long the interview will take, nothing is to be gained by deceiving him.

Occasionally, by chance, an interviewer may have a run of refusals. This can lower morale and prevent a confident approach to new addresses. Refusals may then snowball so it may be best for the interviewer to stop work for a time (at least in that area); otherwise low morale may lead to poor response, carelessness or, occasionally, the temptation to cheat.

Setting the scene
Some surveys require interviews at the roadside or outside shops. In such locations the interview must obviously be short. Similarly, only the briefest of interviews can be carried out successfully on the doorstep. If interviewers are not invited inside early on, an explanation of the need to write down answers (more easily done inside) is usually sufficient to gain entry.

A number of minor points can influence the success of an interview. Most important, interviewers should have all their materials to hand and have them organized so that they can refer to them easily. Interviewers should try to sit facing respondents, but not so near that respondents can start reading the questions instead of listening to them. They should make sure that respondents are comfortable and have their reading glasses, where appropriate, that there is enough light for them to read show cards, and that they are both far enough away from the radio or television to hear each other clearly.

The presence of a third person in the room cannot always be avoided, but the interviewer can suggest that a corner of the room will be quieter, more private and more convenient for the interview. Third persons who interrupt with their own opinions need to be dealt with politely but firmly. This can often be done by suggesting that they give their views afterwards, then concentrating on the respondent with no more than a casual glance at the interrupter. If this fails the interviewer will need to explain why it is important that only the attitudes and behaviour of selected respondents should be obtained.

If the respondent's command of English is poor, it is sometimes possible to find another member of the household who will act as interpreter. But the interviewer must be confident that the respondent's views are obtained, not the interpreter's. In such cases, it is important for the interviewer to note on the front of the questionnaire that the interview has been conducted through an interpreter.

The Interview

Interviewers are trained for their role in an interview. Respondents are not. They need assistance and reassurance in the unfamiliar task they have been asked to perform.

The respondent has to realize that he is taking part neither in an oral examination, nor in an ordinary conversation; if he thinks he is being tested, he may worry that he may give a 'wrong' answer or that he is unqualified to answer certain questions; if he thinks the interview is a friendly chat, he may stray from the subject or try to answer the wrong questions.

Interviewers have to maintain a detached attitude, but ensure that the interview is relaxed and friendly. It is helpful if the interviewer looks at the respondent often, especially just after asking a question, to pick up and deal with signs of worry and bewilderment immediately and to take simple steps to promote informality and co-operation. Too little eye contact may make the interviewer appear uninterested and withdrawn; too much, however, can be embarrassing for the respondent.

Playing a constructive role

The respondent's interest and good will has to be maintained throughout an interview. The interviewer has to ensure, for example, that the pace of the interview suits the respondent. Some people answer quickly and want to get on with the interview as fast as possible. Others need more time to think; the respondent is, after all, hearing the questions for the first time and may be considering ideas that have not occurred to him before.

Whereas in introducing themselves and gaining respondents' co-operation interviewers are generally encouraged to use their own words, in asking the questions they must always use the precise words printed on the questionnaire. Even apparently trivial changes in wording can affect the respondent's perceptions of what is being asked and thus affect his answers.

If a respondent seems to have misunderstood or misinterpreted a question the first time he hears it, it should be repeated slowly. The interviewer should not try to explain it in different words, as these might prejudice the reply. If the respondent asks the interviewer what the question means, the interviewer should first try to find out what the respondent thinks it means. If he is right, the interviewer can then tell him so; if he is wrong, he should be guided towards the correct meaning with no deviation from the original wording.

It is often difficult to keep respondents to the point. If a respondent starts to answer one question by giving information that is asked for in a later question, the interviewer will need to stop him with the explanation that the point occurs later. Even if the respondent appears to be giving a full answer to the later question it is best not to make a forward recording. The subsequent question wording may affect the reply, or an intervening question may remind the respondent of another aspect of the subject. Although the sequence should not be altered, intervening phrases such as 'I'd just like to check,' can be inserted when a question is reached that a respondent has attempted to answer earlier. If a respondent wishes to go back to a previous question to change or add to his answer, the interviewer cannot easily refuse. But for consistency, interviewers should be instructed to make a note beside the appropriate question on the questionnaire rather than change the original coding.

Interviewers can and will add informality to the interview by adding link phrases and comments of their own. But it is important that these phrases and comments have no bearing on the answers given and thus cannot bias the results. This should be stressed to interviewers in their basic training.

Avoiding bias
Respondents' answers can be distorted by faulty memory, embarrassment about sensitive subjects, a tendency to exaggerate where self-esteem is involved or to be evasive where self-criticism is involved. These problems have to be tackled through careful

questionnaire design and piloting. Interviewers cannot wholly counteract biases of this kind.

Respondents' answers can, however, also be distorted by the personal characteristics of the interviewers or by the way they conduct the interview. A number of studies have shown how different interviewers can elicit different replies to the same set of questions from randomly chosen groups of respondents. Interviewers must do everything they can to avoid, or at least minimize, this sort of bias.

In normal conversation, people often bias what they tell another person towards what they think he or she wants or expects to hear. Such responses do much to smooth ordinary social relationships, but have great dangers in an interview. While it is necessary for interviewers to establish an easy, pleasant relationship with respondents, they have to avoid giving them clues about their own attitudes or expectations, or saying anything about their own background, at least until after the interview. They will often be asked about their family or where they live. But the interviewer's answers to even such simple questions as these may lead the respondent to change or modify his answers.

Asked their views on unfamiliar subjects, respondents often reply by asking interviewers what they think. The danger is obvious; in practice interviewers have to find ways of avoiding direct replies and encouraging the respondent to talk instead about himself and his own ideas.

Interviewers must be sure to ask all questions in a neutral, straightforward way and accept the answers in the same manner. A note of surprise or of disbelief or an oversympathetic reaction may easily affect the respondent's subsequent answers. Consistently showing no reaction other than a uniform, polite interest calls for continuous effort. Even apparently trivial reactions can affect answers. For example, following a respondent's reply with the word 'good' can introduce bias in subsequent answers.

Interviewers are sometimes faced with flippancy or facetiousness on the part of respondents. Although it arises only rarely, the best defence is for interviewers to show they are aware of it, usually by breaking off the interview to emphasize the importance of the survey and of the respondent's role in it. Faced by someone who clearly takes interviewing and survey research seriously, only the most determined respondent will persevere with his flippancy.

More often, interviewers are faced with apparent inconsistencies in responses. These can arise because the respondent has misunderstood the question, or because the interviewer has misunderstood the answer, or because the respondent has not expressed himself clearly. If the interviewer notices an outright contradiction in the respondent's answers on a matter of fact, he or she ought tactfully to draw the respondent's attention to it. If, however, the contradiction is in the respondent's views or attitudes, it can remain. Many people genuinely hold views that are contradictory.

Probing

A key interviewing skill is probing: encouraging the respondent to give an answer, or to clarify or amplify an answer. Probing may be non-verbal or verbal. An expectant glance at the respondent or a muttered 'mm' is a probe; so is a direct request such as 'Please tell me more about that', or 'What other reasons?' Probing should always be neutral, as opposed to prompting, which involves suggesting an answer to a respondent. Many questions are designed with specific prompts; this is a matter for the questionnaire designer, and interviewers ought never to prompt on their own initiative.

Several types of probes can be useful for precoded questions. Suppose the interviewer asks, for example, 'How satisfied are you with your present home? Would you say you are very satisfied, fairly satisfied, not very satisfied or not at all satisfied?' the answer may be 'I couldn't really say.' This answer does not usually mean that the respondent has no views but that he is hesitating between the categories offered. In such cases, the interviewer can probe with some such phrase as 'Which comes closest to your views?' and repeat the question. If the answer still does not fit a precode (e.g. 'I suppose it's all right') the interviewer will need to repeat the relevant precodes ('Would you say you are very satisfied, fairly satisfied . . .?' etc.).

Probing is particularly important with open-ended questions, when the respondent is asked to express his views in his own words, and the interviewer has to record them in full. To get the respondent to expand his answer, the interviewer may use whichever of the following probes seems most appropriate; for some questions several may be needed:

an expectant glance
'uh-huh', 'mm', or 'yes' followed by an expectant silence
'What else?'
'What other reasons?'
'Please tell me more about that.'
'I'm interested in *all* your reasons.'

Respondents often use ambiguous words such as 'important' in their answers, or make vague references: 'It is because of my health/my age/the state of the country.' The interviewer needs to seek clarification with probes such as:

'Exactly why do you think this is important?'
'How do you mean it's because of your age?'
'I don't quite understand what you mean by *important*.'
'In what ways does it affect your health?'

Whatever probes are used, the interviewer's task is clear: to draw out all relevant responses from respondents; to ensure that inarticulate or shy respondents have as much chance to give their opinions as articulate or talkative ones; to be neutral, interested and persuasive. Probing is an aspect of interviewing that requires great skill. If carried out poorly it can lead either to loss of information or to the collection of biased information. The skills of probing therefore feature prominently in interviewer training, but it requires experience in the field to refine and develop them.

Recording the answers
Small practical details, such as using the most suitable pen, can assume considerable importance in a large survey employing many interviewers. Writing with a fountain pen, for example, is unsuitable because it smudges in the rain; writing in pencil is better, but it can fade; ballpoint pens are probably best. Colour can be important too. Since the completed questionnaire will be written on later by editors and coders, it is useful to be able to distinguish who wrote what (e.g. blue for interviewers, red for editors). In case they make mistakes in recording the answers to precoded questions, interviewers also need a standard method for cancelling a mistake. Two diagonal lines across the ringed code are preferable to a cross which might be mispunched later as an X code.

Interviewers should record something beside every question they ask. If the answer is 'don't know', 'don't remember' or 'none', this should be coded or written in. Otherwise, the coder and the researcher will be unable to distinguish between questions that have received such answers and questions that the interviewer has forgotten to ask.

Interviewers should indicate where they have used verbal probes. A widely used convention is to write (P) at the relevant point. If the interviewer feels that the precise wording used in probing is necessary to the understanding of what follows, this can be recorded in full, in brackets.

Interviewers should record the answers during the interview as they are given. Trying to remember answers and fill them in later always leads to inaccuracy. Answers to open-ended questions should be recorded in full in the respondent's own words, not summarized or paraphrased. Just as a change in the wording of a question can distort its meaning for the respondent, a summary or paraphrase can distort the meaning of the answer for the coder or researcher.

The only parts of the respondent's answer that can be left out by the interviewer, without risk of distortion, are 'ums', 'ers' and 'you knows', straight repetitions and irrelevant asides.

Accurate verbatim recording of answers is not easy and takes considerable practice. If a respondent speaks very fast the interviewer may have to slow him down, usually by saying 'uh-huh' or 'yes', or by repeating his words aloud at writing speed. When the respondent sees the interviewer trying to take down what he says word for word, he will usually slow down without being asked.

It might seem helpful for the interviewer to abbreviate the respondent's words—for example, 'hsg.' for housing in order to speed up the recording and produce a smoother flow of questioning. However, this can all too easily lead to editing and embellishment by the interviewer when writing up the answer later. Asking the interviewer to write all words out in full and in pen at the time they are spoken is considerably safer.

If the interview presents special difficulties (for example, if the respondent is blind or hard of hearing and the usual method of questioning has to be changed) or if details of the respondent or his household not recorded elsewhere might throw light on his answers, it is helpful for the interviewer to note this at the end of the questionnaire.

Occasionally interviewers are asked by respondents if they may retain a copy of the questionnaire or be sent the survey results. In such cases, it is usually best for the interviewers to put the respondent in direct touch with the researcher who can be more informative and helpful, rather than to attempt to deal with these requests themselves.

Before leaving, interviewers need to check quickly through the questionnaire to make sure that all relevant questions have been asked and the answers correctly recorded. If there was an explanatory letter to be left with respondents they should check that the respondent has it. Finally, respondents should be given a last chance to ask questions and left feeling that their co-operation has been appreciated and that the interview has been worthwhile.

Note on Further Reading
1. Most survey organizations have their own interviewers' manuals, and these give a good guide to the interviewer's task. Among the published manuals are those of the Social Survey Division of the Office of Population Censuses and Surveys (Atkinson, 1968), of the Survey Research Center, University of Michigan (1969), and of the Market Research Society (1974).
2. The books on interviewing by Kahn and Cannell (1957), Richardson *et al.* (1965), Gorden (1975) and MacFarlane Smith

(1972) are all worth consulting. The chapter by Cannell and Kahn in Lindzey and Aronson (1968, Vol. 2) is also recommended. The book by Converse and Schuman (1974) provides interesting insights into survey interviewing: it is based on interviewers' reflections on the interviewing process.

3. There is a sizeable literature on the effects of interviewers on survey results. A classic book in this area is that by Hyman *et al.* (1954), and a recent book by Sudman and Bradburn (1974) reviews the literature. Kish (1962) reports two experiments on variability between interviewers, and reviews three earlier studies. Cannell *et al.* (1968) examine the effects of interviewer and respondent psychological and behavioural variables on reporting health information. A study by Schuman and Converse (1971) compares the results obtained by black and white interviewers in a survey of black respondents in Detroit, and a similar study by Hatchett and Schuman (1975) compares the results for white respondents. Experimental work by Durbin and Stuart (1951) compares the response rates, and Booker and David (1952) compare the results, obtained by experienced and inexperienced interviewers.

Chapter 6. Organizing Fieldwork

Principal contributor: Colin Airey

In some ways, deploying a large interviewing team on a survey involves skills and procedures common to the deployment of any large labour force. It involves training, personnel work, administration, supervision and co-ordination. There are, however, some features of recruitment and fieldwork control that distinguish it from most other forms of person management.

First, interviewers are required to achieve a high standard, working on their own without the aid of continuous supervision or close day-to-day contact with colleagues. Second, the task they perform is not routine: interviewers often have to use a great deal of initiative and effort, for example in searching for obscure addresses, securing appointments and co-operation from reluctant respondents and administering complex questionnaires. Third, although many established professional survey organizations have teams of interviewers to work on national surveys, additional interviewers are often needed to supplement the national fieldforce for large regional surveys. In some instances, large interviewing teams have to be specially recruited from an unskilled pool of applicants to work, say, in one area for a period of two to three months. Within a short time that unskilled labour force has to be capable of achieving high interviewing standards.

For small-scale *ad hoc* surveys, employing a few interviewers, a researcher may decide to recruit, train, organize and supervise the interviewing team himself. But with more than a handful of people, the amount of administration required, particularly for day-to-day contact with interviewers and progress-monitoring, usually justifies appointing a small field control staff. In the structured setting of a survey agency there will be a sizeable field control department often subdivided into staff responsible for training interviewers, staff responsible for control and monitoring, and staff responsible for supervising and checking work in the field. In these circumstances, although interviewers conduct the interview in accordance with the instructions of the researcher, they operate under the direction of the field control staff who deploy the team, provide them with address lists and interviewing supplies, organize their timetables and payments and monitor their work.

The primary aim of this chapter is to explain and illustrate the various functions of fieldwork organization, describing in some detail the processes involved in employing a large interviewing team. Although the organizational structure will vary according to the scale of each survey and the number of surveys handled at any one time, the basic principles apply to all surveys. So those who find themselves faced with the task of carrying out single-handed all the tasks specified here should benefit from the description of the processes involved, without necessarily adopting the same organizational structure.

Recruitment

While there is a range of qualities desirable for interviewers, in practice they vary widely in their personalities, characteristics and approach to interviewing. So there is no rigid set of rules for distinguishing good potential interviewers from bad ones. As with all personnel work, the recruiter's experience and judgement play a large part, but certain qualities or qualifications are well worth looking for. It will be rare, however, for all the qualities mentioned below to be found in any one person.

Qualities needed for interviewing

The wide range of tasks to be carried out by interviewers has been discussed in detail in the previous chapter. It includes securing the co-operation of strangers and conducting interviews to a high technical standard. Successful interviewers need to be able to deal with the occasional aggressive, suspicious or difficult respondent. They have to be capable of gaining co-operation without being domineering. Interviewers do not necessarily have to be from the same background as respondents as long as they are able to communicate easily with people from all backgrounds. Generally, this requires a level of confidence and maturity rarely found in people aged under about twenty.

Conversely, it is rare for people over about fifty to start a successful interviewing career. Interviewers need to be physically fit (there is a great deal of walking and climbing stairs) and willing to spend a lot of time outdoors in all weathers. Though many experienced interviewers continue well into their sixties, survey interviewing is a very demanding task for any but the fittest and keenest to embark on.

At one time almost all household survey interviewing was done by women, largely because the intermittent work made it suitable only for second earners in a family. Nowadays the work is better paid and can often be organized with greater continuity. So more men are joining interviewer teams and most have shown that they can undertake the work as effectively as women. The fear that male interviewers would be regarded more suspiciously by single or elderly respondents, leading to lower response rates, seems to be groundless.

It is almost always essential for interviewers to do some of their work in the evenings or at weekends in order to interview those who are at work during the day. Applicants need to be told this, since the strains of regular evening and weekend work are much greater than people realize in advance. If they have children, the problems are obvious. Relatives and neighbours cannot always be relied on to stand in so that the demands of an interviewing programme can be met. Nor will many husbands or wives tolerate these demands even when there are no children to look after or feed. To prevent interviewers dropping out halfway through the project, applicants need to be encouraged to consider these factors, particularly when evening and weekend work will be the norm rather than the exception.

Other valuable assets for an applicant are the use of a car and a home telephone. Neither is essential, though a car is extremely useful for evening and weekend work and, in certain parts of the country, the absence of a car would prove an almost insuperable handicap. A home telephone is desirable since, on even the best-planned surveys, last-minute changes in schedules or arrangements are often unavoidable. A respondent may want to postpone an appointment; an interviewer who has made an appointment may fall ill and need someone else to act as a substitute. The telephone provides for such emergencies rather better than the post.

Interviewers need to be intelligent, informed and literate. Formal educational qualifications are relevant only insofar as they indicate the presence of these qualities, but their absence should not disqualify applicants. It is, however, essential for interviewers to be well-organized and disciplined if they are to handle their work effectively and economically. They need to be able not only to plan and carry out their schedules, but also to follow the fairly strict survey control procedures laid down for them. They are required, for example, to send questionnaires back and to report progress at regular intervals and to work within rigorous (and not always obviously sensible) constraints. Applicants who lack either the ability or the inclination to work to these rules are unlikely to succeed as survey interviewers.

Advertising for interviewers
Personal contact and word of mouth may be enough to find a few interviewers or applicants for training as interviewers in a small area, but for large-scale survey work in one area or for a national recruitment drive some advertising is likely to prove necessary. For a local survey local newspapers are the obvious medium; several guides* contain details of local papers. For recruitment over a wider area, the national daily and Sunday newspapers provide good coverage, although at a higher cost.

A display or semi-display advertisement of the type illustrated below will normally ensure a good response. The main points to be mentioned include:
    the subject and nature of the survey
    the need for evening/weekend work
    the number of days a week on which successful applicants are
        expected to work

SOCIAL RESEARCH INTERVIEWING

We will be undertaking in March, April and May, a large travel survey in South Hampshire. For the survey we will need to augment our regular panel of freelance interviewers.

The work involves interviewing men and women in their (pre-selected) homes. Some evening and weekend work will be required. All applicants should be able to work a minimum of three days a week for the fieldwork period.

Interviewing experience is desirable but not essential since we will train applicants of the right calibre. Generous fees and all expenses reimbursed.

THE SURVEY AREA INCLUDES:

Southampton	Portsmouth	Winchester
Totton	Twyford	Havant
Hythe	Locks Heath	Fareham
Romsey	Wickham	Fair Oak
Eastleigh	Gosport	Waterlooville

Those interested should apply to: . . .

---

*Useful guides include:
    British Rate and Data, 76 Oxford Street, London, W1.
    Where, Evening Newspapers Advertising Bureau, Victoria House, Vernon Place, Southampton Row, London WC1B 4DS.
    Contact, Weekly Newspapers Advertising Bureau, Suite 401, Steinway Hall, 1/2 St. George's Street, London W1.
The Newspaper Society, 6 Carmelite Street, London EC4 will provide further information.

the duration of fieldwork
whether experience is required or training given
the interviewing areas

Views vary about the best days of the week for advertising but it is widely agreed that Mondays and Saturdays should be avoided. Putting a telephone number in the advertisement is helpful; queries can be answered by telephone and people who have misunderstood the nature of the work or who lack the necessary qualifications (chiefly availability for evening and weekend work) can be filtered out.

Screening and selecting applicants
Each applicant who telephones or writes in can be sent an application form and a detailed description of the work, the hours, the rates of pay and other basic information. These details will discourage some unsuitable applicants and provide a further preliminary screening procedure to minimize the number of applicants to be interviewed. Some organizations send applicants with no interviewing experience a short questionnaire they can use to conduct an interview to see whether they enjoy it. But since these applicants have not at this stage received any training or, more important, the reassurance necessary to conduct good interviews, this practice is of dubious value.

The application form should ask for the basic information—sex, age, previous experience and training (if any), names of referees—needed for screening applicants for any other job. Several other points can be checked at this stage too. Does the applicant have a telephone? Does he or she have unlimited or occasional use of a car? What are the family commitments? For example, are there young children or elderly parents at home? When will the applicant be available for work (days of week, times of day) and what areas will he or she be willing to travel to each day?

As well as considering the information filled in on the returned application form, the recruiter can examine the way the form has been completed: illegible handwriting, an incompletely filled-in form, numerous crossings-out and so on are useful clues to the way in which questionnaires may be completed.

Likely candidates can then be asked to attend for an interview of half an hour to an hour, during which further information is obtained and the details given checked. Since applicants often tend to overclaim their mobility and availability, the recruiter can use this opportunity to emphasize that interviewers will often have to travel some distance and to work in the evenings and at weekends.

A useful device in the interview is to include a reversal of roles, with the applicant interviewing the recruiter from a short, simple questionnaire. The recruiter can then assess how applicants would come across to respondents, how well they adhere to the question wording and how accurately answers have been recorded. The completed questionnaire can also be scrutinized for tidiness and legibility.

The drop-out and rejection rates in interviewer selection are frequently fairly high. Typically, around 60 per cent of those who reply to an advertisement will complete and return the application form sent to them. Eventually, about 50 per cent of those returning an application form may be selected. In some cases only 25 per cent are selected. Additional fall-out can be expected shortly before and after the briefing, and after the first few days' interviewing. Rather less frequently, there is fall-out after supervision or editing has revealed an unacceptably poor performance.

Recruitment involves a great deal of paperwork and administration. Applicants not asked for interview have to be written to, as do applicants rejected after the interview. Recruitment of fifty interviewers may therefore involve correspondence with two hundred applicants and interviews with one hundred.

Training and Briefing

If interviewers are recruited for a single project, their general training and the more specific project briefing will probably be run as one operation. Basic interviewing techniques can then be illustrated by reference to the survey in question. Nevertheless basic training and project briefing have different aims. The latter is chiefly concerned with the particular respondent selection method, questionnaire and instructions for that survey. The former is much wider and has to cover such general topics as securing co-operation, methods of probing and avoiding interviewer bias as well as to prepare interviewers for a varied range of surveys.

Basic training

The main goals of an interviewer's basic training programme are set out in Chapter 5. The topics to be covered fall under three broad headings:

Preparatory work:	planning the work, locating addresses.
Setting up the interview:	introducing the survey, selecting respondents, and gaining co-operation.
Interviewing:	interviewing techniques and methods of recording responses.

Other items to be covered are the administrative procedures that interviewers have to follow when returning their work and reporting their progress, and rudimentary aspects of sampling and data preparation so that interviewers can appreciate their role in the survey.

Whatever training methods are used, interviewers need a set of basic written instructions, as a reference manual for regular use over a long period (often a whole interviewing career). The interviewer needs to assimilate not only the broad concepts of interviewing but also the detailed techniques and classification definitions described in the manual. It is helpful to test interviewers on their knowledge of these techniques and definitions in the training sessions.

The initial training usually takes the form of a conference—a mixture of lectures, practical work, visual displays, demonstrations and discussions. As a rule, formal training sessions of this kind occupy about two days, though, depending on the amount of practical work, some may last for up to five days. At the training conference interviewers should be encouraged to air any doubts about the aims, methods and ethics of interviewing in general. One doubt often expressed concerns the need for (and even the morality of) asking respondents about their income. A discussion of issues like this helps interviewers to appreciate why such data are needed and to convey the need to respondents.

This formal session is the starting-point of the training programme. Many survey practitioners believe that most of the useful training of interviewers is achieved later, by practical field experience under regular supervision. Good interviewing is a craft acquired gradually through an apprenticeship that includes being faced with different types of respondents and questionnaires, different sampling procedures, interviewing situations and researchers. An intensive programme of supervision is therefore essential for inexperienced interviewers. Ideally, new interviewers should be phased into a project a few at a time, so that supervisors can give them sufficient attention and accompany the trainees on their visits. Early on, the supervisors will need to demonstrate the art of interviewing, and give trainees confidence by carrying out interviews themselves. Later on the supervisors can play a more passive role, observing and noting good and bad points for discussion later.

Early supervision can also be used to advise on planning the work, using maps, scheduling calls to maximize response rates, and so on. These points can be covered most effectively by a supervisor accompanying trainees at the start of their work.

The frequency of supervision will depend on the organizational structure and the size of the interviewing and supervisory teams. But some general guidance can be given. For example most inexperienced interviewers need to be supervised at least twice at the beginning of fieldwork. The first supervision is usually on their first day in the field. Its purposes are to instil confidence, to advise, to criticize constructively and where necessary to demonstrate good interviewing techniques. It provides practical examples of explanations and guidance that the trainees have already received. At the next supervision, the supervisor should be able to keep more in the background. The interviewer should by now be more confident and independent, and the supervisor will need to intervene only if serious errors are made. Further supervision can follow according to the overall programme for interviewers or where an interviewer is felt to need special training.

Tape-recordings are increasingly being used as aids in interviewer training. They provide the ideal opportunity for studying aspects of wording and approach which a supervisory visit alone cannot capture. These include nuances of intonation and word selection that can create interviewer bias of the kind referred to in Chapter 5. A particularly useful method of training is to ask a trainee interviewer to record one or more interviews as part of the training conference programme. The tape is studied and assessed by the supervisor or instructor and then used as demonstration material at the conference.

For experienced interviewers, particularly those offered assignments regularly by one organization over a number of years, refresher training schools run along the lines of group discussions can be very useful. Specific topics (e.g. maximizing response rates or probing at open-ended questions) can be dealt with in some depth. The main purposes of refresher schools are to remind interviewers of the need for high standards, to help them recognize any bad habits they may have acquired and to remind them of first principles.

Project briefings

For most large-scale survey projects some kind of project briefing for trained interviewers is required. As mentioned earlier, interviewers recruited for only one project will normally be trained and briefed in one operation; interviewers working regularly on a wide variety of surveys attend a project briefing immediately before each new project. In the latter instance the two processes—training and briefing—are usually handled by different people with different skills: the training by field supervisors or field controllers and the briefing by the researcher who has designed the project.

At the briefing, the researcher will be addressing the interviewers for the best part of a day (or perhaps even longer). To do so successfully he requires to have done a good deal of preparation. The conference programme needs to be structured and a timetable devised to make sure that all relevant points will be covered. The programme might be as follows:

Morning
 Session 1: purpose of survey and general survey method
               (approx. ½ hour)
 Session 2: whom to interview, respondent selection methods
       and use of administrative forms (approx. 1 hour)
 Session 3: general questionnaire coverage and content
               (approx. ½ hour)

Afternoon
 Session 4: dummy interviews   (approx. 2 hours)
 Session 5: issuing supplies, field control procedures
               (approx. ½ hour)

Dummy interviews at the briefing give interviewers practical experience of the questionnaire. An effective method is 'round-the-table' questioning, where each interviewer asks a few questions from the questionnaire with the researcher acting as the respondent. It helps not to discuss questions in advance so that interviewers may make odd mistakes that can then be discussed and corrected. After an interviewer has asked a few questions a short discussion on points arising can follow, before the next interviewer continues with the questionnaire. Choosing interviewers at random increases the attentiveness of all; as a rule, interviewers seem to enjoy this method and respond to it well. It is helpful to have a seating plan so that interviewers can be called on by name.

Usually there is sufficient time to do two complete dummy interviews in this way, working from questionnaires prepared by the researcher in advance of the briefing. Preparation will ensure that the answers are not overcomplicated, and yet that they do draw attention to the main difficulties, filtering, questions that need probing and so on. The balance between ease and complexity is extremely difficult to achieve in a spontaneous dummy interview.

If the questionnaire contains large grids or if a diary record has to be explained these can be dealt with separately; an overhead projector is a useful device for illustrating complex questions and showing how they should be filled in. It is preferable for interviewers to record all answers (not just those to the questions they ask) on blank questionnaires to give them practice in completing the questionnaire as well as in asking the questions.

Not all project briefings lend themselves to this model. Sometimes longer briefings are more appropriate, perhaps with work in the field incorporated into the programme. In other cases where, say, diary records are to be used, the method of briefing for the questionnaire section may differ. But the general principles outlined here are a fairly secure basis for briefing interviewers.

In addition to the briefing, interviewers need as a reference document a set of project instructions which elaborate on the survey definitions, sampling instructions, oddities and exceptions and the way the precodes on the questionnaire should be applied. These instructions need to include a question-by-question explanation of what is being sought and who is to answer. Ease of reference can be achieved by various printing techniques—printing subsections on different colours, linking colours of the instruction pages to colours of questionnaire pages and administrative forms, printing questionnaire pages opposite related instructions, producing a pocket-book supplement of technical definitions, and so on.

It is generally more difficult for the researcher to keep the attention of interviewers if they are given the written instructions either before or during the briefing conference. Preferably he should work from notes or from an annotated set of instructions and distribute the interviewers' copies only at the end of the session.

If the researcher attempts to convey all the project instructions at a personal briefing session he is likely to confuse interviewers and put some of them off. The aim of the personal briefing is not to go over the written instructions; it is to explain the purpose of the survey, to demonstrate to interviewers the broad nature of their task, to show them that they can achieve it, and to engage their interest in and enthusiasm for the project. To some extent, it has to be a public relations exercise, because unless interviewers are sympathetically disposed to a project they are unlikely to give it the necessary commitment. In any case, the briefing session provides an opportunity for personal contact between interviewer and researcher—the essence of the rapport that makes interviewers feel part of the research team.

Although briefings need to be informal and relaxed, the researcher has to appear competent and convey confidence in himself, in his survey and in the interviewers. A good briefer is a good teacher rather than a good interviewer. His aim is to avoid creating a tense atmosphere in which interviewers will be scared of making mistakes. If mistakes are made they can be spotted and corrected, preferably by other interviewers rather than by the researcher.

The briefer should portray the 'average' interview, rather than highly complex exceptions. Complications that may be encountered ought only to be touched upon, and interviewers referred to the project instructions for guidance. The researcher has to remain aware that interviewers will usually be unfamiliar with the background of the survey, the design work, the technical jargon; he needs to bridge both a language and a subject gap. But these aims will not be achieved if he concentrates unduly on the long, complicated points that are covered by the written instructions. The usefulness of a briefing conference as a method of instilling detailed information is somewhat limited. Interviewers need to go away and absorb the information at their own pace, aided perhaps by interviewing a relative or friend.

Field control staff or field supervisors can play a useful role at the briefing by assessing interviewers' performances and helping where necessary to remove doubts and fears. They can raise points that they feel have been misunderstood by interviewers and ask the researcher to clarify them. Most important, they can decide on the follow-up supervisory programme by spotting interviewers who may need immediate practical help in the field, those next in priority for supervisory visits and so on.

Briefing conferences that involve more than about twenty interviewers become unwieldy. For large projects, therefore, it may be necessary to hold a series of briefings, in different locations, to minimize the amount of travelling for interviewers. Briefing conferences are expensive: if sixty interviewers are to work on a survey, three one-day briefing conferences will involve not only at least sixty interviewer days (the equivalent of the cost of conducting about two hundred and fifty long interviews) but a great deal of research and administrative time as well. To minimize overnight accommodation costs it is best to schedule the conferences to start at about 10.30 a.m. and finish at about 4.30 p.m., and to hold them in towns to which good transport links are available (and if possible close to a mainline station).

On a further practical note, a series of briefing conferences involves quite a lot of detailed organization—booking conference rooms (with adequate seating, a blackboard, etc.), preparing supplies of documents for the briefing and getting them to the conference rooms and informing all the interviewers of the time and place.

Field Control

Controlling and co-ordinating the work of a team of, say, fifty or a hundred interviewers working on one project can be a full-time job for one or two field controllers. Much of their time will be spent at the end of a telephone. Their job includes choosing interviewers, arranging the sample of addresses into workable batches, allocating the work, collating supplies and organizing their despatch, monitoring the progress of the fieldwork and taking remedial action where necessary, authorising payment to interviewers and dealing with queries.

Interviewer allocation
In a survey organization that employs a large panel of interviewers, the main criterion for assigning interviewers to a survey will

inevitably be where they live in relation to the sampling areas. In general, the closer to a sampling area that the interviewer lives, the more efficient and economical it is to allocate that area to that interviewer. But other factors have to be taken into account. First, interviewers should not be allocated addresses too close to their homes, since the likelihood is too great that they will know some of their potential respondents. To have interviewers asking their neighbours for confidential information (such as income) is obviously undesirable. Second, in some rural parts of the country, distances may be so great and public transport facilities so limited that having a car may be a more important criterion than living close to the area. Third, where some choice exists within an area, the field controller can match the interviewer's personal characteristics to the task in hand. If a survey is among old people, among the disabled or among mothers of young children, some members of a panel of interviewers may be more suited to the survey than others. Normally interviewers are allocated work that will occupy them in an area for three weeks or more so that there is ample time to call back on those out at earlier calls.

Administrative documents
The work involved in maintaining documents for a large panel of interviewers should not be underestimated. As well as the interviewer's personal file, which generally contains the application form, a report on the recruitment interview, appointment letter, and so on, a card index is useful. Each card contains the interviewer's name, address, telephone number and such basic information as car availability and whether the interviewer can stay away overnight. The same card system might be used to record the initital grading of interviewers at the end of the briefing conferences and the subsequent grading by supervisors. Since location is a key factor, a useful supplement to the card index is a map with flat top pins to identify interviewers; the pins can be colour-coded to indicate various interviewer characteristics. When interviewing begins more documents will accumulate for each interviewer—supervisory reports, progress reports, pay claims, and so on. The clerical work can therefore escalate rapidly.

In notifying interviewers about their fieldwork assignments, usually two to three weeks before the briefing, the details to be transmitted include:

> the title and a brief description of the survey;
> details of the area(s) in which the interviewer is required to work;
> the number of addresses to be issued for the area(s);

details of the categories of respondent: housewives, heads of
household, and so on;

the expected average length of the interview;

the date, venue and arrangements for the briefing;

the starting and finishing dates for fieldwork.

Interviewers need to carry some sort of identity card, preferably
with a photograph, authorized by the survey organization. Supplying
two passport-sized photographs can be made a condition of
acceptance of interviewing work. One photograph can be put on the
personal file and the other on the identity card. An example of an
identity card is given below.

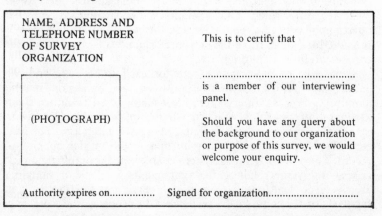

It is also necessary for interviewers to carry a letter from the survey
sponsor or survey organization explaining the nature and purpose of
the survey, reassuring respondents about confidentiality and
explaining how they were chosen for interview. The explanatory
letter can be left with the respondent, in case he wishes to contact the
sponsor or the survey organization after the interview. Even if the
respondent has been sent such a letter in advance, it is helpful for
interviewers to carry copies to show to and leave with respondents
who do not remember the original.

An effective way of stressing the importance of the guarantees
given to respondents about confidentiality is to ask all interviewers
to sign a declaration of confidentiality, undertaking not to disclose
information about respondents that has come into their possession
during the survey.

Monitoring progress

Another field control function is to ensure that the volume of work
carried out each week will allow the project to be completed on

schedule. As well as keeping the documentation up to date, field control must ensure that interviewers remain interested in and enthusiastic about their work. Much of the field controller's time will have to be spent on maintaining morale. Interviewers are isolated from the research and office staff, and easy access to a field controller who is sympathetic to their problems is important. The need to develop close contact between interviewers, supervisors and field control staff is the main reason why some large organizations divide up the field control function by region.

Feedback on the standard of interviewing is also important. If interviewers are not told when they are working well or badly, their standard of work tends to fall. Low morale can lead to careless work, poor response rates, and sometimes to cheating. Completed questionnaires need to be returned to the central office and booked in and edited quickly, so that the performance of each interviewer can be carefully monitored.

Knowledge of the response rate for each interviewer and the pattern of reasons for non-response is also important in the monitoring process. Interviewers are usually asked to return some kind of progress sheet with each batch of questionnaires giving details of unsuccessful calls as well as successful interviews. The field controller can use these returns to update the master booking-in record. This kind of detailed system enables the inevitable fieldwork crises—interviewers falling ill, assignments in difficult sampling areas—to be dealt with. If an interviewer is not sending work in regularly or seems to have a response rate problem, the work may have to be reallocated or a supervisor sent out to help.

During a survey the master record will provide a basis for interim figures on response rates and for checking pay and expense claims. At the end of the assignment interviewers can return all sample issue sheets for cross-checking against the master record in the central office to produce final response summaries.

Maximizing response

A small proportion of the total sample will constitute 'deadwood'; a house may have been demolished, a person may have died. The interviewers cannot do anything about these addresses except report their existence to the field control team. There will, however, be such cases of non-response as refusals, proxy refusals, non-contact with the household, temporary absence and illness; all of these are potentially convertible into interviews.

Although each interviewer needs to work to a fairly well defined timetable, the overall schedule may allow time to reissue some of the unsuccessful addresses, possibly to another interviewer or to a supervisor. This can be done only if the overall fieldwork period

allowed for the project is adequate. Ample time has to be allowed for
the reissue of addresses, particularly during the summer months
when it is essential to allow for a further visit to people initially away
on holiday. In rural areas and bad weather conditions, reissuing and
recontacting may be a very slow process. If the time and resources
are available, more than half of the non-contacts can often be
converted into interviews on reissue. Even refusals, especially proxy
refusals, can be reissued, if they seem to have been caused by
circumstances at the time of interview; often up to a third of these
can be converted into interviews. The field controller should
therefore not only monitor all returns as they come in, but also
scrutinize each interviewer's progress records and decide whether an
unsuccessful address might usefully be reissued.

Paying interviewers
The checking and authorizing of fees and expense claim forms takes
time. The routine work may be done by clerical staff. Some expenses
claimed may have to be disallowed, however, or the amount claimed
as fees increased. Since such decisions affect the relationship
between the interviewer and the central office they need careful
consideration and are best taken by the field controller.

A commonly used payment system is one that is hourly-based in
which the interviewer claims in arrears for the hours worked, no
limit being set in advance. Different rates may be payable according
to the tasks performed: for example, interviewing, attending
briefings, travelling to the interview area, working at home (reading
project instructions, carrying out trial interviews, despatching letters
to respondents in advance—where necessary—and checking
completed work).

The main disadvantage of an hourly-based system is that it does
not allow fieldwork costs to be estimated precisely in advance. An
alternative system used successfully by professional survey
organizations is to calculate in advance a fixed fee per achieved
interview, together with supplementary payments for partially
completed interviews and contacts made. Accurate calculation of the
fees in advance depends on the results of preliminary piloting of
questionnaires and experienced judgements about average interview
length. The system needs to be operated flexibly in order to
distinguish genuine cases of particularly difficult assignments from
other less justified additional claims.

Interviewers who work freelance will be responsible for their own
income tax; it need not be deducted from their earnings. They will
need to distinguish for tax purposes the amount paid to them in fees
and the amount paid in expenses. At the end of the tax year the
Inland Revenue may also require the survey organization to file a

record of payments made to each interviewer. Although freelance interviewers are not classified by the Inland Revenue as employees for the purpose of PAYE, National Insurance deductions have to be made for those interviewers whose fees total more than the threshold currently in operation.

If the fieldwork operation is large, a direct credit transfer system for interviewer payments is simple and efficient. Credit transfer slips are attached to the interviewer's claim form; the interviewer fills in the required details of bank and branch code number and account number; when the pay claim is authorized, office staff enter the amount to be paid and despatch the slips to the bank; only one cheque need then be made out to the bank to cover fees and expenses for all interviewers.

Quality Checks

The quality of interviewing can be checked in various ways. These include personal supervision in the field (which combines training with quality checks), personal recall checks on successful and unsuccessful contacts, postal or telephone checks on respondents, office checking of questionnaires and response rates, and the use of tape-recorders. The different approaches tend to be complementary and all may be used on the same project.

Interviewers ought to be made aware during their basic training of the various procedures that will operate and why. This can be done by stressing the goal of high standards and the necessity for careful monitoring that can identify a drop in these standards.

The supervisor's role

Accompanying an interviewer on fieldwork provides a supervisor with an opportunity to check all aspects of the interviewer's work, to scrutinize all the documents and discuss any problems with him or her. But supervisors have to be used sparingly; most survey projects can afford only one supervisor for every twelve to fifteen interviewers and their initial role will be more concerned with training.

To judge an interviewer's performance fairly, the supervisor needs to observe several interviews, probably amounting to a full day's work, to examine the interviewer's ability to plan and organize the work, to handle selection procedures, to introduce the survey, to conduct the interview accurately, to probe and record answers given, to leave a good impression with respondents, and to maintain progress records. It is helpful for the supervisor to have a standard report form to cover all these points; at the end of the form space can be left for an overall assessment of the interviewer on, say, a five-point scale. For new interviewers, overall assessments of both current and potential performance are useful.

Another task for supervisors is personal recall checking at a selection of addresses. The check may be a simple one to confirm that interviews recorded as productive were carried out; more usefully, however, the supervisor checks other points such as the respondent's recollection of the length of the interview, whether the respondent understood the purpose of the survey and what impression the interviewer left behind. Supervisors may be supplied with a photocopy of part of the questionnaire (usually including some classification items) to check the answers recorded by the interviewer. Recall checks need not and indeed should not be confined to successfully interviewed respondents. Supervisors can also follow up unproductive addresses to see why people refused, to check that the interviewer made every effort to secure a productive interview, and to check that deadwood has been correctly classified. To guarantee objectivity the names of the interviewers whose work is being checked need not be disclosed to the supervisor until after the check.

The addresses at which supervisors carry out recall checks can be selected at random from the interviewer's progress records to cover as great a proportion of the fieldwork period as possible. Personal recall checks on five to ten per cent of an interviewer's work are usual.

Other checking procedures
Personal recall checks can be supplemented by postal checks. Prestamped or reply-paid postcards (precoded with the project number, the interviewer's number and address serial number) are sent to respondents to check whether the interview took place and with whom, approximately how long it lasted and, if appropriate, whether any show cards or other interviewing aids were used.

Normally postal checks are confined to addresses that have yielded an interview, every nth productive address visited by each interviewer being sent a card. Response to postal checks is usually fairly low (40 per cent to 50 per cent), so failure to receive a reply should not be taken as a sign that the interview did not take place. Instances where respondents return cards claiming not to have been interviewed need to be followed up either by a letter describing the survey in more detail (and enclosing a further card) or, preferably, by personal recall. In most cases it will be found that these claims arise because respondents have forgotten about the interview or because someone else has sent the postcard back without checking with the respondent first.

The most important aspect of quality control is the continual monitoring of the interviewer's workload. This operation is usually carried out, along the lines discussed in Chapter 8, by the staff who book in and edit the questionnaires. Three aspects of an interviewer's work can be monitored in this way: communication with the office and return of progress records; ability to achieve co-operation from the sample, and ability to follow instructions and complete questionnaires correctly. Interviewers should be informed of the results of editing checks as soon as possible and, when there have been serious omissions or consistent errors, asked to revisit respondents to correct mistakes. More than any other quality control procedure, monitoring ensures that standards remain high. Vigilance from the field control team almost always finds an echo in vigilance from interviewers. Lack of vigilance is echoed too.

Though tape-recording of interviews is employed mainly in training, it can supplement other quality control procedures. Tapes can provide an accurate record, for example, of deviations in question wording, of omissions in recording and of poor probing. It is, however, an expensive method of quality control, time-consuming for office staff to check items and cumbersome for interviewers. Used selectively, however, tapes provide a better picture of the interview than most other forms of quality control.

Good quality control can never be sporadic. It stems largely from the knowledge of all concerned that there is continuous and rigorous monitoring and reporting. At the end of a project, a report should be prepared on all the quality control procedures employed, the level of supervision and recall, the results of the checks and so on. Quality control is then accepted as an integral part of the survey process rather than as a dispensable extra to be overlooked in times of inevitable fieldwork crisis. The overall quality achieved is a function of the level of training and experience of the interviewing team; a generally high standard can be spoilt by low quality from the poorest group of interviewers. The recruiting, briefing, training and quality control procedures are therefore aimed not only at raising the average level of ability, but also at making sure that the least effective half dozen or so interviewers can conduct sound interviews.

For long field operations, where interviewers' performances can be monitored continuously, it is helpful to rank interviewers according to a range of criteria (response rates, supervisor's gradings, field control reports, etc.) and then to examine very closely those below the lowest quartile. If the same interviewers are repeatedly found in this category, action can be taken (unless it is clear that they are working in particularly difficult areas).

Finally, an obvious function of quality control is to prevent cheating. In practice, very few examples of cheating occur: When cheating is exposed, it is usually a competent interviewer who has hit a moment of crisis, and is tempted not to falsify the entire assignment but perhaps to fill in parts of some questionnaires. Good regular quality control will spot this, although not necessarily immediately. Clearly, however, when cheating is suspected, all that interviewer's work has to be regarded as suspect. It needs to be thoroughly checked in the office and in the field and where necessary redone by other interviewers.

To some extent, an interviewing team has to be remotely controlled and the dangers of the interviewers becoming too isolated are all too obvious. Moreover, good interviewers tend to have strong personalities and to be independent and highly resistant to heavy-handedness. Because of this, field control—and particularly the aspect of it concerned with quality control—requires sensitivity, organizing talent and an ability to work under conditions of strain.

Notes on Further Reading
1. The references on interviewer manuals given in note 1, and those on interviewing given in note 2, of Chapter 5 are also relevant for the topics discussed in this chapter, as are the general textbooks mentioned at the end of Chapter 1.
2. The report of the Market Research Society (1968) describes the fieldwork methods used by commercial organizations, and there are several papers in the Methodological Series of the Social Survey Division of the Office of Population Censuses and Surveys investigating aspects of interviewing and interviewers in relation to the Division's work; the paper by Fothergill and Willcock (1955) is also a useful account of interviewing problems based on experience at the Social Survey Division.
3. The book by Hauck and Steinkamp (1964) contains a good deal of useful information on most of the topics discussed in this chapter. Three of the chapters in Sudman (1967) are also relevant here: they discuss the time allocation of interviewers, the control of interviewing costs, and the cost and quality of interviewers. Cannell et al. (1975) have developed a method for evaluating interviewer performance from tape-recorded interviews.

Chapter 7. Postal Survey Procedures

Principal contributor: Lindsay Brook

Since postal surveys are carried out without the benefit of personal contact between respondents and interviewers (to introduce, complete and return questionnaires), many people assume that they will automatically generate low response levels and poor questionnaire completion. This is not so. Both the level and quality of response are frequently equal to, and in some cases better than, those achieved in interview surveys.

On cost grounds a postal survey has considerable advantages over an interview survey. It normally costs no more than a third of what a comparable interview survey costs; alternatively, for the same cost, the sample size for a postal survey can be perhaps three times as large as that for a comparable interview survey. Moreover, since postal rates do not vary within the United Kingdom, there is no need to cluster a postal survey sample geographically to reduce data collection costs. The efficiency of postal survey samples relative to interview survey samples may therefore be enhanced, as long as an adequate list of addresses exists from which to sample.

A related advantage of postal surveys is that they can reach isolated areas and those members of the population whom interviewers find it difficult to catch at home; they remove the problems of sending interviewers to outlying areas, of having them work in the evenings in inner city areas and of making numerous abortive visits to the homes of those people who are rarely in between 9 a.m. and 9 p.m.

Postal surveys also allow respondents time to reflect on the questions (and possibly to look up records) so that they can give more considered or more precise answers. The presence of an interviewer may inhibit some respondents from taking time to look up information or cause people to answer inaccurately for the reasons discussed in Chapter 3.

Postal surveys can also be used effectively for screening purposes to identify a particular minority group of respondents for subsequent interview, thus reducing the amount of interviewing that needs to be done. Similarly, postal surveys can be used in conjunction with interview surveys; self-completion supplements can be left with respondents at the end of an interview to be returned by post. This can be useful if respondents need to read through some material (e.g. planning proposals) before completing part of the questionnaire or to consult other members of the household who were not at the interview. Alternatively, a self-completion supplement can be a device for extending the questionnaire beyond the length that the researcher regards as reasonable for a personal interview. Whatever their purpose and form, supplements left to be returned by post have usually achieved high response rates—between 80 per cent and 90 per cent of the households interviewed.

But postal surveys have two primary weaknesses. The first is the reliance placed on respondents to complete the questionnaire, aided only by written instructions. The second is that there is only an introductory letter to motivate people to complete and return the questionnaire.

Self-completion Questionnaires
Uses
In considering the role and features of self-completion questionnaires for postal surveys, we can usefully examine more generally the advantages and disadvantages of all kinds of self-completion surveys.

It is sometimes desirable to ask people to record details of their behaviour as it occurs (or soon afterwards) in order to gain accurate information. In these situations self-completion questionnaires are extremely useful. The prime example of the use of self-completion questionnaires in Britain is the Population Census: forms are delivered and collected by enumerators, who provide help to some households in completing the questions. The prohibitive cost of using trained interviewers to interview the entire British population is not the only reason why self-completion methods have been adopted. An important factor is the need to enumerate the population of households on a particular day. Interviewing some weeks later about the composition of each household on census night would lead to gross inaccuracies; training a sufficiently large panel of interviewers to conduct all the interviews within a few days of census night would be impossible.

On a smaller scale, two of the Government's periodic surveys, the

Family Expenditure Survey (Kemsley, 1969), and the National Travel Survey (Brook, 1976), which record details of behaviour as they occur, employ different kinds of self-completion questionnaires. In the first, respondents complete diaries that eventually form part of the questionnaire record for each respondent; in the second, the record maintained by respondents is an *aide-mémoire* referred to when the interviewer subsequently takes the respondent through a structured questionnaire.

In these surveys self-completion questionnaires are used to collect a considerable amount of detailed information. They demonstrate that the approach is not confined either to a small quantity of data or to superficial measurements. But where the data have to be highly structured and where detailed definitions are used (as in the National Travel Survey) interviewers may be needed to go through the self-completion record with respondents and to transfer the information into a structured, coded format. The inability of self-completion questionnaires to convey complex definitions or assist respondents in structuring their answers to questions is a definite limitation of the technique.

Another weakness is that self-completion questionnaires are unsuitable for asking open-ended questions of the type used particularly in attitude research. Self-completion questionnaires cannot probe or ask the respondent to explain a particular answer; they cannot encourage the respondent to be less reticent or to give his own opinions and prejudices rather than slogans or clichés. Most important, perhaps, the more fluent a respondent is with the written word the more likely he is to give full answers, regardless of his strength of feeling. So, where open-ended questions are included to allow respondents an opportunity to comment at length on a subject, the responses must be interpreted more circumspectly than if interviewers had asked the same questions.

A useful design technique for interview questionnaires is the use of question sequence: knowledge questions, for example, usually precede other questions on the same subject, so that respondents are not given information about a subject before their current levels of awareness have been assessed. In self-completion questionnaires, however, question ordering is not effective because respondents can read through the questionnaire before completing any part of it; in any case, they may answer the questions out of sequence. Moreover, knowledge questions pose problems in postal studies because the respondent has the opportunity to look up, or consult others for, the answers. Although respondents can be requested to behave as the researcher wishes them to do, there is no way of exercising control as an interviewer would.

The lack of control extends further. We do not know, for instance, whether the correct respondent has completed the questionnaire, whether the views expressed are his own or his family's, or whether the questionnaire was completed in a tolerably tranquil atmosphere or in one where the respondent's attention was continually distracted. All these variables may affect the quality and nature of the responses.

Where a self-completion questionnaire is used as an adjunct to an interview survey, interviewers may be able to minimize or counter the weaknesses of the technique. In a survey conducted entirely by post, however, there is no personal contact. Nevertheless, for factual surveys, simple behavioural studies and for collecting limited attitudinal data, a postal survey can be very reliable, and particularly useful when a large sample is desirable and only a small budget is available: its limitations have to be recognized, but they are not disqualifications. Where extended attitudinal information is required, despite the cost advantages of self-completion methods, their limitations will generally rule out their use.

Design and layout

By their very nature self-completion questionnaires need to be straightforward enough to be completed by people untrained and inexperienced in filling in forms. As a rule, a self-completion questionnaire of more than about eight to ten sides of A4 paper will put off a sizeable proportion of the population. This need not be so, however, when the sample is made up of people with a special interest in the subject or with a high standard of literacy.

A myth has grown up that a postal survey questionnaire needs to be very short for the survey to obtain a good response rate. Empirical evidence does not confirm this: a complex subject covered by a very short questionnaire is equally wrong. It can appear superficial, especially to special population samples whose members know a great deal about the subject of the study; they might react negatively to what seems to be a cursory or trivial treatment.

More important perhaps than the length of the questionnaire is its appearance. The task required of respondents must appear to be easy and attractive. If the questionnaire looks complex, it is very likely to be set aside and left. A complicated, compressed layout with little space on a page is almost certain to be less inviting than a longer questionnaire with ample space for questions and answers. The actual task required of respondents may well be less important than the perceived task in encouraging or deterring response. Respondents may well glance through or read the whole document before deciding whether to complete and return it. Anything they particularly dislike about the layout, wording or emphasis of the questions may deter them.

The designer of a self-completion questionnaire has, above all, to pay great attention to clarity of wording and simplicity of design. There should be instructions to guide the respondent: should he write in his answer, place a tick in a box, ring one code, ring several codes? Complicated grids generally have to be avoided, however much space they save, because they are likely to put off or intimidate some respondents.

The content of the questionnaire should also be arranged to maximize the chances of co-operation. The content will, of course, be dictated by the purposes of the survey but there are two important tactics available: the first is to include questions that are likely to be of high interest to all recipients; the second is to ensure that early questions do not give any respondents the impression that the study is not intended for them. Either tactic may lead the designer to include extra questions simply to encourage response. In a study of active leisure pursuits, for example, it would be essential to encourage responses from those who take little part in leisure activities in order not to overestimate the proportion of the population actively engaged in each pursuit. So the questionnaire would have to range widely over uses of leisure time to avoid giving the impression that the study was concerned only with regular participants in those activities. If that impression were created, some people might pass on the questionnaire to apparently more suitable friends and others might throw it away as not applicable to them.

There is also often a case for including attitude questions that allow respondents to express their views rather than merely describe their behaviour and characteristics. These questions can be precoded or open-ended, interspersed throughout the questionnaire or grouped. Their value lies in preventing boredom and frustration, and in providing space for comments that might otherwise be written all over the questionnaire. The answers may not be analysed in full if they are peripheral to the aims of the study.

At a more detailed level, some well-tested methods of self-completion questionnaire design and layout seem to produce both a high quality and a high volume of response. Seven of these conventions are as follows:

First, self-completion questionnaires are generally type-set and, when they are long, are more elaborately printed than interview questionnaires. They may contain coloured pages to clarify the structure, or colour printing to distinguish instructions from questions or to emphasize filtering (which should be used only if it is essential).

Second, it is usual to ask respondents to record their answers by placing ticks in boxes rather than following the interviewer's convention of ringing codes. The justification for this practice is the need for clarity: some respondents do not understand what code numbers are for and look for other meanings in the numbers. Placing ticks in boxes is a familiar enough process and is probably less confusing. For reasons of economy, the relevant code numbers are, however, frequently preprinted (in very small print) in the boxes, and the relevant column numbers preprinted in the margin, so that card punchers can work directly from questionnaires. The resultant layout, which must be as consistent as possible throughout the questionnaire, will often be something like this:

Q.4(a)   On what day of the week did this questionnaire arrive in the post?

	Office use
PLEASE TICK ONE BOX	Col.
Monday [1]	
Tuesday [2]	
Wednesday [3]	
Thursday [4]	
Friday [5]	
Saturday [6]	
I do not remember [7]	(56)

Third, on a long questionnaire, it is common practice to use sublettering with question numbers, e.g. Q.4(a), (b), (c), (d), etc., since high question numbers may deter a recipient who looks at the back page and sees, say, Q.110. Sublettering can also be used to group questions on similar subjects, and this may well make the questionnaire easier to complete.

Fourth, self-completion questionnaires need to include explicit instructions, and to repeat them as necessary. With self-completion questionnaires, one person untrained and inexperienced in interviewing fulfils the roles of both interviewer and respondent. Instructions cannot therefore be abbreviated as they often are in interview questionnaires; they need to be distinguished clearly from questions by their type face, usually using large bold or italic type.

Fifth, since questionnaire completion is a learning process with which the respondent will become increasingly at ease as he proceeds, the more difficult questions should come in the middle or towards the end. The first few questions should ideally be simple, of high and general interest and of obvious relevance to encourage the recipient to start. The last few questions should also be of high interest to all respondents so that they are encouraged to return the completed questionnaire. Other than in these respects, however, question-ordering cannot be used as a design tool in self-completion studies for the reasons already mentioned.

Next, the wording of questions in self-completion surveys is even more crucial than in interview surveys, since there is no intermediary between researcher and respondent to clarify ambiguities or explain intricacies. So, pretesting is crucial for self-completion questionnaires. The results of pretests can be used both to improve wording and to refine layout. Even though the main survey will be by self-completion methods it helps if interviewers can watch respondents complete the pretest questionnaires and ask them what difficulties they have encountered, what they understood by certain questions, and so on.

Finally, it is helpful to include some notes at the end of a self-completion questionnaire: a request to respondents to check that no answers have inadvertently been left out; an invitation to comment on the subject of the study or the questionnaire; a message of thanks, and (for postal studies) a plea for a prompt return of the questionnaire.

Maximizing Response Levels
The most daunting problem in a postal survey is to ensure that the response level will be high enough to give confidence that the respondents are reasonably representative of the total population sampled. The contact letter, questionnaire and reminders have to achieve co-operation on their own.

Not surprisingly, response levels are more variable for postal surveys than for interview surveys. Although high response rates (i.e. over 70 per cent) are frequently achieved in postal enquiries, they sometimes drop to around 50 per cent for reasons that are not always clear. The likely response level should therefore be checked in at least one pilot survey (perhaps on a split-run, so that more than one approach can be assessed). A pilot may involve monitoring the response to, say, two versions of a contact letter and questionnaire from about a hundred recipients. Reminders may be issued, if the initial response is low; if it is high enough, it may be felt that enough evidence exists to justify the approach without monitoring the effect of a reminder. If the response level remains low after reminders have been sent, a second pilot survey, with modifications and perhaps on a smaller scale, may be necessary.

In any event, the researcher must be persuaded on the basis of the preliminary work (including pretests of the questionnaire) that the presentation and approach will achieve an acceptable volume and quality of response. The pilot work will also give a useful indication of how fast response is likely to be—another factor that varies from one postal survey to another. The approximate timing of reminder letters can then be provisionally arranged before the initial mailing.

As already mentioned, the questionnaire itself can have a crucial effect on response levels. It defines the subject matter of the survey, it tells respondents of the task required of them, and its appearance acts as either an incentive or deterrent to completion. There are, however, several other factors that influence response rates in postal enquiries, each of which is discussed in turn in the following pages:
—the initial mailing
—the covering letter
—reminders and follow-ups
—use of incentives.
Not all of these factors are equally effective. The use of reminders, for example, is by far the most productive. All four factors are, however, separately and cumulatively relevant to the design and planning of any postal survey.

The initial mailing
The first requirement is that the recipient should be persuaded to open the envelope. Packaging is therefore very important. Good quality envelopes and neat labelling should always be used and, if possible, envelopes should be addressed to a named person. Where, as often, this is not possible, special care must be taken that the envelope does not look like a promotional circular of the type that often gets discarded unopened.

First-class postage helps (but adds considerably to the costs of a large survey). Stamping rather than franking the outward envelope is also recommended unless the scale of the operation renders it impracticable: the difficulty and time involved in buying, say, 20,000 stamps and sticking them onto envelopes are considerable. Use of commemorative stamps or several small denomination stamps may also help. Although none of these ploys has been shown consistently to improve response rates, they inject a sense of importance and urgency into the initial approach.

An addressed envelope must be enclosed for the respondent's reply and there is a case for stamping it rather than using the reply-paid system. Stamped return envelopes have frequently been shown to boost response, probably because recipients do not like to throw them away. A first-class stamp on the return envelope also emphasizes the sense of urgency that the researcher needs to get across, on the sound principle that the longer a questionnaire remains uncompleted, the less likely it is to be completed at all.

Some studies have used the tactic of recorded delivery, which seems—and almost certainly is—excessive, except perhaps in rare instances, for the second reminder letter. The most prudent course of action is to resort to it only when less elaborate and less expensive methods have failed. Recorded delivery letters can cause inconvenience to recipients and may create an atmosphere of drama out of proportion to the importance of an average postal study.

There is slight evidence that, for general population samples, a Thursday mail-out elicits a quicker (if not a higher) response than a mailing on any other day, probably because respondents complete the questionnaire over the weekend. By contrast, a Monday or Tuesday mailing seems to increase and hasten response from organizations. The differences in response to mailings sent on different days of week will, however, probably be marginal.

More important than day of week is time of year. December is a disastrous month for postal surveys for obvious reasons; the dates of wake weeks and annual factory shut-downs in certain areas need to be checked to avoid mailings when many people will be away from home. The timing of the initial contact and the survey period has therefore to be planned well in advance. Giving respondents a deadline for completion and return is usually inadvisable: it may slow rather than hasten response since some recipients will wait for the deadline date instead of completing the questionnaire immediately; others who miss the date may throw away a completed questionnaire rather than return it late.

One final detail, often overlooked, warrants special mention. It is important to consider the weight of the envelope once the questionnaire, the contact letter, the return envelope (and, occasionally, an incentive) are inside. A little extra on the weight of each envelope can increase postal costs on a large survey by hundreds of pounds. Even worse, unless the correct weight is established, recipients may be asked to pay extra postage when the letter is delivered, a situation guaranteed to produce a derisory response rate.

The covering letter
The covering letter explains the aim of the survey to recipients and

provides assurances about confidentiality. It must convey the importance and urgency of the study as cogently as possible and needs to be composed with a clear view of the recipients in mind. Since it is the main means of persuading people to take part, it must anticipate likely causes of non-response and encourage recipients to reply.

The letter should contain references, where appropriate, to the purpose of the project, stressing the importance of co-operation. In a general population sample, for instance, it will normally contain specific reference to the need to have answers from those who know a lot about the subject as well as from those who know less about it. Where the sample is drawn from specialized groups (for example, nurses or teachers or graduates) the attention of recipients may be directed towards the importance of the study to their profession or discipline, the importance of achieving a balanced sample of grades, degrees of experience, and so on.

The relevance to the sample of the covering letter—its tone, its content, its vocabulary—is always critical. Various stylistic ploys can be used with some effect. For example, Roeher (1963) conducted an experiment into the status of the signatory of the covering letter and its effect on response. The results suggest that the more senior the signatory is in his organization the more likely it is that response will be high. In the United States a practice grew up during the 1960s of using female signatories in the belief that this also boosted response. But this practice seems to have been abandoned there and has (fortunately) never been adopted in Britain. The use of facsimile handwritten postscripts pleading for high levels of co-operation, was also fashionable at one time but has become less so.

Appeals to altruism based on the social value of the study, have also been tried with little success. The social value of a study may help to secure a high response level among some groups, but appeals to altruism are probably best left unsaid; getting across the importance of the study is sufficient.

The survey designer can do little about the recipient's image of the sponsoring organization. There is some evidence (Scott, 1961) that response rates vary according to how prestigious or relevant to the subject respondents believe the sponsor to be. When he conducted his experiments Scott found that the response rate was slightly higher in a government-sponsored study than in a privately-sponsored study with the same questionnaire, but this may no longer be true. The sponsor's name should be mentioned in the covering letter and it will probably have most impact if it appears in the letterhead as well as in the body of the letter. The researcher has to decide—preferably on the basis of a pilot—how much prominence to give the sponsor's name in relation to that of the research

organization. Where the sponsor cannot be mentioned at the outset
for fear of biasing the results, a postal survey approach should
probably not be used. Delicate circumstances require the presence of
an interviewer.

While some experimental studies have suggested that a
personalized approach can raise response levels, the available
evidence is equivocal. If the sample consists of named individuals
rather than unknown heads of households, letters can be personally
addressed to 'Dear Mr_____'. In these cases the instruction
'PLEASE FORWARD IF NECESSARY' should feature prominently on the outward envelope. Where personalization is
impracticable, the covering letter generally starts with 'Dear
Sir/Madam', with the envelope addressed to 'The Occupier'. In
either case the letter itself is generally framed in a fairly formal but
persuasive style.

Most important, the letter should contain a reference to the
confidentiality inherent in all sample surveys, pointing out that
names will never be associated with responses, that the serial
numbers on the questionnaires are solely to identify those to whom
reminders (or letters of thanks, or both) are to be sent, and that
names and addresses will never be passed to third parties. The
name, address and telephone number of a person who can be
contacted by respondents should also be prominent in the letter.

Having suggested various points to include in the covering letter,
it may seem perverse to recommend that it should nonetheless be
fairly short—certainly not more than one side of a page. Instructions
for completing the questionnaire or further explanations can always
be printed separately or, preferably, be included in the
questionnaire. If the letter is long, complicated or pompous it is
unlikely to be read and is certainly unlikely to be persuasive.

Experimental evidence (listed by Linsky, 1975, p. 84) suggests that
a pre-survey contact with members of the sample, advising them of
the study and leading them to expect a questionnaire, can raise
response rates, in some cases substantially. Unfortunately pre-survey
contact by telephone call is not usually possible in Britain unless the
sample comprises, say, businessmen or some other special group
with a high incidence of telephone ownership. In rare cases,
pre-survey contact can be carried out by interviewers but, because
of the cost, there have to be special reasons for recommending
it—for example, where subsidiary observational material is
required, say about the state of repair of the sampled person's
dwelling. In general, however, an interview survey would be done in
these cases in preference to a postal survey.

Reminders and follow-ups

To raise response levels in postal surveys a reminder letter (or telephone call) to recipients who have not yet returned the questionnaire is essential. In most surveys, a second reminder enclosing a copy of the original questionnaire and another return envelope is necessary. Alternatively, a telephone follow-up (sometimes employing a shortened version of the questionnaire to collect basic information) can be tried. More rarely, a personal follow-up is employed. But reminder letters are by far the most common method for boosting response; follow-ups tend to be used as a last resort when an unusually high proportion of recipients is recalcitrant. The mechanics and timing of reminders are discussed in a later section; the focus here is on their tone, content and likely effect on response.

Most of the rules or conventions that apply to the covering letter apply with even greater force to reminder letters. They must certainly re-emphasize both the urgency and the importance of a response, on the prudent assumption that any impact of the covering letter may have faded. They should not look like circulars: since the first letter has failed to produce results, the reminders have to make more impact.

The serial numbers of returned questionnaires need to be recorded to identify those who have replied so that reminder letters are sent only to those who have not. Sending reminders to all, including those who have co-operated, is not only gratuitous and intrusive, but probably creates an impression that the researcher is unable to distinguish respondents from others. Even when reminders are sent only to non-respondents they should contain an apologetic phrase acknowledging that they may have crossed in the post with the completed questionnaire.

Above all, reminders should never give the impression that non-response is normal or that many people have yet to co-operate. The tone of disappointment, concern and surprise generally adopted in reminder letters helps to convey to the recipient who has not replied that he is atypical in his unco-operativeness. The use of the second person singular also helps to imply this sense of isolation, e.g. 'We are very disappointed that you have not yet replied; perhaps your questionnaire went astray; could you give it your urgent attention, so that your views will be included in the study?' These tactics can be used to excess (as the combination of the examples above uses them) but the principle is sound.

The second reminder needs to contain a copy of the questionnaire and a return envelope in case the originals failed to arrive or have been mislaid or thrown away. But a check then has to be made later

to ensure that two questionnaires have not been completed and
returned by the same respondent.

Use of incentives
Some postal surveys make considerable demands on respondents,
either because the questionnaires are long or the tasks (such as diary
completion or reference to past records) are arduous, or perhaps just
because the subject is of low interest to the majority. In these cases,
consideration should be given to the use of what are commonly
referred to as incentives, or, more pompously, 'techniques of
economic persuasion'.

The use of incentives is rare in British social surveys. They are
used somewhat more in commercial research but, even there, not
very frequently. They are essentially a last resort measure, adopted
when the pretests have shown that the combination of other
techniques generates too low or too slow a response. Even small
incentives can add appreciably to the costs of a survey, particularly if
they increase the postage on the outward envelope or necessitate a
separate mailing.

Incentives can certainly reduce non-response, sometimes
substantially (Scott, 1961; Scott Armstrong, 1975); to be most
effective they should be enclosed with the initial mailing rather than
promised as a reward for a completed questionnaire. The sense of
obligation this creates seems to be a more effective psychological
spur than the alternative of withholding rewards until proof of
goodwill has been established. In any case, the incentives are
generally too small to be held out as much of a reward.

Various types of incentive have been employed successfully. If
money is sent it is often in the form of a postal order to the value of
50p. Since the incentive is described in the covering letter as a token
of appreciation rather than payment for time, a token sum is usually
appropriate. Books of postage stamps or fibre-tipped pens are also
commonly used, partly because they are inexpensive, partly because
they are somehow appropriate to the task requested of recipients,
and partly because they are small enough to insert in the outward
envelope.

The type of incentive is important, since an ill-considered choice
can increase the risk of non-response bias. Trading stamps, for
instance, may appeal more to some sections of the population than
to others and may even offend some recipients. When incentives are
planned, they should be selected to be as neutral as possible.

Coping with non-response
Despite all the efforts at maximizing response levels, some recipients
will not reply. In fact, non-response in postal surveys takes two

forms: failure to return the questionnaire, and failure to answer one or more of the questions. The latter is usually referred to as item non-response. The reasons for it will seldom be clear but if the questionnaire has been well-designed and pretested it is unlikely to occur frequently. We concentrate here on the more common and more important problem of failure to respond at all.

Non-response is peculiarly important in postal surveys because there are generally no clues about the characteristics of non-respondents and how they differ from respondents. In field surveys, interviewers can often collect limited information about non-respondents such as approximate age, house type, type of area. Moreover, the evidence available suggests that respondents and non-respondents to postal surveys do differ in several respects.

Respondents (and particularly early respondents) tend to be:
    favourably disposed towards the survey's aims or involved in the
        survey subject
    politically or socially active
    in the higher socio-economic groups
    receptive to new ideas
    rapid decision-makers
    high achievers, especially educationally
    used to communicating by post.
Non-respondents and late respondents are more likely to:
    be elderly, disengaged or withdrawn
    live in urban, rather than suburban or rural areas
    feel that they may be judged by the responses that they make
    feel that they will be inadequate at supplying the information
        requested.
References to some of the many studies dealing with the characteristics of non-respondents are given in the Notes on Further Reading at the end of this chapter.

It is to mitigate some of these potential biasing factors that the initial contact with recipients is so important. But no matter how much effort is made to encourage response, the likelihood of more resistance (in postal and indeed in interview surveys) from most of the types of people listed above is very great indeed. And if the subject matter is related in any way to the characteristics associated with non-response the results will contain some element of bias.

Two kinds of checks on non-response can be carried out on most postal surveys. First, an analysis can be made of answers to key questions by date of reply (which should be coded onto the questionnaire). Early returns often yield a higher proportion of positive answers to one or more of the key questions than do later replies. By plotting the proportion of positive answers over time, an estimate can be made, by extrapolation, of the likely responses of those who did not respond at all. Second, the profile of respondents can be checked against known characteristics of the population that has been sampled; in a general population sample, for instance, checks can be made against the census distributions of age and urban/rural populations.

A third check is available in rare cases when further information about the sample can be gained from independent records (chiefly the sampling frame) which may provide a more definitive picture of the characteristics of non-respondents.

When the characteristics of non-respondents can be established, consideration could be given to weighting the final sample by an appropriate factor in an attempt to reduce the bias, as discussed in Chapter 4. Or, if it seems necessary and resources permit, a further reminder letter could be used to secure further returns. Where non-response is suspected of having a particularly damaging effect on the validity of the findings of a postal survey, the designer may need to conduct follow-up interviews with all or with a subsample of non-respondents, using a full or a shortened version of the questionnaire.

Mechanics of Postal Surveys

A large-scale postal survey (with, say, 1,000 or more recipients) requires a great deal of preparation and planning. Arrangements for the bulk purchase of stamps and for printing return envelopes must be made well in advance, the size and weight of the questionnaires must be established early on, the local post office appreciates being informed in good time of the intended mailing date, the internal procedures for monitoring response and timing reminders have to be set up and working in time to cope with early replies. The following paragraphs contain some practical guidance on the principal organizational requirements for postal surveys.

Supplies required

In ordering supplies for the initial mailing, it is economical to arrange for extra quantities to cover the reminder mailings. So assumptions need to be made about how many reminders are likely to be required. A rule of thumb is that 300 to 400 envelopes and stamps and 160 questionnaires may be needed for every 100 people in the sample (200 of the envelopes—outward and return—being used in the first mail-out).

The figures below chart the rough average pattern of response on a survey that yields a 70 per cent response level, together with the mailing requirements at each stage. It should be noted, however, that the average pattern conceals wide variations between surveys.

Initial mail-out to 100% (two envelopes and stamps per person—outward and return—and one questionnaire)

First reminder to 60% (one envelope and stamp per person, no questionnaire)

Second reminder to 40% (two envelopes and stamps per person—outward and return—and one questionnaire)

Letter of thanks to 70% (one envelope and stamp per person)

The exact quantity of supplies required depends largely on the likely level and speed of response, which a pilot will generally indicate. The following table shows the volume of supplies required, given various expected response levels, and assuming two reminders but no letter of thanks.

Overall expected response level	50%	60%	70%	80%	90%
Approximate number of envelopes required per 100 sample members	380	360	340	320	300
Approximate number of questionnaires required per 100 sample members	160	150	140	130	120

Even if a high response is anticipated, however, it is unwise to budget for less than about three-and-a-half times as many envelopes and stamps and about one-and-a-half times as many questionnaires as there are original recipients. A letter of thanks would increase the envelope and stamp requirements to over four times the number in the sample. Obviously this last mailing is a luxury, but when respondents have had to spend a lot of time on the questionnaire it may nonetheless be desirable.

The budget should also allow for the cost of address labels and, where appropriate, incentives. These calculations emphasize the benefits to be gained if the weight of the outward envelope does not exceed the limit for standard postage rates; they also indicate that the greater the response to the initial mail-out, the smaller will be the cost per completed questionnaire.

Preparation of the mail-out
In considering the staff and administrative requirements for postal surveys, the flow chart overleaf may be helpful.

For booking-in completed questionnaires and for sending reminders respondents have to be identified. To maintain confidentiality this is best done by identity or serial numbers. It is best to have serial numbers on all documents contained within the outward envelope—the questionnaire, the covering letter and the return envelope—in case a recipient sends back, say, the covering letter or questionnaire with comments, but with no other legible identification. In this case the recipient can be identified by his serial number.

Address labels for the outward envelopes have the considerable cost and time advantage of being available in carbonized pads: the name and/or address can be typed direct from the sampling frame onto the labels in quadruplicate—the top copy for the outward envelope, two copies for possible reminders and the last copy for office monitoring and control purposes. If a letter of thanks is to be sent, an extra copy will be needed.

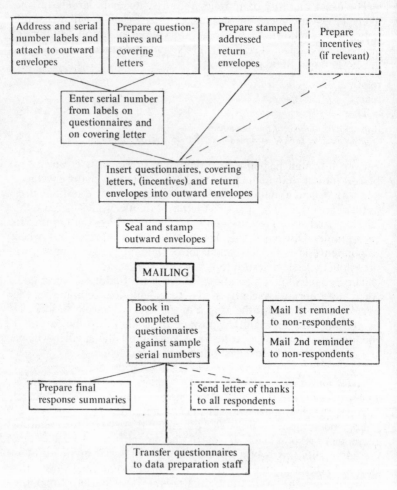

Attention needs to be paid to the typing requirements for the labels, for instance whether recipients are being addressed by name. In the case of surveys of organizations, the researcher must decide on the appropriate recipient and how to address him, e.g. Managing Director (for limited companies), Manager (for shops or banks), Chief Executive, Town Clerk or Clerk to the Council (for local authorities), Establishment Officer (for Government Departments). The decision about whom to address will naturally be based on the subject of study: for example, a Borough Treasurer may be more appropriate as the recipient in some local authority surveys.

Monitoring response and issuing reminders

A rigorous yet simple method of monitoring response to postal surveys can be based on the pads of labels, the top copies of which have been used for the initial mailing. A simple coding system on the remaining copies (ideally kept in identity number order for ease of reference) can be used so that a full record of response, including reasons for non-response (where known), can be maintained.

The system works roughly as follows:

TOP LABEL used on outward envelopes.

SECOND LABEL used for control, then first reminder. When a completed questionnaire is returned, the second label is ticked. The mark is transferred through the carbon to the third and fourth labels. Similarly, when an envelope is returned undelivered by the Post Office or a definite refusal comes in, an appropriate code is entered. At the time of the first reminder mailing, the unmarked second labels represent the section of the sample eligible for first reminders; the marked second labels are discarded.

THIRD LABEL used for control, then second reminder. Some third labels are already marked as a result of the ticks on the second copies. The unmarked ones are then used as above for control purposes until the next reminder mailing. Again the labels remaining unmarked at the end of this phase represent the sample for the reminder; the marked ones are discarded.

FOURTH LABEL used as final control record. The final receipts are marked off as before. Unmarked labels indicate unexplained non-response. All details are now available for the final response summary.

The only problem with a label control system is that, in some surveys, correspondence with recipients precedes the return of the completed questionnaire or the final refusal. This happens particularly in surveys among businessmen or members of a profession. Since the labels may still have to be used for reminders, it is difficult to mark them with a code indicating, say, 'letter sent', without rendering them unusable. Yet it is important to know with whom correspondence is taking place because reminders to them would probably be inappropriate. The best compromise is to use an unobtrusive coding system, like a dot or a comma, or to keep a separate list by serial number.

A daily tally needs to be kept of returned questionnaires, possibly with separate counts within subgroups of the sample (e.g. large and small firms); these subgroups can be identified from, say, the first digit of the serial number. This control makes it possible to determine the best moment for sending each of the reminders. The tallies can usefully be plotted on a graph to provide a direct visual guide along the following lines.

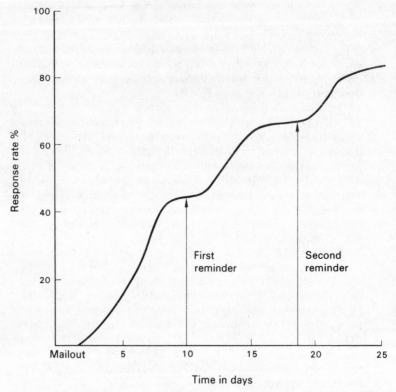

Time in days

As the graph suggests, the optimum time for sending reminder letters is at the point when the curve begins to flatten—commonly about ten days to two weeks after the mailings. Before this, sending reminders is wasteful and unnecessarily intrusive.

In most postal surveys two reminders will suffice to produce acceptable response rates and a reasonably representative coverage of the sample. The bias arising from non-response is thus usually minimal. The reason for this is mainly that preliminary testing and piloting in postal surveys is comparatively inexpensive; so by the time the main postal survey is embarked upon the researcher has usually been able to establish that the quality and size of response will be comparable to those achieved in interview surveys.

Notes on Further Reading

1. There is a large literature on mail questionnaires, much of it reporting the results of experiments comparing different methods of improving response rates. The journal *Public Opinion Quarterly* contains many article on this subject.

2. Several useful articles reporting and commenting on experiments with the use of mail questionnaires have been published. An important article is that by Scott (1961) in which he reports on some experiments by the Government Social Survey, reviews the literature and provides an extensive bibliography. An article by Linsky (1975) on increasing response rates updates Scott's article in this area; and one by Scott Armstrong (1975), reviewing the effects of using monetary incentives, is also useful. The article by Blumberg *et al.* (1974), reporting on an experiment designed to test a wide variety of techniques for raising response, and a review article by Kanuk and Berenson (1975), are also worth consulting.

3. Among the many articles on the characteristics of late respondents and non-respondents to mail questionnaires, the following may be noted: Mayer and Pratt (1966), Schwirian and Blaine (1966), Wells and Andapia (1966) and Ognibene (1970).

4. Some experimental work comparing the responses obtained from self-completion and other data collection techniques has been carried out. Among the articles that may be noted are: Cannell and Fowler (1963) and Hochstim (1967). The article, in two parts, by Nolan (1971) is also useful.

5. Less has been written about the design of mail questionnaires. The book by Berdie and Anderson (1974) covers the design and use of mail questionnaires and includes an annotated bibliography. The article by Nolan (1971) also contains some practical advice on design. The book on mail surveys by Erdos (1970) covers all aspects of conducting a postal survey (illustrated mainly with market research studies) and has many hints on survey and questionnaire design as well as advice on how to secure high response rates.

Chapter 8. Data Preparation

Principal contributor: David Walker

During the data preparation stages of a survey the completed questionnaires have to be checked and transferred into a format suitable for computer analysis. The main functions that follow data collection and precede data analysis are editing and coding—functions that vary in complexity and magnitude but that require to be carried out by skilled and experienced specialist teams.

The Processes Involved

For very small surveys of, say, fewer than 100 interviews and a handful of questions, it might be easy and practicable to analyse the data by going through the questionnaires and counting up answers. But most surveys are too large and complex to be analysed in this way; the researcher cannot cope with the volume of answers and needs a system by which the responses can be transferred onto a computer file for aggregation and statistical analysis. Before this can be done, all responses have first to be translated into numerical codes.

Much of the translation of answers into numerical codes has already been carried out by the interviewers; for precoded questions they circle the code numbers corresponding to respondents' answers. In some cases, however, the final coding has to be done after fieldwork as part of a data preparation task. However, data preparation involves a good deal more than coding. Its various components are typically:

> *Booking-in.* To monitor the interviewer's progress, and to allow response rates for the survey to be compiled, each questionnaire has to be cross-checked against the original sample list of addresses or people. This process is known as booking-in. For postal surveys the booking-in is part of the mailing process as described in Chapter 7.

Clerical edit. Once booked in, the questionnaire has to be examined (or 'edited') for errors. The editors look for consistent errors by an interviewer who may have misunderstood an instruction, for individual errors arising from carelessness, and for universal errors that indicate a fault in the questionnaire. They also check that the document is complete and that any supplementary questionnaires, diaries or self-completion records are present.

Response listing. Almost all questionnaires contain some open-ended questions (discussed in Chapter 3) that are not assigned numerical codes before the interview because the range of answers is not known at that stage. A listing of responses on, say, the first 100 completed questionnaires has to be done so that the researcher can examine the range of responses obtained and draw up a coding frame.

Coding. The open-ended responses on each questionnaire then have to be assigned numerical codes according to the coding frames, and certain standard coding operations, such as occupation coding, will have to be performed. A few summary codes may also have to be added at this stage to assist in the analysis, although most of these will be done later by computer.

Punching. The coded questionnaires are then ready to be transferred onto a computer file. The method of transfer varies: as a rule, punched cards are produced as an intermediate step; in some cases, however, the information on the questionnaire is transferred directly to tape or disk.

Computer editing. For most surveys the clerical edit of completed questionnaires is reinforced by a more extensive and detailed computer edit. An edit specification is prepared which instructs the computer to check, as it reads the data, for certain possible errors and inconsistencies. Errors are identified and corrections have to be made before the record is resubmitted. Only records that pass all the edit checks are accepted onto the computer file; data analysis cannot begin until all records have been 'cleaned'.

Organization of the work

In an organization that has separate field control and data preparation departments, booking-in is normally handled by the field control team. That team may also be involved in some initial clerical editing as part of the quality control associated with fieldwork, although normally data preparation encompasses some further quality control checks. In any event, the clerical editing needs to start soon after the beginning of fieldwork in order to fulfil its quality control role.

For surveys on which the amount of coding on each questionnaire is limited, editing and coding can be combined. As the editors scan the questionnaires for errors and omissions, they code the few open-ended questions by reference to the coding frames. But for surveys involving a lot of coding work and for items of information that are complicated to code, it is generally more efficient to separate the functions and treat coding as a specialist task.

Several teams of people may therefore be working independently on batches of questionnaires. One team does the editing and some minor coding operations along the way. When a batch of questionnaires is completed it is passed to a second team responsible for, say, occupation coding. From there the batch is passed to a third team responsible for coding open-ended questions, and so on. Each team of editors or coders will require a detailed manual of instructions and a personal briefing to enable them to carry out their part of the operation.

With a sequential operation involving several teams, a convenient practice is to arrange questionnaires into batches of twenty-five or fifty with a record slip attached to each batch.

This batch has been:	
Edited by_____	checked by_____
SEG coded by_____	checked by_____
Open-ended coded by_____	checked by_____
Passed to punchers [ ] on (date) ___ / ___ / ___	
(tick)	

The questionnaires stay in their batches throughout the various operations until each batch is ready for punching. The batches are then stored in the order in which they are punched so that they can be referred to easily if the computer edit identifies any errors.

Quality control

It is important to distinguish between training of editors and coders and the quality control of their work. The work of new staff will require to be checked in full as part of the training and supervision function. In addition, before each major coding operation, even experienced coders will need to be trained in the application of the particular coding frame. This training, to ensure uniformity and accuracy, might consist of dummy coding and duplicate coding. Obviously, the more complex the coding operation the more important it is to include trial coding, consistency checks and comprehensive verification.

In a large survey the data preparation process in some ways resembles a production line, with individual workers (or small groups) assigned specialized tasks, each of which contributes to the end product. The quality of work can easily fall in these circumstances unless it is continually monitored. It is therefore advisable to introduce rigorous quality control checks similar to those used in industry. A system of random spot checks is commonly employed to determine whether each member of the team is continuing to operate to a high standard. One method employs batch checking in which, say, three questionnaires are selected at random from each batch of twenty-five and thoroughly examined. By keeping a systematic record of the errors detected in each coder's batch it is possible to determine, from these sample checks, whether the required standard is being achieved. Clearly odd errors (or failures to correct interviewer errors) will be found in the randomly selected questionnaires (which can be corrected), but a complete batch would be inspected only if the error rate based on the sample exceeded the predetermined standard.

This system of batch checking allows errors on the non-sampled questionnaires in a batch to go undetected. But the failure to spot and correct every coding error must be offset against the cost of rechecking every item on every questionnaire. An error rate kept down to about one or two per cent of items by a system of batch checking is usually acceptable given time and budgetary constraints.

The main point to note is that, throughout the data preparation process, supervision and checking should be both systematic and continuous. The results of all checks should, if possible, be documented and summarized in a technical report on a survey. This will help to ensure, whatever the pressures on time, money or labour, that the quality of the work will be high.

Quality control of card punching can be achieved by having all of one operator's punching verified by another. Verification involves repunching to check whether the original punching was in the correct position on each column. Verification does not eliminate all punching errors; a badly written 3 may still be punched and verified as an 8; the puncher and verifier may both make the same basic error in reading from a grid. Nevertheless, verification ensures that punching is a very minor source of survey error; the few errors that do slip through are usually of the kind that will be spotted and corrected in the subsequent computer editing.

Data transfer
Before examining editing and coding in detail, we deal briefly with the system of data transfer to which all editing and coding is directed. As we have mentioned, the object of data transfer is to turn

all answers into a series of numerical codes that can be statistically analysed by computer. Take, for example, the following three items that might appear on a questionnaire:

Sex:	Male . . . . . 1 Female 2	column 1
Age:	Under 15 . . . . .1 15-24 . . . . . 2 25-34 . . . . . 3 35-44 . . . . . 4 45-64 . . . . . 5 65 and over 6	column 2
Do you have a full driving licence to drive a car?	Yes . . . . . 1 No 2	column 3

The answers of two respondents can be summarized by replacing their questionnaires with small cards such as those shown below. The circles on each card summarize the response patterns to the three items.

Respondent A

Man, aged 46, with
a full driving licence
to drive a car

column 1	column 2	column 3
①	1	①
2	2	2
	3	
	4	
	⑤	
	6	

Respondent B

Woman, aged 27, without
a full driving licence
to drive a car

column 1	column 2	column 3
1	1	1
②	2	②
	③	
	4	
	5	
	6	

If instead of the three questions asked of each respondent there had been fifty questions, each questionnaire would probably have been seven or eight pages long. But we could still summarize the answers for each respondent on a fairly small card containing fifty columns.

This is the basic principle of a punched card system. Every card has eighty columns with ten code positions printed on each column (from 0 to 9).* Instead of a circle being drawn around the appropriate code number a hole is punched into the card. So for Respondent A in the example above there would be a hole in code 1 position on column 1, a hole in code 5 position on column 2 and a hole in code 1 position on column 3, as in the card reproduced below:

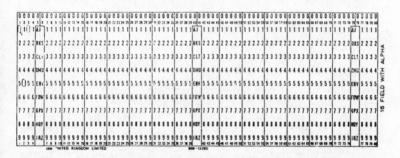

A second card would be used for the second respondent with codes 2, 3 and 2 punched on columns 1 to 3 respectively, and so on.

Since in most surveys dozens of questions are asked of each respondent, many if not all of the eighty columns are normally used, and often more than one card per respondent is necessary. How these cards are identified so that they can be linked to one another and to the appropriate questionnaire is discussed in a later section.

Once all the data have been punched onto a set of punched cards, they can be transferred to a computer file (either a tape or a disk). Cards are used only as an intermediate process since the computer can analyse from tape or disk more efficiently. The cards are passed through a reader that identifies the position of each hole and reproduces an equivalent code on a computer tape or disk. So the computer reads the punches in much the same way as a clerical editor reads the circles around a code number on a questionnaire.

A more recent development is to punch directly onto a computer file. This overcomes the restriction of cards to eighty columns: a questionnaire that would spread onto four separate punched cards (with all the attendant need for cross-identification) can therefore be

---

*Two more code positions can be used on each column, although they are not printed on the card. These are referred to variously as the X and Y, X and A, X and V, — and +, or — and & positions.

punched as a continuous record onto the computer file, followed by the second record and the third, and so on. The disadvantage of this direct transfer system occurs at the computer editing stage, particularly when there are large, complex data sets that need a lot of correction. Whereas each card (or group of cards) provides a discrete set of responses for each questionnaire that can be corrected individually, a continuous record of responses makes individual identification and correction (on a large scale) a more difficult operation. The card system is more common (partly because of the way data analysis developed from mechanical counting and sorting equipment) but both systems are workable, and the users of each tend to be strong advocates of their own.

A third system of data transfer involves the use of special optical scan equipment. With this system, a page of a questionnaire is transferred visually (using special equipment) to the computer file. Punching is eliminated, with the result that, in theory at least, speed and efficiency are increased and errors minimized. It is a system best suited to very short questionnaires with very large samples. On other types of survey the system is difficult and expensive to apply: optical scan requires questionnaires with special design and printing, special training of interviewers, care in completing difficult questionnaires, and special editing to remove from each page extraneous marks that would spoil the visual record. Where optical scan is employed, the initial design of the survey has to be carefully geared to its use. But the system is still developing and, as improvements are made and familiarity with it increases, it may be possible to extend its use further.

Whatever the system adopted, however, the principles of data preparation and data transfer remain much the same: questionnaires require clerical editing; some responses need to be coded before any mechanical, photographic or computer transfer is done; when the transfer has taken place, by whatever process, the data should be computer-edited so that errors can be corrected by referring back to questionnaires.

Editing
One part of the editing function is to check on interviewing quality. An examination of the initial batch of work of each interviewer will show whether consistent errors are being made. The results of these first checks can be used by field supervisors in their contact with interviewers and by field controllers in helping to detect interviewers who may need to be retrained or rejected. Lessons learned from the editing need to be transmitted to the field in time to be acted upon, as discussed in Chapter 6.

The other part of the clerical editing function is correcting such errors as occur even when all interviewers are operating to a consistently high standard. The errors may be minor: circling of some codes may have been ambiguous; a filter instruction may have been misunderstood; an answer to an expenditure question may have been entered as, say, £1.24 when it should have been entered as 01.24, and so on.

Editing functions
Since an interviewer's workload may consist of about thirty interviews each of forty-five minutes' duration, each questionnaire comprising fifteen or twenty pages (a total of 450-600 pages), it would be very surprising if there were no errors or omissions.

Most clerical editing is a routine operation to make the documents clear and consistent enough for punch operators to work with at high speeds. The main source book for the editor is the interviewer's project instructions. These, with the questionnaire, should contain all the necessary information about valid codes, filter checks and the way responses should be entered. In addition, specific editing instructions will normally have to be compiled to deal with items such as logic checks and how to cope with missing data.

The questionnaire layout should be such that the editing task is clear and easy. Usually a questionnaire that has been well laid out for interviewers along the lines specified in Chapter 3 will also be efficient for editing. For example, using the right-hand column for filter instructions makes it easy for editors to check that the filters have been correctly applied. Similarly, where there are boxes on the questionnaire for code numbers (for example where exact numerical information such as expenditure or times is to be entered) missing entries can readily be identified. For clarity, editors should use different coloured pens from those used by interviewers and take care not to obscure any previous entries. An editing supervisor or researcher can then see what the interviewer has done and what changes or insertions have been made by the editors—a useful practice for assessing not only interviewers' performances but also the quality of the questionnaire.

Editing problems can arise where responses have been omitted. If the omission is an isolated or minor one, it would be inappropriate to send the interviewer back to the respondent. These omissions have to be dealt with by the insertion of a 'not answered' code (unless the answer is obvious from other information in the questionnaire). On the other hand, more serious or widespread omissions can be corrected only by a follow-up interview. Distinguishing these serious omissions from others requires judgement and experience on the part of editors.

There are some situations where the editor can deduce an answer that has been omitted, for example when a 'total' figure has been left blank but all components of the total have been provided, or where it is obvious from other information that a zero has been left off an entry. Attempting to impute missing bits of information, however, by inserting codes at random or by some form of guesswork is risky. The better and safer policy is to use the 'not answered' code. The researcher then has various options for dealing with the missing data in his interpretation. And at least it will be explicit that the data are deficient in various (usually trivial) ways. Imputation at the editing stage removes the researcher's options and is bound to cause concern about the volume of information that has been inserted artificially rather than collected from respondents.

Since in most surveys there is both a clerical and computer edit, some double-checking is inevitable. Although this might seem wasteful, to dispense with the clerical edit would lead to a lower standard of interviewing since, carried out concurrently with interviewing, clerical editing helps prevent errors. It would also result in an expensive and laborious punching stage with punch operators having to sort out ambiguities and, in many cases, making decisions without proper reference. Moreover, it is helpful to detect errors earlier rather than later: errors detected at the computer edit, for example, are generally tedious and expensive to correct. The latter process involves finding the questionnaires from the identification numbers on the print-out, re-examining them, finding the error from the column numbers on the print-out, correcting the errors, and, either repunching and submitting the corrected or new cards or directly changing the image in the computer file. It is generally preferable to spot and correct as many errors as possible beforehand.

In any case, clerical editing fulfils functions that computer editing could fulfil only at much greater cost. Trained editors can cross-relate bits of information on questionnaires and spot inconsistencies difficult to detect by computer; reading through questionnaires, they may remember items that jar with later items, even though precise instructions to check one against the other have not been given. In the clerical editing of expenditure information, for example, a skilled editor may well spot a pattern of expenditure that seems surprising in view of the circumstances of the household and establish that an extra digit has been added in error. This sort of check relies on the experience and skill of an editor rather than on precisely specified logical checks. Although, technically, sophisticated checks of this kind could be built into a computer edit program, in practice the scope is severely limited. A clerical edit, however brief, is a necessary component of almost every survey.

Why, therefore, since a clerical edit is desirable and overlaps with a computer edit, can we not dispense with the latter? There are two main reasons. First, there may be several hundred important but simple checks that would be both tedious and uneconomic to handle clerically—for example, checking that every code number is within the range of codes allowed for each question. The editors would, in any case, miss some of these checks whereas the computer edit can be comprehensive. Second, the data preparation stages themselves can introduce errors, made by editors, coders or punchers, and a final check is necessary, before the analysis, to ensure the data are 'clean' so that expensive machine time at the analysis stage is not wasted.

Checks to be made

Five principal types of editing checks are performed clerically and/or by the computer. These are as follows:

Structure checks: These are undertaken primarily to ensure that all the information sought has been provided. In the clerical edit a check is made that all documents for a record are together and correctly labelled. For example, a household questionnaire and separate questionnaires for each person in the household may have to be identified and linked. Similarly, in the computer edit, checks are made that all the punched cards are present for a record (i.e. the complete data set for the person or household being interviewed).

Valid coding range checks: The range of possible codes for each column is known. In some cases only codes 1, 2 and 3 are possible; in others, codes 1 to 9 may be used. The edit function in this case (mainly done by computer) is to check that no code outside the valid range has been punched and, where applicable, that more than one code has not been punched on a column.

Filter checks: For each question that should have been answered by only a subsection of the sample, two checks need to be made: first, that those who should have answered the question (by virtue of a particular answer to an earlier question) have done so; second, that no-one else has.

Checks for omissions: As mentioned, dealing with omissions generally involves inserting a 'not answered' code, although it is sometimes possible for the editor to deduce the correct answer from other items of information.

Logic checks: In some cases precise logic checks can be specified in advance. For example, a person under 16 cannot be married or have a full driving licence; a housewife not in paid employment should not have an occupation code. In other cases, scrutiny may be advisable to pick up very unlikely occurrences—for example, a person who seems to have travelled 2,000 miles by car in a week, or a family of fifteen people. They may be genuine or they may be the result of misunderstanding or incorrect transcription. But it is worth checking to see if there is a clue to the appropriate entry. Occasionally, as already indicated, editors carry out some logic checks that have not been specified in spotting apparent inconsistencies.

The data transferred to the computer file for analysis may contain errors that have not been detected even after a comprehensive clerical and computer edit. If, for example, a respondent's age has been incorrectly entered on the questionnaire by the interviewer, the error will pass undetected unless it is obviously inconsistent with other items (such as marital status or possession of a driving licence). Editing can identify only noticeable errors; it can correct items of information wrongly given by respondents or wrongly transcribed by interviewers only when there are clues that point to the error and provide the solution.

Computer edit procedures

Records are transferred to the final computer file only after they have passed through all the computer edit checks without a failure. A record that fails on even one check is not transferred. Instead the questionnaire number is printed out together with a coded message or series of messages to indicate the errors. Reference is then made to the questionnaire, errors are put right and the record is resubmitted to the edit routine. If it fails again because the errors have not all been eliminated or because correcting one error has exposed or created another, then it will be rejected again and the process will be repeated.

The method of correcting errors on the computer file varies according to the data transfer system. If punched cards are being used, the cards comprising the failed record are normally withdrawn by hand, repunched where necessary and resubmitted. When the scale of the survey demands it, this is done sequentially: as the field-work and data preparation progress, batches of cards are computer edited; records that fail in the first batch are resubmitted with the second batch, and so on. Developments in computer technology have made it possible for direct transfer of corrections to a record (through a computer terminal) to the original computer file to replace items of information in error. This system is likely to be used increasingly in the future, at least for the final stages of correction. With any system of correction, however, it is important that the corrections are also noted on the questionnaires so that they remain consistent with the computer file.

The first and most fundamental check to be made in computer editing is the structure check. If one card is missing from a record so many errors would be printed out (one for each valid column) that the computer edit for that record would automatically stop after reporting the omission. In other cases, however, it is inefficient for editing of a record to stop every time an error is located in it. Usually, therefore, all the errors contained in a record are identified and printed out together so that all corrections can be made at the same time.

The other main checks to be built into the computer edit fall under the headings discussed earlier—range checks, filter checks, checks for omissions and logic checks. With data sets based on long interviews there will naturally be a great number of composite checks to be made, for example, that on, say, column 43, either a code 1, 2 or 3 must be punched and nothing else (i.e. that it was single-punched and only a code within the valid range was present); or that column 44 must be blank if code 1 or 2 was punched on column 43, but coded 1 to 5 if code 3 was punched on column 43. For economy, the print-out from a computer edit is normally cryptic: the error messages are usually in a simple code (e.g. LC 17/24=logic check between columns 17 and 24; R1.31= range check on card 1, column 31). The listing usually comprises the record number of each failed record together with an indication of the checks that the record has failed.

Since a whole record fails if one code is mispunched or one column incorrectly left blank, the initial rejection rate of records will often be fairly high. Not uncommonly with an average-length interview survey, between a third and a half of all records fail at the first submission. In longer interviews such as the 1975/76 National Travel Survey (Brook, 1976), where some 15,500 records were submitted to a detailed computer edit, an even higher rejection rate at the first submission may be anticipated. The average number of cards per record in this case was very high at just over 30; there were thus approximately half a million punched cards involved. The edit programme failed 57 per cent of records at the first submission; yet only 4 per cent of cards and 0.2 per cent of columns were in error.

At the end of the computer edit stage all records will have been passed successfully onto the computer file ready for data analysis, although for the reasons mentioned earlier, they will not be entirely error-free. They should, however, be internally consistent.

Coding

As indicated earlier, answers given by respondents have to be reduced to numerical codes before the data can be punched and processed. For most questions the coding frame is devised before the main interviewing begins and can therefore be printed on the questionnaire. The interviewer then circles the code number corresponding to the respondent's answer as indicated in Chapter 3.

Not all precoded frames are straightforward, but for most questions the instructions give an adequate guide to coding. Moreover, the standard instruction to interviewers in doubt about precodes is that they should write the answers on the questionnaire in full so that they can be dealt with by coders later. An 'other answer' code is often added to the end of a coding frame with space for interviewers to write the answer in full. A response coded 'other answer' by the interviewer and written in may be reclassified at the coding stage into one of the predetermined categories.

There are, however, other questions requiring office coding. First, some responses cannot be coded in the field even though the coding frame is known at the outset. The coding of occupations into socio-economic groups or addresses into geographical zones are two of the most common examples. An interviewer could not possibly choose during the interview the appropriate code for a particular occupation from the many thousands classified by the Office of Population Censuses and Surveys. Later, however, each occupation can be identified from the appropriate manual, as discussed in Chapter 9, and coded. Interviewers collect and insert full details of occupations; specialist coders then fit the answers into a specified socio-economic classification.

Address coding, used mainly in travel or mobility studies, requires a similar procedure. Interviewers obtain full postal addresses from respondents; coders then refer to gazetteers, maps or Post Office microfiche postal codes that can be used to classify addresses geographically. The gazetteers and maps may be insufficiently comprehensive as a coding frame and may need to be supplemented by lists of establishments such as pubs, cinemas, hospitals and major stores, the names of which are often referred to by respondents as their destinations instead of the exact addresses. In addition, it is helpful to engage a small team with detailed local knowledge to deal with the more difficult queries. They will be familiar with nicknames and local abbreviations for places that will be recorded in questionnaires.

A second form of coding can be achieved without the aid of a coding team. For some variables, such as household composition, it is more efficient and accurate to produce a summary code at the computing stage from detailed information collected by interviewers. In this case the full details recorded in the household composition grid are punched directly from the questionnaire and the computer is programmed to construct summary codes by grouping them in a specified way. Formation of age groupings from exact ages recorded by interviewers is also often done by computer summary coding.

The third main type of coding requirement is to deal with responses to open-ended questions for which coding frames cannot be compiled in advance because too little is known about the range of possible responses or their likely frequency. The coding frames in these cases have to be compiled on the basis of the range of answers given.

Compiling a coding frame
In large-scale surveys the researcher cannot look at every response to an open-ended question before compiling a coding frame. He can, however, usually learn enough about the range and grouping of responses from the first hundred or more questionnaires to arrive from the field (provided that they are a reasonably unbiased sample of all questionnaires). If no immediate pattern of answers is apparent, the number must be increased; on some surveys, researchers work to a rule that ten per cent of the sample should form the basis for the coding frame.

It is unwise to compile a coding frame without taking into account the frequency with which different answers occur. Flicking through the returns can be very misleading: unexpected answers that may occur only once or twice will catch the eye and more frequent but less surprising answers may be overlooked. A more systematic approach is needed, such as a listing of responses as in the example overleaf. In this case the question used for illustration might well have been precoded, since it is not difficult to anticipate the likely range of answers. For more complex questions the range of answers may occupy four or five pages.

Each new kind of answer identified by coders is written on the listing sheet, but answers that have occurred before can be entered simply by adding a 1 to the count column. When responses from all the selected questionnaires have been listed, the frequency of each category listed would be totted up and entered. Each marginally diferent kind of answer should be entered separately by the coder, so that it leaves the researcher free to adopt any kind of grouping.

An examination of a hundred questionnaires will not always produce a hundred responses to all questions. The illustration overleaf is based on the assumption that the question was filtered and applied only to respondents in car-owning households who travelled to work by train. Moreover, it is based on the fact that a few respondents gave more than one answer to the question. So two hundred questionnaires were needed to find one hundred separate answers to the question. If there is any reason to believe that the

LISTING SHEET: Number of questionnaires examined **200**

Question No. **1(b)** - Column No. **17**

Q. **Why do you travel to work by train rather than by car?**

Code		Count	Total
	Unable to drive	꠰꠰꠰꠰ ꠰꠰꠰꠰ ꠰꠰꠰꠰ ꠰	16
	Car used by wife during day	꠰꠰꠰꠰ ꠰꠰꠰꠰ ꠰꠰꠰	13
	Nowhere to park the car	꠰꠰꠰꠰	5
	Parking costs too expensive	꠰꠰꠰꠰ ꠰꠰꠰꠰ ꠰꠰꠰꠰ ꠰꠰꠰꠰ ꠰꠰	22
	Takes too long by car	꠰꠰꠰꠰ ꠰꠰꠰꠰	9
	Driving is too tiring	꠰꠰꠰	3
	Like to relax + read the paper	꠰꠰	2
	Don't like driving in the rush-hour	꠰꠰꠰꠰	5
	Carpark is too far from work	꠰꠰꠰	3
	More pleasant journey by train	꠰꠰꠰꠰ ꠰꠰꠰꠰ ꠰꠰	12
	Don't have driving licence	꠰꠰꠰꠰ ꠰꠰	7
	Quicker to go by train	꠰꠰꠰꠰ ꠰꠰꠰	8
	Frustrating sitting in traffic jams	꠰꠰	2
	Like company of other people on train	꠰꠰꠰	3
	Would have long walk from carpark	꠰꠰	2
		Total	112

initial batch of questionnaires was a biased subgroup, for instance that it contained an unduly high proportion of part-time employees (because they are more readily found at home), the listing will have to be delayed until a greater number (and a better cross-section) of questionnaires has arrived.

Having studied the listing sheets the researcher would then compile the coding frame, based partly on the frequency with which types of answer occur and partly on the importance he attaches to a category for analysis purposes. In the example cited, the coding frame might be:

Response type	Code
Cannot drive/no licence	1
Car not available/used by someone else	2
Quicker by train/too long by car	3
More pleasant/less tiring journey by train	4
Difficult to park/parking too far away	5
Cost of parking too high	6
Other answer	7

The researcher would normally code the responses on the listing sheet to make sure the frame works and to show the coding team how each type of answer corresponds to each code. As a safeguard it is useful for coders to apply the coding frame to a further subsample of questionnaires—say another hundred or more. These should be inspected by the researcher to ensure that the frame works and that it is being applied properly. If, for instance, more than about ten per cent of responses are being coded as 'other answer', the frame should probably be extended before full coding begins. Getting the coding frame right at the outset is important; once coding is in progress it is difficult and time-wasting to accommodate changes—even minor ones.

The ideal coding frame is unambiguous enough to be applied uniformly by all members of a coding team. Once the team has been trained in its use it should be possible to apply it consistently. In practice, however, some element of judgement is inevitable and the aim must be to minimize its possible effects. So the coding frame should not demand that subtle variations or fine differences in response are detected. If it does, differences of application between coders will introduce bias.

However good the coding frame, some responses will be difficult to code. Instead of allowing the coders to force them into one of the categories, these oddities are more effectively dealt with by 'tabbing' the questionnaire in which they occur—that is, stapling a piece of paper to it so that it can easily be spotted later. Then, perhaps at the end of coding, the researcher can make decisions about each query.

Multi-coding

Before computers were used for the analysis of survey data, the process was carried out mainly on mechanical card-sorters and counters. It was then usual practice to squeeze the information comprising one record onto the fewest number of cards to facilitate the analysis. For example, if sex was punched on a column using code positions 1 (male) and 2 (female), the remaining codes on that column would generally have been used to signify an entirely different variable—possibly marital status. Nowadays, this practice is avoided, partly because it unnecessarily squeezes unrelated pieces of information onto the same column, and partly because many computer programs, particularly statistical analysis programs, will accept only one code per column; multi-coded columns are rejected as invalid.

Multi-coding is also sometimes used when a respondent legitimately gives more than one answer to a question. He may, for example, mention two reasons for using a train for his journey, e.g. 'Parking is too difficult' (Code 5) and 'It's quicker by train' (Code 3). These codes could reasonably be (and often are) punched onto the same column as long as the computer program contemplated can cope with multi-punching. Otherwise the researcher would find himself faced with the tiresome operation of transforming the multi-punched responses into a single-punch format.

Many survey agencies routinely use complex multi-punched data sets, and have access to tabulation programs to handle them. Unless such programs are available to the researcher, it is best to avoid multi-punching as it can reduce flexibility in the choice of the most appropriate program. The column layout will thus have to allow, say, two or three columns for answers to some questions so that a respondent who gives several answers can be provided for. His first answer will be punched on, say, column 17, his second on column 18, and so on. For respondents who give a single response, column 18 is left blank or coded 'not applicable'. So a decision needs to be made in advance of fieldwork as to how many columns to leave for each open-ended question: if too few columns are allowed some answers will have to be disregarded. Where practicable, the column allocation should be generous. In any event, the coding of responses requires prior knowledge of the analysis program envisaged or at least prior communication with those responsible for the programming.

There are various ways of avoiding multi-coding for multiple answers but the simplest is to allow several columns.

Linked codes
Although there are twelve coding positions on a single column, 0 to 9 and X and Y, many computer programs do not accept X and Y positions as valid individual codes. For many purposes, therefore, a single-column 'field' limits the coding frame to ten items; for a frame that requires more than ten possible answers (including 'Don't know' and 'Other answer'), a two- or more-column field has to be used. If two columns are linked—so that the responses are coded 00, 01, 02, 03 . . . up to 99—there are 100 positions. A three-column field will provide for 1,000 positions, and so on.

Linked coding frames are used most often for items such as

expenditure or times. Exact figures can then be punched and there is no need for summary codes. For instance 99p can be punched as 099 on three consecutive columns; 7.15 p.m. can be punched as 1915 on four consecutive columns, and so on. With linked codes, answers can never be multi-coded because there is no way of distinguishing one pair of digits from another.

Identification codes

When data have been reduced to a series of numerical codes, and transferred to cards or tape, it is essential that each record can be identified and related to its questionnaire by an identity or questionnaire number. If punched cards are used, with more than one card for each respondent, we also have to be able to identify which card corresponds to which section of the questionnaire; and if we want to be able to say that these cards or tapes correspond to a particular research project, that project has to be given an identity number that is punched onto all the records.

The system of identification needs to be carefully planned. Apart from the project number, which will be common to all records, and usually punched on the first or last few columns, the two main considerations are the identity link between the computer records and questionnaires, and the corresponding link between the various punched cards that together form one record.

When addresses or individuals' names are issued to interviewers, or listed for postal despatch, each address or person is usually given a serial number for easy reference. Serial numbers are also a means of achieving confidentiality, since names and addresses can be left off the questionnaire without losing the connection—necessary for quality checks—between questionnaires and respondents. Serial numbers also help to relate documents from the same household or organization.

Except in very small-scale surveys the issued serial numbers are, however, not usually the means by which computer records are matched to questionnaires, even though they may appear on both. Questionnaires are not returned from the field in serial number order. The order of return will depend on the interviewers' success at different addresses, and sorting, say, 5,000 questionnaires from the field into serial number order would be a major task. In any case, the editing, coding and data transfer functions usually begin before all questionnaires have been returned. It is convenient, therefore, to batch questionnaires as they are edited and coded (say, into groups of 25) and to number them sequentially for example from 0001 for a sample of between 1,000 and 9,999. The computer record is then identified by this questionnaire or record number. If an error occurs in record 0371 it is then easy to find the appropriate questionnaire since they will have been batched and stored in numerical order.

For long interviews where the record consists of several cards per person, there may, for instance, be a wide range of questions about current employment and a similar range about past employment. One punched card might record the answers to the current employment questions and a second the answers to the historical questions. All the 'current' cards would then have a code 1 punched on a particular column and all the 'historical' cards would have a code 2 punched on the same column. By relating the record identity numbers and the card identity numbers we can select the two cards for any one respondent and distinguish between the two data sets. In practice, however, separate punched cards do not always conform to separate topic sections. They do not need to. The computer will treat these separate cards as one long record at a later stage and the subdivision into topic areas will be carried out in the analysis.

The same principle applies to different questionnaires relating to the same record. For example one household questionnaire and several individual questionnaires may form a data set for one household. The household questionnaire may then be punched as card type 1, and each individual questionnaire from that household as card type 2. With this kind of structure, it is always useful to include a check for completeness: one such check is to enter on the household card how many individual person cards there should be for that record.

Several columns may in the end be taken up on each card by the basic identification codes, for example:

Columns 1-3   codes 246 punched to indicate that the card belongs to project number 246

Columns 4-7   codes 0371 punched to indicate the question-naire number (i.e. record number) for the respondent

Column 8   code 3 punched to indicate that it is the third card for the respondent

Columns 9-12   codes 0274 punched as a record of the issued address serial number for the respondent.

Although the column layout and the definitions of various administrative and identity codes will be familiar to all at the time of the data preparation operation it is important to remember that the data may continue to be analysed for a year or two afterwards. Documentation is therefore an important part of data preparation. Anyone who wants to analyse the data will need a full description of what each code on each column means. For most of the record this is clear from the questionnaire (or at least from an annotated version); but certain types of information, including identity codes and codes for open-ended questions, will have been added. These must be

documented in full alongside all the other coding instructions that
have been followed.

Notes on Further Reading
1. The texts by Lansing and Morgan (1971), Moser and Kalton
   (1971) and Warwick and Lininger (1975) contain good
   discussions of preparing survey data for analysis.
2. The coding manual edited by Muehl (1961) and the editing and
   coding manual of the World Fertility Survey (1976) are
   useful contributions on this subject. Downham (1955) and
   Harris (1955) describe the work involved in the coding
   operation.
3. There have been several studies of the reliability of coding,
   including Durbin and Stuart (1954), Woodward and Franzen
   (1948), Crittenden and Hill (1971), Kammayer and Roth in
   Costner (1971), Sussman and Haug (1967), Morrissey (1974)
   and Duncan and Evers in Land and Spilerman (1975).
4. Kemsley (1972) describes the pre-computer editing procedures
   used with the complex budget data obtained in the Family
   Expenditure Survey; the coding procedures for this survey are
   described in Kemsley (1969a). Computer editing of census and
   survey data is discussed by Stuart (1966), Pritzker *et al.* (1966),
   Freund and Hartley (1967), Fellegi and Holt (1976), and
   Hocking *et al.* (1974).

Chapter 9. Classifying Respondents

A major feature of survey analysis is the search for variation in responses between subgroups of a sample. Attempts are made to associate variations with differences in the age or sex, region or type of area, income, education or occupation of respondents. These and a great many further demographic, socio-economic and other classifications can be used as a basis for subdividing respondents in the analysis. A number of these classifications will be found in almost all large-scale surveys and the questions and coding frames for classification data have been extensively developed. Moreover, the Population Census has provided an invaluable testing ground for some of the items: its comprehensive coverage means that the classifications have to cover even the smallest minority groups.

The extensive development of survey classifications has not, however, resulted in universal agreement about every detail. Whereas some categorizations, for instance male/female, are presumably beyond dispute, most others, for example educational qualifications or housing tenure have several variations. Standardization across surveys and with the census (although the latter, as a self-completion form, is not always an appropriate model for household survey definitions) has several advantages: it makes comparisons easier; it helps to check the representativeness of the achieved sample against census and other survey data; it helps interviewers and coders to become familiar with detailed points of definition, which can only improve the quality of their work.

On the other hand the precise form of classification must obviously take account of the specific purpose of each survey. For some samples or subjects familiar classifications may need to be adapted. It would be wrong to put standardization and conformity above all other considerations. The aim of this chapter is not to lay down a set of rigid rules for classification variables; in any case, conventions or definitions tend to change in response to new circumstances. Instead, we consider a selection of important and widely used variables and illustrate the way in which these can be categorized. We also illustrate the need for detailed points of definition.

The items covered here are those that are probably the most widely used classifications for population surveys: we do not deal with business survey classifications or less commonly used social groupings such as religion or political allegiance. We have, however, tried to illustrate the range and structure of classifications by providing examples from four major categories of variable.

Individual classifications, such as demographic, employment and educational variables.

Household classifications, such as family composition, socio-economic and mobility variables.

Accommodation classifications, such as type of accommodation, space and amenity variables.

Geographical classifications, such as area and regional variables.

Individual Classifications
Sex, age and marital status
Whereas the classification of respondents into males and females offers no problems special to survey research and can usually be done without asking a question, it is risky to classify other members of the household who are not present simply on the basis of their first names. Each person's sex must be asked. The division into age categories is a little more difficult. The question most commonly used is:

'What was your/his/her age last birthday?'

Usually exact age (in years) is recorded by interviewers and groupings are subsequently formed for analysis, normally beginning, for comparability with census data, with the years ending in 0 or 5

i.e. 30 but less than 35
    35 but less than 40, and so on.

There must be no ambiguity over the end points of each range; in this case 35 is obviously included in the second of these two groups. Groupings of ages can be achieved most efficiently at the analysis stage after a preliminary tabulation to show a detailed age distribution. This can then be collapsed to provide appropriate age groups as the final classification variable for analysis.

The age categorization of children usually conforms in a general way to pre-school, primary school and secondary school ages:
1. less than 5 years
2. 5 but less than 12 years

3. 12 but less than 17 years

Adults may be grouped into approximate stages of the life cycle, for example:

4. 17 but less than 25 years
5. 25 but less than 45 years
6. 45 but less than 65 years
7. 65 years and over

Or they may be grouped simply into ten-year or twenty-year categories.

The marital status classification is fairly straightforward. The sort of question used is:

'Are you single, married, widowed, separated or divorced?'

1. Single
2. Married (including common law marriages)
3. Widowed
4. Separated or divorced

Activity status

The classification of respondents according to whether or not they are in employment is usually done before details of occupation are sought. A simple three-way split is often used (working full-time, working part-time, not working) instead of the more extensive classification given below:

1. Working full-time (over 30 hours per week)
2. Working part-time (10 to 30 hours per week)
3. Seeking work
4. Sick
5. Retired
6. Student
7. Housewife
8. Other persons not working

A number of points of definition for this classification need to be considered:

(a) The two 'working' categories are usually taken to include those on strike, on holiday and temporarily sick.
(b) A person who works for less than the lower number of hours used to define part-time working (sometimes 6 or 8 hours, more usually 10 hours per week) has to be coded as 'not working' unless a special extra category has been allowed. The alternative would be to have no lower limit on part-time hours.
(c) Retired people who have taken up a new full-time or part-time job are normally coded on the basis of that job.

(d) The 'retired' category does not usually include women who give up work to marry or to have children; they are coded as housewives.

(e) Apprentices on sandwich courses organized as part of their employment are usually coded into the working categories (not as students).

(f) The student category includes schoolchildren and those following full-time further education.

(g) The 'other' category will normally be used for children of pre-school age, for adults who have never worked and for adults working less than 10 hours per week who are not seeking work, sick or retired.

Personal income

Although a broad categorization of personal income is useful it presents problems. First, questions on income attract a higher refusal rate than other questions; not uncommonly, between one-fifth and one-quarter of respondents who have answered other questions refuse to provide details of their income. Second, they can cause resentment, even among those who do answer the question. Third, income is very difficult to define precisely; its accurate measurement requires a long and complex series of questions (*see*, for instance, the income schedule used in the Family Expenditure Survey—Kemsley, 1969a). The measurement of income based on short and simple classification questions is therefore somewhat crude and imprecise. Attempts should nonetheless be made to distinguish between gross and net income; most classifications employ gross income (i.e. before tax and National Insurance deductions).

The conventional and fairly satisfactory approach to income classification is to ask the respondent to choose a category, corresponding to his gross income, from a list of ranges on a printed card. Each range is identified by a code letter so that respondents can simply mention the letter.

The card shown to respondents normally has weekly income and annual income ranges side by side. It also includes the words that the interviewer has to repeat and footnotes containing guidance on how the respondent should define his income. An example of an income card is shown overleaf.

A similar classification can be used in enquiring about household income. In this case the total gross household income would be the basis for the classification. Since personal income is coded in broad ranges, total household income cannot be computed simply by adding the personal income codes of all members of the household.

PLEASE INDICATE THE GROUP THAT INCLUDES YOUR OWN
PERSONAL INCOME FROM ALL SOURCES OUTSIDE YOUR
HOUSEHOLD. THIS SHOULD BE YOUR GROSS INCOME BEFORE
INCOME TAX AND NATIONAL INSURANCE HAVE BEEN DEDUCTED

Weekly income	Group	Annual income
Less than £23	M	Less than £1,200
£23 but less than £33	K	£1,200 but less than £1,700
£33 but less than £43	D	£1,700 but less than £2,235
£43 but less than £53	T	£2,235 but less than £2,750
£53 but less than £68	G	£2,750 but less than £3,535
£68 but less than £83	P	£3,535 but less than £4,300
£83 but less than £98	W	£4,300 but less than £5,100
£98 but less than £113	E	£5,100 but less than £5,875
£113 and over	Q	£5,875 and over

Include: overtime, bonuses, unearned income, pensions, social security
        benefits
Exclude: payments from other members of the household

Usually the head of household has to be asked to indicate the group
corresponding to the total household income. Where there is more
than one wage-earner the head of household may have difficulty in
providing the information and consultation with other people in the
household may be necessary. A question about total household
incomes may well produce a lower percentage of definite answers
than a question about personal incomes.

Because people are sensitive about income questions they are
usually left until the very end of the interview. And the information
is not usually obtained second-hand, i.e. from one member about
another, except where the head of household is providing gross
income figures for his or her household.

Education
The difficulty with education variables is that the classifications
have to be applicable to respondents educated at very different times
during this century. The variation between areas of the United
Kingdom (particularly between Scotland and England), between
courses followed by different generations and between different
systems of education makes the detailed definition of each variable
rather cumbersome. There are two main education variables in
use—terminal age of full-time education and educational
qualifications. Of these, terminal education age is the easier to deal
with. It is most accurately obtained by asking the following three
questions:
    (a) How old were you when you left school?
    (b) Did you follow any other full-time education course at a

university, a polytechnic or a further education college?
IF 'YES' ASK (c)

(c) How old were you when you finished your last full-time education course?

Interviewers can record age in individual years so that the classification can be formed at the analysis stage. A classification related to 'A' level and higher education courses might be adopted, for example:

1. 14 years of age or under
2. 15 years but under 17 years
3. 17 years but under 19 years
4. 19 years but under 24 years
5. 24 years and over

Two further categories would widen this classification to cover the entire population:

6. Still receiving full-time education
7. Below school age

Details of educational qualifications are usually collected in full by interviewers and coded subsequently by the office coding team. Interviewers need to probe for course attended, examinations passed, qualifications and certificates obtained and completed apprenticeships. A general-purpose qualification classification is usually done by priority coding on the basis of the highest attainment in the list.

The following categorization of qualifications illustrates the detail often required to code respondents into appropriate groups. Even then, some respondents will be unclassifiable without further checking of their qualifications. As long as full details of all qualifications or courses are recorded by the interviewer, checks can be made with appropriate educational authorities so that each course or certificate can be allocated to the most appropriate attainment category.

1. University degree or above — includes higher degrees (PhD etc.) and full medical qualifications.

2. Professional institute—final examination — e.g. actuarial, accountancy, architecture, business courses, insurance, statistics, surveying.

3. Higher National Certificate or Diploma

4. Teachers' training certificate — i.e. non-graduate teaching qualification.

5. GCE 'A' Levels — including Higher and Senior leaving certificates for Scotland, the Scottish Universities Preliminary Examination at the

		Higher Grade and the Scottish Certificate of Education at the Higher Grade.
6.	Professional institute intermediate examination	i.e. below final level.
7.	Intermediate	intermediate Arts or Science, Attestation of Fitness (in Scotland), State Registered Nurse (SRN).
8.	Full industrial apprenticeship	i.e. trade apprenticeship to an acknowledged standard and length for diploma or certificate.
9.	GCE 'O' Level, CSE and secretarial	including Matriculation, General School Certificate, Certificates of Secondary Education, secretarial diplomas and certificates, Lower and Junior Leaving Certificates in Scotland, the Scottish Certificate of Education at the Ordinary Grade.
10.	Ordinary National Certificate or Diploma	Including City and Guilds.
11.	Other qualifications	Trade certificates and diplomas, including Forces educational certificates, and others not covered elsewhere.
12.	No qualifications	

Household Classifications

Household size and structure

To classify a household the interviewer has first to identify which persons resident at an address (or temporarily away) are members of the same household. The most common survey definition, that follows the approach used in the Population Census, is based on a 'catering' rule. It is usually defined as follows:

A household is a group of people who live regularly at the same address and who are all catered for by the same person.

If other people living at the address cater for themselves (or are catered for by someone else), they form a separate household (or several separate households).

To apply this classification interviewers need more rigorous definitions of terms. For example, 'regularly' is usually taken to mean at least four nights a week at the address. 'Catering' is usually taken to apply to at least one meal per day (when in residence).

Interviewers will also need a more detailed set of rules to guide them in special cases e.g.:

A spouse working away from home:	the 'regularity' rule is normally relaxed here to once per week instead of the four nights per week.
A fisherman or merchant seaman at sea:	normally included if he returns, say, every six weeks.
Someone in the armed forces or at university/college	normally excluded from the household if stationed/living away from home.
A child (under 16 years) at boarding school:	normally included in the household (despite not fulfilling the 'regularity' rule).
Temporary visitors to the household:	normally included only if they have been resident at the household for six months or more.
Boarders and lodgers:	boarders are usually defined as those people staying with the household and being catered for by the household: they are included as part of the household; lodgers cater for themselves and therefore form separate households.
Students sharing rooms:	students (and others) sharing a room but catering for themselves are normally defined as separate one-person households.

When details of each household member are required, a recording grid of the kind shown on p. 173 is commonly used. Each person occupies one row in the grid, with the head of household conventionally entered on the top line. The head of household is defined according to rules that can be uniformly applied. Some of these rules are increasingly under attack on the grounds of their male chauvinistic bias and the fact that they are anachronistic: in households that contain a husband and wife, for example, the former is normally defined as the 'head of the household', regardless of their respective working status. Nevertheless, current practice is still to define the head of household as the husband or, in the absence of a husband, as the person who is the owner of the accommodation, or who is legally responsible for paying the rent, or who holds the tenancy by virtue of a job or for some other reason.

Under this definition the rule of precedence is central: a husband is head of household even when the wife owns the property or has her name in the rent book. If two members of the same sex fulfil the various requirements equally, age is usually taken as the deciding factor (i.e. the older one is deemed to be the head of household).

From the household recording grid, various household composition and structure classifications can be derived, ranging from a simple measure of household size to a composite classification based on the family structure, age and size. These classifications can be determined either at the data preparation stage (by coders) or at the analysis stage (from a computer coding operation). An example of a detailed household composition classification is given below. The categories can (and almost always would) be collapsed to provide the smaller number of groups sufficient for most purposes.

1. Single person under 30
2. Single person 30-59
3. Single person 60 or over
4. Young married couple with no children—with head of household under 30
5. Small households with an infant—households containing one or two adults with one or two children, at least one of whom is under 5
6. Other small households with children—other households containing one or two adults with one or two children
7. Larger adult groupings with one child—three or more adults with one child under 16
8. Larger households with children—households containing three or more children or two children with two or more adults
9. Other larger adult groupings—households of three or more adults
10. Elderly couples—two-person households with at least one person 60 or over
11. Small adult-only households not included in categories 4 or 10.

Socio-economic group

It is common practice to use some kind of social class or socio-economic grouping to distinguish between households with differing backgrounds. 'Social grade' is the most common market research classification, based primarily on the chief wage earner's occupation (managerial, white collar, skilled manual, etc.). Interviewers apply the classification themselves, largely because market research relies heavily on quota sampling where the interviewer's quota is defined partly by 'social grade' controls: interviewers are usually required to find a prescribed number of respondents from households whose

HOUSEHOLD COMPOSITION RECORDING GRID

Name	Relationship to Head of Household	Sex M	Sex F	Age last birthday	MARITAL STATUS Single	Married	Widowed	Divorced	ACTIVITY STATUS Working Full-time	Working Part-time	Seeking work	Sick	Retired	Student	Housewife	Other not working
1. Mr A Head of H/hold		(1)	2	42	1	(2)	3	4	(1)	2	3	4	5	6	7	8
2. Mrs E Wife		1	(2)	39	1	(2)	3	4	1	2	3	4	5	6	(7)	8
3. Miss I Daughter		1	(2)	15	(1)	2	3	4	1	2	3	4	5	(6)	7	8
4. Mr M. Boarder		(1)	2	24	1	2	(3)	4	(1)	2	3	4	5	6	7	8
5.		1	2	..	1	2	3	4	1	2	3	4	5	6	7	8
6.		1	2	..	1	2	3	4	1	2	3	4	5	6	7	8
7.		1	2	..	1	2	3	4	1	2	3	4	5	6	7	8
8.		1	2	..	1	2	3	4	1	2	3	4	5	6	7	8
9.		1	2	..	1	2	3	4	1	2	3	4	5	6	7	8
10.		1	2	..	1	2	3	4	1	2	3	4	5	6	7	8
11.		1	2	..	1	2	3	4	1	2	3	4	5	6	7	8
12.		1	2	..	1	2	3	4	1	2	3	4	5	6	7	8

chief wage earners are in each of the following grades:

AB Managerial, administrative or professional occupation (at a senior or intermediate level)

C1 Supervisory or clerical occupation (i.e. white collar) and junior managerial, administrative or professional

C2 Skilled manual worker

DE Semi-skilled and unskilled manual workers and state pensioners, widows (with no other wage earner in the household) and casual workers.

In social research the classification is usually based on the OPCS socio-economic group classification according to the occupation of the head of household, or occasionally to the occupation of each respondent. The interviewer is required to collect the following items of information about the head of household's occupation:

(a) The name of the job
(b) A description of the activity involved
(c) The degree of skill and qualifications held
(d) The degree of responsibility involved, including any supervision of others (and the number supervised)
(e) Management responsibilities (and the size of the establishment)
(f) Employment status (i.e. employee, self-employed)

The description of each occupation needs to be precise enough to be pinpointed to one of the 30,000 or so entries in Classification of Occupations (OPCS, 1970).

The task of determining the socio-economic classification needs to be performed by experienced coders; interviewers merely collect the detailed information that forms the basis of the office coding. The classification manual works well and is fairly easy to use once the coding team has become familiar with its indexing system. Initially coders may have to spend some time looking up particular occupations in four or five different places in the manual before finding the appropriate classifications. Each occupation is allocated a code number in the classification which can be arranged initially into about 200 occupational groups. These, in conjunction with employment status and number of employees at the establishment, can be used to form 16 socio-economic categories, and, grouped still further, to form the sort of classification given below:

Classification	Socio-Economic Group No.
1. Professional workers	3/4
2. Employers, managers	1/2/13
3. Other self-employed	12/14
4. Skilled workers and foremen	8/9
5. Non-manual workers	5/6

6. Service workers, semi-skilled and agricultural workers	7/10/15
7. Armed forces	16
8. Unskilled	11

Retired persons and those who are temporarily ill or unemployed are normally classified into the group corresponding to their last full-time occupation.

Household vehicle ownership

Information about vehicle ownership is often collected as a classification variable, particularly in investigations of travel patterns, use of local facilities, holiday behaviour and so on. The classification is usually obtained from the question:

'Does anyone in the household own or have the regular use of any kind of motor vehicle?'

A number of points of definition not conveyed by this question need to be introduced by the interviewer. It is necessary to make clear first whether, as is usually the case, household vehicles include those owned and registered in the name of an employer but generally available for use by the household. Second, are vans or lorries to be included as household vehicles (irrespective of ownership) if they are used for passenger trips? The usual rule is that they are. Third, a vehicle temporarily out of action for repair but currently taxed and insured is normally included as a household vehicle if it is intended for use again shortly. Fourth, vehicles available to the household on a long-term hire or loan are usually taken to be household vehicles.

For most purposes it is sufficient to classify households into two groups (those who have use of a motor vehicle and those who do not). In some cases an extended classification (including pedal cycles) might be more appropriate, subdivided according to the type of vehicle owned and, perhaps, the number of vehicles. Respondents can then be asked to indicate on a card whether anyone in the household owns or has the regular use of any of the vehicles mentioned and, if so, how many in each category.

1. Van/lorry, etc.
2. Car (including estate cars and three-wheeled cars)
3. Motorcycle combination (i.e. with sidecar)
4. Motorcycle
5. Scooter, moped
6. Pedal cycle

Accommodation Classifications

Tenure

For certain studies, details of a household's accommodation (i.e. dwelling unit) may provide useful classification material. The most commonly employed variable of this kind is housing tenure, usually categorized in the following way:

1. Owner-occupied
2. Rented from council
3. Rented privately—furnished
4. Rented privately—unfurnished
5. Rent-free (including tied to employment)

The owner-occupied category includes households that are buying their property on mortgage or loan and those with leases that were initially for at least twenty-one years. Shorter leases are usually included in the rented categories; the rented categories are usually used even when someone outside the household actually pays the rent (e.g. a son on behalf of his mother). Council rented usually includes New Town and Housing Association tenancies as well as local authority tenancies.

The tenure classification can be derived either from sequential questioning, i.e.

'Do you own or rent your accommodation?'
IF RENTED
'Is it rented from the council or privately?'
IF PRIVATELY
'Is it rented furnished or unfurnished?'

Or respondents can be asked to choose the appropriate category from a show card.

Type of accommodation

Type of accommodation is sometimes classified on a priority basis giving precedence to those types of accommodation that occupy an entire building (house, bungalow, etc.), then to those that occupy a self-contained dwelling unit forming part of a building (flat, maisonette, etc.) and then to those that share a dwelling unit (bedsitters, apartments, etc.) as follows:

1. Shared dwelling unit
2. Converted self-contained flat
3. Purpose-built flat/maisonette/tenement
4. Terraced house/bungalow (including end terrace)
5. Semi-detached house/bungalow
6. Detached house/bungalow
7. Prefab
8. Temporary dwelling, e.g. caravan
9. Other accommodation

To qualify as self-contained, a dwelling unit has to satisfy certain conditions, most commonly:

(a) It must have its own front door;

(b)   It must have direct access either to the street or to a public hall or staircase, without the need for occupants to pass through anyone else's living quarters;

(c)   Other persons must not have access through that accommodation;

(d)   Bedsitters qualify if they contain both cooking and bathroom facilities and meet the other criteria; a self-contained dwelling unit need not include a w.c.

To qualify as 'shared', a dwelling unit has to be occupied by at least two households. If a household has sublet one or two rooms to different tenants who live as part of the main household, the accommodation is not shared, since it contains only one household. A house converted into separate self-contained flats (i.e. dwelling units) will not be classified as 'shared'.

Persons per room

A persons per room index is also sometimes used as a classification to identify the degree of crowding within the dwelling unit. Various types of indices exist, but all are usually compiled by computer from the separate pieces of information collected by the interviewer. Interviewers need first to identify both the household and the relevant dwelling unit. They can then record the number of persons in the household according to the rules previously discussed. Finally they have to establish the number of rooms in the dwelling unit. The initial question normally used is:

'What rooms (excluding bathrooms and lavatories) does your accommodation consist of?'

Interviewers will need to follow this question with a series of specific probes and to refer to more detailed notes in odd instances. The points to be noted are as follows:

Living rooms, bedrooms and kitchens are usually included whether or not they are furnished at the time of interview;

Attics, cellars and storage rooms are usually included only if they have windows and are habitable without further modification;

Sculleries are usually included if they are used for cooking;

Bathrooms, toilets, washrooms and laundry rooms are not included, nor are landings, halls, lobbies and recesses;

Rooms that can be effectively subdivided by a fixed partition or sliding/folding doors normally count as two rooms; rooms separated by a curtain, furniture or other flimsy and temporary divider count as a single room;

Rooms used solely for business purposes are excluded;

Prefabricated rooms and extensions normally count as separate rooms as long as they satisfy the other conditions, although a conservatory that provides the sole source of natural light and fresh air to another living area does not.

Amenities
For some surveys it is useful to compile a more detailed picture of the amenities that form part of the dwelling unit. To obtain these data, the question generally allows for a three-way classification— sole use, shared use or no use of various named amenities:
'Does your household have the use or shared use of the following?'
The individual items vary, but the most common are:
a fixed sink (i.e. with a fixed water pipe) with running water
a cooker (or cooking stove with an oven)
piped hot water (including Ascot-type geysers)
a fixed bath or shower with running water
an inside w.c. (i.e. in the building, not necessarily in the householder's accommodation unit)
an outside w.c.

Geographical Classifications
Region
There are various ways of classifying respondents in terms of the region of the country in which they live, depending on the purpose of the survey. Sometimes the purpose predetermines the classification (e.g. television regions or regional health authority areas). More commonly the Economic Planning Regions of the country are used, the definitions of which are contained in Appendix 1 of the Annual Abstract of Statistics (CSO, 1976).

The following list contains this classification, commonly referred to as Standard Regions. Although Greater London is not specified separately, its size and significance in most surveys usually warrant separate classification, thus increasing the number of separate regions to eleven.
1. *Northern:* Cleveland, Cumbria, Durham, Northumberland, Tyne and Wear
2. *Yorkshire and Humberside:* Humberside, North Yorkshire, South Yorkshire, West Yorkshire
3. *East Midlands:* Derbyshire, Leicestershire, Lincolnshire, Northamptonshire, Nottinghamshire
4. *East Anglia:* Cambridgeshire, Norfolk, Suffolk
5. *South East:* Bedfordshire, Berkshire, Buckinghamshire, East Sussex, Essex, Greater London, Hampshire, Hertfordshire, Isle of Wight, Kent, Oxfordshire, Surrey, West Sussex
6. *South West:* Avon, Cornwall, Devon, Dorset, Gloucestershire, Somerset, Wiltshire

7. *West Midlands:* Hereford and Worcester, Salop, Staffordshire, Warwickshire, West Midlands
8. *North West:* Cheshire, Lancashire, Greater Manchester, Merseyside
9. *Wales:* All counties
10. *Scotland:* All counties

Type of area
On a smaller scale than region, the area in which a respondent lives can be classified at different levels (county, constituency, ward, census enumeration district). Constituencies and local authority areas—particularly since the reorganization of local government—are often too large and heterogeneous to be useful classification variables. An index based on the characteristics of a local authority would not for instance discriminate between respondents living in deprived areas and those living in other areas. Researchers frequently have to make use of finer measures, sometimes building up their own area indices from census ward data or from other published material.

The Census of Population is the main source for area classifications; examples of area indices that can be compiled include:

Percentage of households in the area with no car
Percentage of households in the area with head in socio-economic groups 1 to 4 or 13
Percentage of households in the area living in rented accommodation

A common area classification is based on population density, linking the size of population (or electorate) to amount of land (measured in acres or hectares).

There are also other data sources for certain area classifications, such as the Census of Production and Distribution, or the voting figures of the last election—from which, for example, constituencies can be classified according to the percentage of their electorate who voted Labour.

Asking Classification Questions
Placing most classification questions at the end of the interview is sound practice: by the time the respondent gets to them he has seen the purpose and coverage of the survey and has some rapport with the interviewer. Questions on age, marital status, income and so on are then less likely to seem impertinent. Some classification items, for example those that seek to subdivide respondents into behavioural groups, may, however, fit more naturally with other questions on behaviour in the body of the questionnaire.

For some surveys a 'contact sheet' containing some classification items forms the front page of the questionnaire. It records administrative details such as the interviewer's name and identity number, the duration of the interview, the serial number of the address, whether there was multi-occupation, and so on. Area and region classification codes are often transferred from the sample issue sheets to this page. When the contact sheet is also used to record the respondent's name and address it should always be detached from the questionnaire at the earliest opportunity, to preserve anonymity.

Survey organizations that use the same trained interviewers for a variety of studies tend to use a standard classification page containing abbreviated headings and the minimum of definitions. The interviewers work to a set of house rules laid down in a basic training manual. This practice is risky, however, with a less experienced team because the essence of classification questions is the need to adhere to strict and complex points of definition.

Notes on Further Reading
1. Standard classification questions are usually discussed in interviewers' manuals: the *Handbook for Government Social Survey Interviewers* by Atkinson (1968) contains a particularly thorough treatment of these questions and the definitions adopted. The *Handbook for Interviewers* of the Market Research Society (1974) discusses standard classification questions in general, and pays particular attention to the social grading classification used widely in market research. Standard classifications are also discussed by Hoinville and Jowell (1969) and in the Market Research Society's booklet edited by Wolfe (1973). The classifications of education, family and household, income and occupations are discussed in considerable detail in the book edited by Stacey (1969); housing and locality are similarly discussed in the book edited by Gittus (1972).
2. The definitions used in the Censuses of Population are described by Benjamin (1970). The report by Gray and Gee (1972) on the quality check of the 1966 Sample Census discusses the errors that were found to arise in collecting Census data according to these definitions.
3. The *Handbook on the Family Expenditure Survey* by Kemsley (1969a) contains definitions of the classification items included in that survey. Income is a major variable in the FES, and the *Handbook* gives the questionnaire and definitions used to collect precise income information. Elsewhere Kemsley (1969b) has proposed a simplified version of the FES income questions for use in other surveys.

4. The *Introductory Report on the General Household Survey*, OPCS (1973) contains details of the classifications used for that survey.
5. Goldthorpe and Hope (1974) comment on the standard classification of social class and discuss a new 'social grading of occupations'.

Chapter 10. Caveats and Conclusions

It would be inappropriate to end without adding a cautionary note on the application of sample surveys. We have tried to show that survey research is not, and cannot be, a precise measuring instrument; that, despite its scientific base, it is not an exact science. In varying degrees, surveys underestimate the complexity of human behaviour and attitudes; they can generally paint only a sketchy picture of society since their results are subject to errors of commission and omission.

In contrast, we hope we have demonstrated that systematic sample surveys can give more accurate measurements of a population's characteristics, attitudes and behaviour patterns than could be obtained by casual observation; that they provide a means of aggregating information collected from a representative sample of the population; that they can illuminate variations in behaviour and attitudes. We believe that surveys can and do provide a context for better-informed judgements and better-directed decisions.

Throughout, we have tried to suggest ways in which the advantages of surveys can be maximized and the disadvantages minimized by the application of procedures, practices and conventions that form part of a growing body of knowledge in a comparatively young discipline. Almost regardless of the rigour with which survey methods are applied, however, some defects will remain and individual survey results will—and should—continue to be viewed with circumspection. So many unseen factors can affect the accuracy of a survey that its validity must be demonstrated rather than accepted as an act of faith. Some of these factors have been discussed, for instance that poor design or faulty execution can lead to errors. What has not been covered, however, is the hazard of faulty interpretation, a subject that properly belongs to a volume on data analysis, but that should at least be signalled here as an immeasurably large potential source of error.

Faulty interpretation arises partly from the tendency to demand too much of surveys. On the surface, behavioural data, for example, should be easier to interpret than attitudinal data, since most people can describe what they do rather more accurately than they can communicate what their values are. Yet, for the reasons mentioned in Chapter 3, this is not always so: memory can be faulty, definitions can be ambiguous, answers can be deceptive. Moreover, wrong conclusions can be drawn if insufficient account is taken of the factors governing behaviour and their relationship with the survey purpose. People who have a low tolerance of noise, for instance, will not be found in their true population proportions living near an airport or on a noisy road. A survey of residents around an airport could not therefore be used to describe the noise tolerance levels likely to be found in the rest of the population. Nor could a survey that showed that airport residents were as tolerant of their noise levels as residents of a country village were of theirs be used to conclude that airport noise causes no special annoyance. It would probably mean that the majority of people now exposed to high noise levels consists of those best able to tolerate or adapt to them.

Interpretation becomes still more problematical in surveys that attempt to collect data about intended or future behaviour. Whereas many people can answer with confidence how often, say, they play tennis, or when they last played, or when they first took it up, most people are demonstrably bad at predicting how often they would play if more tennis courts were available, or if a new sports complex were built in their area. Their answers, however confident, are little better than guesses. Changes in circumstances or priorities will render their forecasts inaccurate. Moreover, people do not generally possess sufficient knowledge to make reliable forecasts: they cannot know in advance of the event how a new sports complex will affect the use of other local amenities or the extent to which it will release a latent demand for tennis in the area, either of which could change their propensity to use the facility.

In these circumstances researchers sometimes attempt to incorporate an educational element into their surveys. They may, for example, provide respondents with detailed information about the new sports facility and the way in which other facilities have worked in other areas in the hope that the implications will be absorbed quickly enough for respondents to make informed and balanced judgements about their future behaviour. The approach should not be belittled, but it can hardly overcome the inherent weaknesses in asking respondents to forecast their likely behaviour patterns.

There are similar inherent weaknesses in attempting to make forecasts by extrapolating from existing behaviour patterns and characteristics. Detailed information about present behaviour will offer suggestions about the future, but it cannot be used for precise forecasts because it takes no account of which aspects of present behaviour are governed by the facilities available, which by choice, which by habit, which by fashion, and so on.

For all these reasons, surveys should be regarded essentially as a means by which we can document, analyse and interpret past and present attitudes and behaviour patterns. By exposing trends, they will certainly provide clues about the future, but they are only clues.

In attitudinal research also, the primary cause of errors in interpretation is the temptation to read too much into the data or to ignore their shortcomings. A newspaper report that merely quotes an opinion poll finding that, say, 50 per cent of the population support capital punishment or abortion law reform, makes the extraordinary assumption that public opinion is well formed and dichotomous on those issues. The opposite is usually true of most political and social issues. People's views are ambivalent, sometimes because they feel they lack the information or understanding to make proper judgements, sometimes because they cannot decide between the attractions of competing arguments, mostly because they have not been required to consider the issue seriously or to come to any conclusion about it. Given more information, more discussion, more opportunity for reflection and more experience of the alternatives, their conclusions might well differ from their spontaneous reactions. A warning of the limits of interpretation that ought to be placed on the answers to single opinion questions is provided by Davis (1971, p. 20) who observes: 'It is well known that the distributions of answers on attitude and opinion questions will vary by 15 or 20 per cent with apparently slight changes in question wording.'

Any interpretation of survey data that ignores these considerations is bound to be suspect. For this reason comprehensive attitudinal surveys include questions on knowledge and experience so that expressed views can be placed in a wider context and assessed accordingly. They include questions that elicit strength of feeling, which is at least as important as the direction of feeling in relation to an issue. They try to take account of the variation in people's expectations created by their different experiences and different backgrounds: old people, for example, tend to express greater satisfaction with (or is it resignation about?) their living conditions or incomes than young people in similar circumstances do. The researcher also has to interpret attitudinal data in the context of social and environmental conditions that can substantially alter people's outlooks: those who live in very poor housing conditions, for instance, are likely to be so obsessed by their immediate problem as to appear indifferent to more abstract issues. The interpretation of survey data should ideally take all these factors, and others, into account before it can inspire confidence.

These strictures on some of the interpretational difficulties of surveys are not meant to suggest that they are a wholly subjective form of measurement. On the contrary, sample surveys are an attempt to apply scientific disciplines to the measurement of social phenomena. To some extent they fail, partly because the phenomena are too abstract and changeable to be measured precisely. To a large extent they succeed. But potential users of data should not demand from surveys a degree of precision or the fulfilment of purposes that they are inherently incapable of meeting. And researchers have a responsibility to those who make use of their data not to claim characteristics for surveys that they do not and cannot possess.

Researchers also owe a responsibility to their potential respondents on whose co-operation survey research depends. Respondents are often asked to give up a good deal of time to answer questionnaires but are rarely offered payment for their time; the results of surveys are usually neither promised nor sent to them; only brief details about the purpose of the survey and the *bona fides* of the sponsor can usually be conveyed to them. Yet surprisingly few refuse their co-operation. This makes it even more important that respondents are properly protected from the excesses of survey researchers and that the assurances given to them are honoured, as discussed in *Survey Research and Privacy* (SCPR, 1973).

At each stage in the survey process, issues of privacy or intrusion can arise:

—The use of a particular source list for sampling may constitute an invasion of privacy.

—The interviewer's visit to the sampled person at home may constitute an intrusion, particularly if the interviewer is unduly persistent.

—The sampled person may be misled as to the purposes or sponsorship of the interview, or may wrongly be led to believe that co-operation is obligatory.

—Questions may be asked that cause the respondent embarrassment or offence.

—Information about an individual or family may be disclosed to third parties during a survey (either by the interviewer or by someone else with access to the identifiable data).

—Personal data might be identifiable in the published statistics of a survey.

—Subsequent disclosures may occur when data are stored on computer tapes or on other documents and records.

Sample surveys are not, and should not be, concerned with individual identities. Unlike administrative records which do have to distinguish between individuals, surveys use aggregated or statistical data to describe the characteristics, attitudes or behaviour of groups. They are indifferent to the names of those comprising the group; the questions to be answered by surveys are 'How many?' or 'What proportion?', not 'Who?'; surveys seek co-operation from respondents with a promise of anonymity.

Unfortunately, however, the distinction between individual data (such as tax records, electoral registers, medical files, bank accounts, telephone directories) and statistical data is blurred because the individual is often the starting point for the collection of statistics. Individuals may be sampled by name and, although there is no need for the name to be retained after the interview, the danger exists that the promise of anonymity will not be honoured.

One method of safeguarding anonymity is to separate the identifying material from the questionnaires. The interviewer often needs to be supplied with a name and address, serially numbered. But once the questionnaire has been completed, only the serial number need appear on it while it goes through checking and analysis. The questionnaire can then be identified only by consulting the sampling list in order to decode the serial number. Sampling lists and questionnaires need to be kept separately and securely. The sampling lists in particular—containing as they do the key to the identity of respondents—should never be allowed to come into the hands of unauthorized people.

In a sample of major British manufacturers, data on tape about numbers of employees, turnover, geographical location and nature of product might be sufficient to identify individual manufacturers. But in a normal population survey, identification by such means would be impractical. Like fingerprints, data about an individual may be unique, but the size of the population covered means that finding the possessor of a particular set of attributes would be almost impossible.

Preserving anonymity is the first aspect of respondent protection that should exercise survey researchers. The second aspect is 'intrusion'. A common objection to surveys is that people have a right to be left alone and that survey research, by its very nature, violates this right. Although partly true, it is not generally felt that telephoning, writing to or calling upon people constitutes a serious invasion of privacy unless—and it is an important proviso—the method or extent of contact is excessive. The Report of the Committee on Privacy (HMSO, 1972) concluded that the normal activity of a survey interviewer was sufficiently restricted by the right of the person interviewed to refuse to take part or to terminate the interview at any stage.

Survey research depends essentially on information being freely given without duress, obligation or deception. The doctrine of 'informed consent' (explicitly used in the United States as a cardinal rule of survey practice) requires that the respondent should be told at the outset that co-operation is voluntary and be given explanations of the purpose and sponsorship of the research. Fulfilling either of these requirements can be difficult. Since the success of surveys depends largely upon the level of response, it may be naïve to assume that interviewers will invite a refusal from someone who might conceivably feel that he was obliged to participate. And as for announcing the precise purpose of the survey, a bias may immediately be created if respondents are then influenced by this purpose to give the answers they think are wanted. To obtain valid responses it is sometimes necessary to give a general explanation which, though accurate, is broad enough to avoid the problem. Alternatively, to prevent bias, the interviewer can explain to respondents that the name of the sponsor or purpose of the survey will be communicated only at the end of the interview at which point the respondent will have the right to insist that the record of his answers be destroyed.

The doctrine of informed consent becomes even more important when interviewing is being done within an institution such as a school, factory or prison. In these cases a feeling of obligation is often created in respondents simply by the fact that an authority figure has agreed on the respondent's behalf to the interview. In all such cases, the absolute right to refuse should be asserted.

A third and somewhat different aspect of public interest that survey research has been held to threaten concerns the issue of 'manipulation'. The proponents of this view argue that by agreeing to disclose information about their attitudes and behaviour to social scientists, the public is providing the establishment with the tools it needs to maintain the *status quo* by means of its knowledge of the public's fears, aspirations and weaknesses. This view is in direct contrast to the now more common conviction that survey research is an integral feature of a participatory democracy, a means of involving the public in decision-making by allowing it to express its views to policy-makers without binding them to those views (as referenda usually do). In any case, there is no answer to the assertion that survey research is automatically dangerous and divisive save that, in our view, a systematic and anonymous observation of the way in which society is changing is a great advance on the unsystematic messages that would otherwise reach us from self-selected elements in the system.

Bibliography

AIREY, C., BROOK, L. and SMITH, D. J. (1976). *A technical report on a survey of racial minorities.* Social and Community Planning Research, London.

ANDERSON, T. R. and ZELDITCH, M. (3rd ed. 1975). *A basic course in statistics with sociological applications.* Holt, Rinehart and Winston, New York.

ARGYLE, M. (1967). *The psychology of interpersonal behaviour.* Penguin Books, London.

ATKINSON, J. (1968). *A handbook for interviewers.* Government Social Survey (No. M136), HMSO, London.

BABBIE, E. R. (1973). *Survey research methods.* Wadsworth, Belmont, California.

BACKSTROM, C. H. and HURSH, G. D. (1963). *Survey research.* North-Western University Press, Evanston, Illinois.

BANNISTER, D. (1962). Personal construct theory: a summary and experimental paradigm. *Acta Psychologica*, Vol. 20, pp. 104-120.

BARNETT, V. (1974). *Elements of sampling theory.* English Universities Press, London.

BARTON, J. A. (1958). Asking the embarrassing question. *Public Opinion Quarterly*, Vol. 22, pp. 67-68.

BELSON, W. A. (1962). *Studies in readership.* Business Publications, London.

BELSON, W. A. (1968). Respondent understanding of survey questions. *Polls*, Vol. 3, pp. 1-13.

BELSON, W. A. (1975). *Juvenile theft: the causal factors.* Harper and Row, London.

BELSON, W. A. and DUNCAN, J. A. (1962). A comparison of the check-list and the open response questioning systems. *Applied Statistics*, Vol. 2, pp. 120-132.

BELSON, W. A. and THOMPSON, B. A. (1973). *Bibliography on methods of social and business research.* Crosby Lockwood, London.

BENJAMIN, B. (1970). *The Population Census*. Heinemann, London.

BERDIE, D. R. and ANDERSON, J. F. (1974). *Questionnaires: design and use*. Scarecrow Press, Metuchen, New Jersey.

BLALOCK, H. M., Jr. (2nd ed. 1972). *Social statistics*. McGraw-Hill, New York.

BLUMBERG, H. H., FULLER, C. and HARE, P. A. (1974). Response rates in postal surveys. *Public Opinion Quarterly*, Vol. 38, pp. 113-123.

BLUNDEN, R. M. (1966). Sampling frames. *Commentary (Journal of the Market Research Society)*, Vol. 8, pp. 101-112.

BLYTH, W. G. and MARCHANT, L. J. (1973). A self-weighting random sampling technique. *Journal of the Market Research Society*, Vol. 15, pp. 157-162.

BOGARDUS, E. S. (1933). A social distance scale. *Sociological and Social Research*, Vol. 17, pp. 265-271.

BOOKER, H. S. and DAVID, S. T. (1952). Differences in results obtained by experienced and inexperienced interviewers. *Journal of the Royal Statistical Society*, Series A, Vol. 115, pp. 232-257.

BROOK, L. L. (1976). *National Travel Survey 1975-1976: technical report*. Social and Community Planning Research, London.

CANNELL, C. F. and FOWLER, F. J. (1963). Comparison of a self-enumerative procedure and a personal interview: a validity study. *Public Opinion Quarterly*, Vol. 27, pp. 250-264.

CANNELL, C. F., FOWLER, F. J. and MARQUIS, K. H. (1968). The influence of interviewer and respondent psychological and behavioral variables on the reporting in household interviews. *Vital and Health Statistics*, Series 2, No. 26, US Government Printing Office, Washington DC.

CANNELL, C. F., LAWSON, S. A. and HAUSSER, D. L. (1975). *A technique for evaluating interviewer performance*. Survey Research Center, Institute for Social Research, University of Michigan, Ann Arbor.

CANTRIL, H. ed. (1944). *Gauging public opinion*. Princeton University Press, Princeton.

CARTWRIGHT, A. (1963). Memory errors in a morbidity survey. *Milbank Memorial Fund Quarterly*, Vol. 41, pp. 5-24.

CENTRAL STATISTICAL OFFICE (1976). *Annual abstract of statistics*. HMSO, London.

COMMITTEE ON PRIVACY (1972). *(Younger Committee) Report*. HMSO, London.

CLUNIES-ROSS, C. W. (1967). Simplifications to survey statistics. *Commentary (Journal of the Market Research Society)*, Vol. 9, pp. 68-76.

CONVERSE, J. M. and SCHUMAN, H. (1973). *Conversations at*

random: survey research as interviewers see it. Wiley, New York.

CORLETT, T. (1963). Rapid methods of estimating standard errors of stratified multi-stage samples: a preliminary investigation. *The Statistician,* Vol. 13, pp. 5-16.

CORLETT, T. (1965). Sampling errors in practice. *Commentary (Journal of the Market Research Society),* Vol. 7, pp. 127-138.

COSTNER, H. L. ed. (1971). *Sociological Methodology, 1971.* Jossey-Bass, San Francisco.

COSTNER, H. L. ed. (1974). *Sociological Methodology, 1973-1974.* Jossey-Bass, San Francisco.

CRITTENDEN, K. S. and HILL, R. J. (1971). Coding reliability and validity of interview data. *American Sociological Review,* Vol. 36, pp. 1073-1080.

DANIEL, W. W. (1975). Nonresponse in sociological surveys: a review of some methods for handling the problem. *Sociological Methods and Research,* Vol. 3, pp. 291-307.

DAVIS, J. A. (1971). *Elementary survey analysis.* Prentice-Hall, Englewood Cliffs, New Jersey.

DAWES, R. M. (1972). *Fundamentals of attitude measurement.* Wiley, New York.

DEMING, W. E. (1944). On errors in surveys. *American Sociological Review,* Vol. 9, pp. 359-369.

DOWNHAM, J. S. (1955). The function of coding. *The Incorporated Statistician,* Vol. 5 (Supplement), pp. 73-81.

DURBIN, J. and STUART, A. (1951). Differences in response rates of experienced and inexperienced interviewers. *Journal of the Royal Statistical Society,* Series A, Vol. 114, pp. 163-205.

DURBIN, J. and STUART, A. (1954). An experimental comparison between coders. *Journal of Marketing,* Vol. 19, pp. 54-66.

ERDOS, P. L. (1970). *Professional mail surveys.* McGraw-Hill, New York.

ERICKSEN, E. P. (1976). Sampling a rare population: a case study. *Journal of the American Statistical Association,* Vol. 71, pp. 816-822.

FELLEGI, I. P and HOLT, D. (1976). A systematic approach to automatic edit and imputation. *Journal of the American Statistical Association,* Vol. 71, pp. 17-35.

FESTINGER, L. and KATZ, D. ed. (1953). *Research methods in the behavioral sciences.* Holt, Rinehart and Winston, New York.

FISHBEIN, M. ed. (1967). *Readings in attitude theory and measurement.* Wiley, New York.

FISHER, R. A. and YATES, F. (6th ed. 1963). *Statistical tables for biological, agricultural and medical research.* Oliver and Boyd, Edinburgh.

FOTHERGILL, J. E. and WILLCOCK, H. D. (1955). Interviewers

and interviewing. *The Incorporated Statistician*, Vol. 5 (Supplement), pp. 37-56.

FREUND, R. J. and HARTLEY, H. O. (1967). A procedure for automatic data editing. *Journal of the American Statistical Association*, Vol. 62, pp. 341-352.

GITTUS, E. (1972). *Key variables in social research. Volume 1: religion, housing, locality*. Heinemann, London.

GLASER, B. G. and STRAUSS, A. L. (1967). *The discovery of grounded theory*. Aldine, Chicago.

GLOCK, C. Y. ed. (1967). *Survey research in the social sciences*. Russell Sage Foundation, New York.

GOLDMAN, A. E. (1962). The group depth interview. *Journal of Marketing*, Vol. 26, pp. 61-68.

GOLDSTEIN, H. (1968). Longitudinal studies and the measurement of change. *The Statistician*, Vol. 18, pp. 93-117.

GOLDTHORPE, J. H. and HOPE, K. (1974). *The social grading of occupations*. Oxford University Press, London.

GORDEN, R. L. (rev. ed. 1975). *Interviewing: strategy, techniques, and tactics*. Dorsey Press, Homewood, Illinois.

GRAY, P. G. (1955). The memory factor in social surveys. *Journal of the American Statistical Association*, Vol. 50, pp. 344-363.

GRAY, P. G. and GEE, F. A. (1967). *Electoral registration for parliamentary elections; an enquiry made for the Home Office*. Government Social Survey (SS 391), HMSO, London.

GRAY, P. and GEE, F. A. (1972). *A quality check on the 1966 ten per cent Sample Census of England and Wales*. Government Social Survey (SS 391), HMSO, London.

GRAY, S. (1970). *The electoral register: practical information for use when drawing samples, both for interview and postal surveys*. Government Social Survey (No. M151), London.

GUTTMAN, L. (1944). A basis for scaling qualitative data. *American Sociological Review*, Vol. 9, pp. 139-150.

HANSEN, M. H., HURWITZ, W. N. and MADOW, W. G. (1953). *Sample survey methods and theory. Vol I: Methods and applications. Vol. II: Theory*. Wiley, New York.

HARRIS, A. I. (1955). The work of a coding section. *The Incorporated Statistician*, Vol. 5 (Supplement), pp. 82-92.

HATCHETT, S. and SCHUMAN, H. (1975). White respondents and race-of-interviewer effects. *Public Opinion Quarterly*, Vol. 34, pp. 523-528.

HAUCK, M. and STEINKAMP, S. (1964). *Survey reliability and interviewer competence*. Bureau of Economic and Business Research, University of Illinois, Urbana.

HEDGES, B. M. (1972). *Sampling minority groups*. Silver medal award paper, Thomson Organisation, London.

HEDGES, B. M. (1973). Random samples of individuals. *Journal of the Market Research Society*, Vol. 15, pp. 233-235.

HENRY, H. (1963). *Motivation research*. Crosby Lockwood, London.

HOCHSTIM, J. R. (1967). A critical comparison of three strategies of collecting data from households. *Journal of the American Statistical Association*, Vol. 62, pp. 976-989.

HOCKING, P. R., HUDDLESTON, H. F. and HUNT, H. H. (1974). A procedure for editing survey data. *Applied Statistics*, Vol. 23, pp. 121-133.

HOINVILLE, G. (1971). Evaluating community preferences. *Environment and Planning*, Vol. 3, pp. 33-50.

HOINVILLE, G. and COURTENAY, G. (1977). *Measuring consumer priorities*. Occasional paper, Social and Community Planning Research, London.

HOINVILLE, G. and JOWELL, R. (1969). *Classification manual for household interview surveys in Great Britain*. Social and Community Planning Research, London.

HYMAN, H. H. and others (1954). *Interviewing in social research*. University of Chicago Press, Chicago.

JOWELL, R. (1975). *A review of public involvement in planning*. Occasional paper, Social and Community Planning Research, London.

JAHODA, M. and WARREN, N. (2nd ed. 1973). *Attitudes: selected readings*. Penguin Books, London.

KAHN, R. L. and CANNELL, C. F. (1957). *The dynamics of interviewing; theory, technique and cases*. Wiley, New York.

KALTON, G. (1966). *Introduction to statistical ideas for social scientists*. Chapman and Hall, London.

KALTON, G. and BLUNDEN, R. M. (1973). Sampling errors in the British General Household Survey. *Bulletin of the International Statistical Institute*, Vol. 45 (3), pp. 83-97.

KALTON, G. and LEWIS, S. M. (1975). Sampling error in OPCS's *The General Household Survey 1972 (Chapter 7)*. HMSO, London.

KANUK, L. and BERENSON, C. (1975). Mail surveys and response rates: a literature review. *Journal of Marketing Research*, Vol. 12, pp. 440-453.

KELLY, G. A. (1955). *The psychology of personal constructs*. W. W. Norton, New York.

KEMSLEY, W. F. F. (1966). *Sampling errors in the Family*. Expenditure Survey. *Applied Statistics*, Vol. 15, pp. 1-14.

KEMSLEY, W. F. F. (1969a). *Family Expenditure Survey: handbook on the sample, fieldwork and coding procedures*. Government Social Survey (M.146), HMSO, London.

KEMSLEY, W. F. F. (1969b). *Income questions—a simplified*

version of the FES questions for use in other surveys. Government Social Survey (M.147), London.

KEMSLEY, W. F. F. (1972). Pre-computer editing of budgets for the Family Expenditure Survey. *Applied Statistics*, Vol. 21, pp. 58-64.

KISH, L. (1949). A procedure for objective respondent selection within the household. *Journal of the American Statistical Association*, Vol. 44, pp. 380-387.

KISH, L. (1957). Confidence intervals for clustered samples. *American Sociological Review*, Vol. 22, pp. 154-165.

KISH, L. (1962). Studies of interviewer variance for attitudinal variables. *Journal of the American Statistical Association*, Vol. 57, pp. 92-115.

KISH, L. (1965). *Survey sampling*. Wiley, New York.

KISH, L., GROVES, R. M. and KROTKI, K. P. (1976). *Sampling errors for fertility surveys.* Occasional Paper No. 17, World Fertility Survey, London.

KRAUSZ, E. (1969). Locating minority populations: a research problem. *Race*, Vol. 10, pp. 361-368.

LAND, K. C. and SPILERMAN, S. eds. (1975). *Social indicator models.* Russell Sage Foundation, New York.

LANSING, J. B. and MORGAN, J. N. (1971). *Economic survey methods.* Survey Research Center, University of Michigan, Ann Arbor.

LANSING, J. B., WITHEY, S. B. and WOLFE, A. C. (1971). *Working papers on survey research in poverty areas.* Survey Research Center, University of Michigan, Ann Arbor.

LAURENT, A. (1972). Effects of question length on reporting behaviour in survey interviews. *Journal of the American Statistical Association*, Vol. 67, pp. 298-305.

LEGGATT, T. ed. (1974). *Sociological theory and survey research: institutional change and social policy in Great Britain.* Sage Publications, London.

LEMON, N. (1973). *Attitudes and their measurement.* Batsford, London.

LIKERT, R. (1932). *A technique for the measurement of attitudes.* Columbia University Press, New York.

LINSKY, A. S. (1975). Stimulating responses to mailed questionnaires: a review. *Public Opinion Quarterly*, Vol. 39, pp. 82-101.

LINDZEY, G. and ARONSON, E. (2nd ed. 1968). *The handbook of social psychology, Vol. 2: research methods.* Addison-Wesley, Reading, Massachusetts.

MCFARLANE-SMITH, J. (1972). *Interviewing in market and social research.* Routledge and Kegan Paul, London.

McKENNELL, A. C. (1974). Surveying attitude structures: a discussion of principles and procedures. *Quality and Quantity*, Vol. 7, pp. 203-294.

MARCHANT, L. J. (1970). A method of sampling small minorities: suggestions and objections. *Journal of the Market Research Society*, Vol. 12, pp. 248-251.

MARKET RESEARCH SOCIETY (1974). *A handbook for interviewers*. Market Research Society, London.

MARKET RESEARCH SOCIETY WORKING PARTY (1968). *Fieldwork methods in general use*. Market Research Society, London.

MARKET RESEARCH SOCIETY WORKING PARTY (1976). Response rates in sample surveys. *Journal of the Market Research Society*, Vol. 18, pp. 113-141.

MAYER, C. S. and PRATT, R. W. Jr. (1966). A note on nonresponse in a mail survey. *Public Opinion Quarterly*, Vol. 30, pp. 637-646.

MILES, G. (1970). A method of sampling small minorities. *Journal of the Market Research Society*, Vol. 12, pp. 181-189.

MORRISSEY, E. R. (1974). Sources of error in the coding of questionnaire data. *Sociological Methods and Research*, Vol. 3, pp. 209-232.

MORTON-WILLIAMS, J. (1971). Research on the market for national savings (case study No. 3) in M. K. Adler ed. *Leading cases in market research*. Business Books Ltd., London.

MORTON-WILLIAMS, J. and HINDELL, K. (1972). *Abortion and contraception—a study of patients' attitudes*. Broadsheet No. 536, Political and Economic Planning, London.

MORTON-WILLIAMS, J. and STOWELL, R. (1974). *Small Heath Birmingham: an inner area study*. (Report 1AS/B/5), Department of the Environment, London.

MOSER, C. A. (1952). Quota sampling. *Journal of the Royal Statistical Society*, Series A, Vol. 115, pp. 411-423.

MOSER, C. A. and KALTON, G. (2nd ed. 1971). *Survey methods in social investigation*, Heinemann, London.

MOSER, C. A. and STUART, A. (1953). An experimental study of quota sampling. *Journal of the Royal Statistical Society*, Series A, Vol. 116, pp. 349-405.

MUEHL, D. ed. (1961). *A manual for coders: content analysis at the Survey Research Center, 1961*. Survey Research Center, University of Michigan, Ann Arbor.

MUELLER, J. H., SCHUESSLER, K. F. and COSTNER, H. L. (2nd ed. 1970). *Statistical reasoning in sociology*. Houghton Miffin, Boston.

NATIONAL OPINION POLLS (1975). *Effects of alternative*

wording on the outcome of the EEC referendum. National Opinion Polls, London.

NETER, J. and WAKSBERG, J. (1965). *Response errors in collection of expenditures data by household interviews: an experimental study.* US Department of Commerce, Technical Paper No. 11, US Government Printing Office, Washington, DC.

NOELLE-NEUMANN, E. (1970). Wanted: rules for wording structured questionnaires. *Public Opinion Quarterly*, Vol. 34, pp. 191-201.

NOLAN, J. (1971). Self-completion questionnaires: new uses for an old technique (part 1). *The European Marketing Research Review*, Vol. 6(1), pp. 59-81; (part 2) ibid, Vol. 6(2), pp. 67-84.

OFFICE OF POPULATION CENSUSES AND SURVEYS (1970). *Classification of Occupations.* HMSO, London.

OGNIBENE, P. (1970). Traits affecting questionnaire responses. *Journal of Advertising Research*, Vol. 10, pp. 18-20.

OPPENHEIM, A. N. (1966). *Questionnaire design and attitude measurement.* Heinemann, London.

OSGOOD, C. E., SUCI, G. J. and TANNENBAUM, P. H. (1957). *The measurement of meaning.* University of Illinois Press, Urbana.

PARTEN, M. B. (1950). *Surveys, polls and samples: practical procedures.* Harper, New York.

PAYNE, S. L. (1951). *The art of asking questions.* Princeton University Press, Princeton.

PICKETT, K. G. (1974). *Sources of official data.* Longman, London.

PIGOU, A. (4th ed. 1932). *The economics of welfare.* Macmillan, London.

PRESCOTT-CLARKE, P. and HEDGES, B. M. (1976). *Living in Southwark.* Social and Community Planning Research, London.

PRESSER, S. and SCHUMAN, H. (1975). Question wording as an independent variable in survey analysis: a first report. *Proceedings of the Social Statistics Section, American Statistical Association*, 1975, pp. 16-25.

PRITZKER, L., OGUS, J. and HANSEN, M. H. (1966). Computer editing methods—some applications and results. *Bulletin of the International Statistical Institute*, Vol. 41, pp. 442-473.

RAJ, D. (1972). *The design of sample surveys.* McGraw-Hill, New York.

RICHARDSON, S. A., DOHRENWEND, B. S. and KLEIN, D. (1965). *Interviewing: its forms and functions.* Basic Books, New York.

ROEHER, G. A. (1963). Effective techniques in increasing response to mailed questionnaires. *Public Opinion Quarterly*, Vol. 27, pp. 299-302.

SAMPSON, P. (1967). Commonsense in qualitative research.

Commentary (Journal of the Market Research Society), Vol. 9, pp. 30-38.

SCHUMAN, H. and CONVERSE, J. M. (1971). The effects of black and white interviewers on black responses in 1968. *Public Opinion Quarterly*, Vol. 35, pp. 44-68.

SCHWIRIAN, K. P. and BLAINE, H. R. (1966). Questionnaire-return bias in the study of blue-collar workers. *Public Opinion Quarterly*, Vol. 30, pp. 656-663.

SCOTT ARMSTRONG, J. (1975). Monetary incentives in mail surveys. *Public Opinion Quarterly*, Vol. 39, pp. 111-116.

SCOTT, C. (1961). Research on mail surveys. *Journal of the Royal Statistical Society*, Series A, Vol. 124, pp. 143-205.

SELLTIZ, C., JAHODA, M., DEUTSCH, M. and COOK, S. W. (revised one-volumed ed. 1959). *Research methods in social relations*. Holt, Rinehart and Winston, New York.

SLONIM, M. J. (1968). *Guide to sampling*. Pan Books, London.

SMITH, G. H. (1954). *Motivation research in advertising and marketing*. McGraw-Hill, New York.

SOCIAL AND COMMUNITY PLANNING RESEARCH (SCPR) WORKING PARTY (1973). *Survey research and privacy*. Occasional paper, Social and Community Planning Research, London.

SOCIAL SURVEY DIVISION, OPCS (1973). *The General Household Survey: introductory report*, HMSO, London.

SPEAK, M. (1967). Communication failure in questioning: errors, misinterpretations and personal frames of reference. *Occupational Psychology*, Vol. 41, pp. 169-181.

STACEY, M. ed. (1969). *Comparability in social research*. Heinemann, London.

STEPHAN, F. F. and McCARTHY, P. J. (1958). *Sampling opinions: an analysis of survey procedure*. Wiley, New York.

STUART, A. (1963). Standard errors for percentages. *Applied Statistics*, Vol. 12, pp. 87-101.

STUART, A. (1968). Sample Surveys II. Nonprobability sampling. *International Encyclopaedia of the Social Sciences*, Vol. 13, pp. 612-616, Macmillan and Free Press, New York.

STUART, A. (2nd ed. 1976). *Basic ideas of scientific sampling*. Griffin, London.

STUART, W. J. (1966). Computer editing of survey data—five years of experience in BLS manpower surveys. *Journal of the American Statistical Association*, Vol. 61, pp. 375-383.

SUDMAN, S. (1966). Probability sampling with quotas. *Journal of the American Statistical Association*, Vol. 61, pp. 749-771.

SUDMAN, S. (1967). *Reducing the cost of surveys*. Aldine, Chicago.

SUDMAN, S. (1972). On sampling very rare human populations.

Journal of the American Statistical Association, Vol. 67, pp. 335-339.

SUDMAN, S. (1976). *Applied sampling.* Academic Press, New York.

SUDMAN, S. and BRADBURN, N. M. (1973). Effects of time and memory factors on response in surveys. *Journal of the American Statistical Association*, Vol. 68, pp. 805-815.

SUDMAN, S. and BRADBURN, N. M. (1974). *Response effects in surveys: a review and synthesis.* Aldine, Chicago.

SUMMERS, G. F. ed. (1970). *Attitude measurement.* Rand McNally, Chicago.

SURVEY RESEARCH CENTER, UNIVERSITY OF MICHIGAN (1969). *Interviewers' manual.* Institute for Social Research, University of Michigan. Ann Arbor.

SUSSMAN, M. S. and HAUG, M. R. (1967). Human and mechanical error—an unknown quantity in research. *American Behavioral Scientist*, Vol. 11, pp. 55-56.

THURSTONE, L. L. and CHAVE, E. J. (1929). *The measurement of attitudes: a psychophysical method and some experiments with a scale for measuring attitude toward the church.* University of Chicago Press, Chicago.

US BUREAU OF THE CENSUS (1974). *Indexes to survey methodology literature.* Technical paper No. 34, US Government Printing Office, Washington, DC.

WARWICK, D. P. and LININGER, C. A. (1975). *The sample survey: theory and practice.* McGraw-Hill, New York.

WARNER, S. L. (1965). Randomized response: a survey technique for eliminating evasive answer bias. *Journal of the American Statistical Association*, Vol. 60, pp. 63-69.

WELLS, D. E. and ANDAPIA, A. O. (1966). Adoption proneness and response to mail questionnaires. *Rural Sociology*, Vol. 31, pp. 483-487.

WESTOBY, A., WEBSTER, D. and WILLIAMS, G. (1976). *Social scientists at work.* Society for Research into Higher Education, University of Surrey, Guildford.

WOLFE, A. R. ed. (1973). *Standardised questions: a review for market research executives.* Market Research Society, London.

WOODWARD, J. L. and FRANZEN, R. (1948). A study of coding reliability. *Public Opinion Quarterly*, Vol. 12, pp. 253-257.

WORLD FERTILITY SURVEY (1976). *Basic documentation No. 7: editing and coding manual.* World Fertility Survey, London.

YATES, F. (3rd ed. 1960). *Sampling methods for censuses and surveys.* Griffin, London.

YOUNG, P. V. (4th ed. 1966). *Scientific social surveys and research: an introduction to the background, content, methods, principles, and analysis of social studies.* Prentice-Hall, Englewood Cliffs, New Jersey.

ZARKOVICH, S. S. (1966). *Quality of statistical data.* Food and Agricultural Organisation of the United Nations, Rome.

Appendix. Examples of Questionnaires

Three questionnaires are included here for illustration.

A depth interview guide. The guide included here was employed by SCPR in a study, carried out among abortion patients in three clinics during early 1971, to identify the circumstances that led to the abortion and the patients' attitudes towards it (Morton-Williams and Hindell, 1972). The guide illustrates the unstructured nature of the interview, leaving as much as possible to interviewers' discretion and outlining only broad information requirements. The order of topics discussed was allowed to vary.

An interview survey questionnaire. Selected pages (nine out of twenty-seven) of a questionnaire are included here to illustrate both layout considerations and methods of handling different types of questions: for example, open-ended questions, filter instructions, monetary information, household composition, classificatory data. The full questionnaire was employed in a study of housing characteristics and behaviour in the London Borough of Southwark during 1975 (Prescott-Clarke and Hedges, 1976).

A postal survey questionnaire. The example here was used in a study of social science graduates, carried out jointly by SCPR and the Higher Education Research Unit of the London School of Economics in 1971/72 and reported on by Westoby *et al.* (1976). Since the sample was highly literate, the questionnaire was more demanding than would be advisable among a general household sample, but it is included here for guidance on layout, presentation and approach.

EXAMPLE OF DEPTH INTERVIEW GUIDE

 SOCIAL & COMMUNITY PLANNING RESEARCH

16 Duncan Terrace, London, Nl 8BZ.   Telephone: 01-278 6943

P.181   PATIENTS' ATTITUDES TO ABORTION - DEPTH INTERVIEW GUIDE

Introduction

From S.C.P.R. - an independent research organisation.
We are doing a study on women's attitudes to having an
abortion (stress confidentiality).

Background data

Age
Marital status, number and ages of children
Type of home, household composition, respondent's position
   in household
Work status and occupation of respondent and head of
   household
Education level
Nationality, length of residence in U.K.

I THE ABORTION

1.   Is this her first abortion? At what point in the pregnancy
     was the abortion performed?

2.   How did she set about getting an abortion? When?
     How easy was it to arrange? If private, cost and
     who paid?

3.   Who was involved in organising the abortion?
     Who gave advice, information, help? Was G.P. involved?

4.   Who knew about the pregnancy and the abortion (friends,
     family, colleagues etc.) - What were their attitudes?

5.   The father - who is he, what is/was the nature of her
     relationship to him? What was his reaction to the
     pregnancy and the abortion?

EXAMPLE OF DEPTH INTERVIEW GUIDE (continued)

II HER SEXUAL RELATIONSHIPS

1. What is her normal pattern of sexual relationship,
    if any?

2. How satisfactory are her relations with the man or
    men in her life? Attitudes to fidelity etc.

3. If unmarried, what are her attitudes towards marriage,
    her hopes and plans.

III CONTRACEPTION

1. What was the situation that led to her getting pregnant?
    Was contraception used? If so, what? If not, why not?

2. Her history of contraceptive usage
        Methods used.
        How chosen and when; sources of advice and
            information.
        Use of family planning clinics and G.P. and
            attitudes towards them.

3. Satisfactoriness of methods used: effectiveness, side
    effects, convenience, comfort, availability.

4. Knowledge of other methods.
    Why other methods not used.

5. Attitudes to all methods:-
        What do her friends use?
        What sort of people use the various methods?
        Advantages and disadvantages of each

    (Condom, cap, pill, IUD, withdrawal, rhythm, vaginal
     creams and tablets, vasectomy)

6. Is abortion considered as a method of contraception
    or a last resort?

EXAMPLE OF DEPTH INTERVIEW GUIDE (continued)

IV   ATTITUDES OF OTHERS

1.   Sex education: how and when learnt about sex;
      attitude of parents during childhood towards sex
      and contraception.
      How did she first learn about contraception and
      what learnt?

2.   Attitudes of parents towards her current sex life.
      How open is she with them? Do they know all about
      it or does she keep things private from them?

3.   Attitudes of her parents towards abortion in
      general. Do they know about her abortion? What
      are their reactions?

4.   Attitudes of her friends and colleagues. Is her
      sex life similar to that of her peers or more or
      less conventional?
      What was their reaction to her pregnancy and to
      the abortion?
      Have others that she knows had abortions?
      Is abortion usual way of dealing with unwanted
      pregnancy in her group. How usual is unwanted
      pregnancy among them? Are there conflicting
      groups in her life with opposing views on sex,
      pregnancies and abortion?

5.   How does she think that men feel about pregnancy
      and abortion? Are they sympathetic, helpful or
      do they want nothing to do with it?
      How does her husband/lover/father of child feel
      about pregnancy and abortion. Have their/his
      attitudes changed at all as a result of the
      abortion?

V   ATTITUDES TO ABORTION, SEX and CONTRACEPTION

1.   How does she feel about the abortion:-
         a) physically
         b) emotionally (relieved, guilty, regretful?)
      Has her view of abortion changed as a result of this
      pregnancy? (Did she ever think beforehand that she
      might have an abortion? Would she have another?)
      Religious implications of abortion.
      If unmarried, what is her attitude to pregnancy and
      abortion inside and outside marriage?

2.   What are her attitudes to sexual relations inside and
     outside marriage? (Religious connotations).
     Is there any clash between her and her husband/
     boyfriend in attitudes towards sex, purpose and
     permissibility of sexual relations in and out
     of marriage? Does she regard him as considerate,
     demanding?
     Have her views on sexual relations and marriage
     changed as a result of the abortion?

3.   What form of contraception will she use in the future?
     What advice, if any, will she seek?
     Have her views on contraception changed as a result
     of the abortion?

VI   ATTITUDE TO THE CLINIC

1.   Opinions about treatment received.

2.   Any improvements she would like to see.

VII   INTERVIEWER REPORT

Respondent Number:

Date of Interview:

Private/NHS:

Present living situation:

Present occupation (full/part-time):

Religion:

EXAMPLE OF INTERVIEW QUESTIONNAIRE

SOCIAL & COMMUNITY PLANNING RESEARCH

16, Duncan Terrace, London N1 8BZ   Telephone: 01-278 6943

P.362   SOUTHWARK HOUSEHOLD SURVEY 1975   April 1975

                           INTERVIEW QUESTIONNAIRE   (1-4)

(5)

Household Code ☐   (6)

                                                    Card ☐2

(7)(8)(9)   (10)(11)

Ward/P.D. Code ☐☐☐   Serial Number ☐☐

Interview Type: Head of Household ☐1   *As*   Time interview started:
                                    → *entered*
              Housewife ☐2   *on*   WRITE IN:
                                    S.I.S.

		Col./ Code	Skip to
1a)	What is the name of this district you live in, that is, what do you call it? WRITE IN NAME _____ CODE IN PRECODED LIST IF POSSIBLE, OTHERWISE ASK b) IF NAME NOT ON PRE-CODED LIST ASK b) AND THEN CODE SHOW CARD A b) I have on this card the names of the various parts of the Borough of Southwark; in which of these do you live?	Bermondsey The Borough Camberwell Dulwich Dulwich Village East Dulwich West Dulwich Herne Hill Honor Oak Newington Nunhead Peckham Rotherhithe Walworth	(12-13) 01 02 03 04 05 06 07 08 09 10 11 12 13 14	
2.	How long have you lived in .... (<u>CODED</u> DISTRICT NAME)?	Under 6 months 6-11 months 1 year, but less than 2 years 2 years, but less than 3 years 3 years, but less than 5 years 5 years, but less than 10 years 10 years, but less than 20 years 20 years or more All my life	(14) 1 2 3 4 5 6 7 8 9	

<u>EXAMPLE OF INTERVIEW QUESTIONNAIRE</u> (continued)

		Col./ Code	Skip to	
3.	I would like to hear wnat you like and dislike about living in .... (<u>CODED</u> NAME OF <u>DISTRICT</u>). First can you tell me what you <u>like</u> about .... (<u>CODED</u> NAME OF <u>DISTRICT</u>) as a place to live? PROBE FULLY, INCLUDING "Why do you say that?" AND "What else?" UNTIL FINAL "No".	(15) (16)		
4.	What do you <u>dislike</u> about .... (<u>CODED</u> NAME OF <u>DISTRICT</u>) as a place to live? PROBE FULLY, INCLUDING "Why do you say that?" AND "What else?" UNTIL FINAL "No".	(17) (18)		

EXAMPLE OF INTERVIEW QUESTIONNAIRE (continued)

CARD 2

			Col./ Code	Skip to
20 a)	Turning now to your home itself, do you have a fixed bath or shower with hot water supply?		(46)	
		Yes	A	
	IF YES AT a) - CODE A	No	1	Q.21
	b) Is this in a proper bathroom?	Yes	2	
		No	3	
	c) Do you have the sole use of the bath/shower, or do you share with any other households?		(47)	
		Sole use	1	
		Shared use	2	
21a)	ASK ALL Apart from a sink in a kitchen, do you have a wash-hand basin with running water?	Yes	(48) A	
	IF YES AT a) - CODE A	No	1	Q.22
	b) Do you have the sole use, or do you share with any other households?	Sole use	2	
		Shared use	3	
22a)	ASK ALL Do you have a flush toilet?	Yes	(49) A	
	IF YES AT a) - CODE A	No	1	Q.23
	b) Do you have the sole use, or do you share with any other households?	Sole use	2	
		Shared use	3	
	c) Is the entrance to it ....READ OUT		(50)	
		..... inside your accommodation	1	
		outside your accommodation but inside the building	2	
		or, outside the building?	3	
23a)	ASK ALL How many bedrooms do you have, including bedsitting rooms and spare bedrooms?	NUMBER OF BEDROOMS	(51)	
b)	Do you have the sole use of all these bedrooms or are any shared or sub-let to other households?	Sole use of all	(52) 1	Q.24
		Some or all shared/sub-let	2	
	IF SOME/ALL SHARED/SUB-LET AT b) - CODE 2 c) COMPLETE BOXES:	NUMBER OF BEDROOMS FOR SOLE USE	(53)	
		NUMBER OF BEDROOMS SUB-LET	(54)	
		NUMBER OF BEDROOMS SHARED	(55)	
		NUMBER OF HOUSEHOLDS BEDROOMS SHARED WITH	(56)	

EXAMPLE OF INTERVIEW QUESTIONNAIRE (continued)

			CARD 2	
			Col./Code	Skip to
26.	ASK IF A FLAGGED ( ) SHARED USE ENTRY MADE, EITHER AT Q.23c), Q.24d), OR Q.25d). OTHERS SKIP TO Q.27		(68)	
a)	Thinking of the rooms you share, are the households you share with relatives of yours, by birth or marriage, or other people?	Relatives	A	
		Other people	1	Q.27
	IF RELATIVES AT a) - CODE A			
	b) Are any of these your children or children-in-law?	Yes	2	
		No	3	
27a)	ASK ALL Would you say your house/flat here has too many rooms for your needs, too few for your needs, or about the right number?	Too many	(69) 1	
		Too few	2	
		About right	3	
b)	What about the size of the rooms, you live and sleep in, in general, are they too large for your needs, too small for your needs, or about the right size?	Too large	(70) 1	
		Too small	2	
		About right	3	
28.	Would you say your home here is in a good or in a poor condition as a building? Is its condition...READ OUT	..... very good	(71) 1	
		fairly good	2	
		fairly poor	3	
		or, very poor?	4	

29a)	NOTE LEVEL OF MAIN LIVING ROOM IN ACCOMMODATION:	(72-73)	

Basement	0X	4th floor	04
Ground floor	00	5th floor	05
1st floor	01	6th-9th floor	06
2nd floor	02	10th-14th floor	10
3rd floor	03	15th or more floor	15

			Col./Code	Skip to
b)	SHOW CARD C . How satisfied are you with living at ....floor level (NAME LEVEL)?		(74)	
		Very satisfied	1	Q.30
		Fairly satisfied	2	
		Not very satisfied	3	
		Not at all satisfied?	4	
	IF 'FAIRLY', 'NOT VERY' OR 'NOT AT ALL SATISFIED' - CODES 2, 3 OR 4 AT b)			
	c) Why are you not satisfied at living at this level? PROBE AND RECORD FULLY		(75)	

	362	(78-80)

EXAMPLE OF INTERVIEW QUESTIONNAIRE (continued)

			Col./ Code	Skip to
	CARD 3			
	QUESTIONS 38-43 TO BE ANSWERED BY OWNERS ONLY. RENTERS SKIP TO Q.44		(29)	
38.	Is this the first property the head of your household has ever bought or not?	Yes, first	1	
		No, not the first	2	
39a)	Is your accommodation freehold or leasehold?	Freehold	(30) 1	
		Leasehold	2	
b)	Do you own your home outright now or are you paying off a loan or mortgage at the moment?	Own outright	(31) 1	Q.40
		Paying off loan/mortgage	2	
	IF PAYING OFF LOAN/MORTGAGE - CODE 2 AT b)			
c)	Where did you obtain the loan/mortgage from?		(32)	
		Building Society	1	
	IF MORE THAN ONE SOURCE, CODE LENDER OF LARGEST PART OF LOAN	Insurance Company	2	
		London Borough of Southwark	3	
		G.L.C.	4	
	Other answer (WRITE IN)_____		5	
d)	How much are your regular repayments? £_____ per_____	OFFICE USE ONLY — Annual	(33-36)	
40a)	Do you get any rebate on your rates?	Yes	(37) 1	
		No	2	Q.41
	IF YES AT a) - CODE 1			
b)	How much rebate do you get a year? £_____ per annum	OFFICE USE ONLY — Annual	(38-41)	
41a)	Apart from rates and mortgage, do you pay any other regular amounts, such as ground rent or service charge for your accommodation?	Yes	(42) 1	
		No	2	Q.42
	IF YES AT a) - CODE 1			
b)	How much do you pay a year? £_____ per annum	OFFICE USE ONLY — Annual	(43-46)	

EXAMPLE OF INTERVIEW QUESTIONNAIRE (continued)

CARD 4

Col.

ASK ALL

60a) How many people live in your household, including yourself?   NUMBER [   ] (38-39)

b) How many are babies <u>aged 2 or less</u>?   NUMBER - Boys [   ] (40)
                                                        - Girls [   ] (41)

c) How many are young children <u>aged 3 or 4</u>?   NUMBER - Boys [   ] (42)
                                                            - Girls [   ] (43)

d) How many are children <u>aged 5 to 9</u>?   NUMBER - Boys [   ] (44)
                                                      - Girls [   ] (45)

e) How many are older children <u>aged 10-15</u>?   NUMBER - Boys [   ] (46)
                                                           - Girls [   ] (47)

f) How many are people aged 16 or more?   NUMBER [   ] (48)

g) CHECK TOTAL WITH NUMBER ENTERED IN BOX AT a) ABOVE

IF AT LEAST ONE CHILD AGED 5-15 - SEE Q.60d) AND e)
61 Do any of the children aged 5-15 receive free school meals?   NUMBER [   ] (49)
   IF 'NO' WRITE '0' IN BOX

IF AT LEAST ONE CHILD AGED 3-9 - SEE Q.60c AND d)
62a) Which of the children aged 3 to 9 will next have a birthday?   (50)
                    NAME OF CHILD _____

b) Where does...(NAME OF CHILD) <u>usually</u>   Private garden   1
   play when he/she is not inside your   Public/communal garden   2
   house/flat? DO NOT READ OUT CODES   Playground/special play space   3
                                                            On balcony   4
       RING ONE CODE ONLY   In corridor   5
                                                             In street   6
          Other answer (WRITE IN) _____   7
                                            Does not play outside home   8

                                                                       (51)
c) SHOW CARD C. How satisfied are you with   Very satisfied   1
   ...(READ OUT PLACE CODED ABOVE) as a   Fairly satisfied   2
   place for them to play?   Not very satisfied   3
                                                  Not at all satisfied   4

EXAMPLE OF INTERVIEW QUESTIONNAIRE (continued)

		Col./Code	Skip to
63.	**ASK:** IF RESPONDENT IS A WOMAN AND THERE IS A CHILD AGED ☐0-4☐ IN HOUSEHOLD - SEE QUESTIONS 60b) AND c)	(52)	
a)	Are you the mother of the child/children aged 4 or under? Yes, of at least one No	1 2	 Q.64
	IF YES AT a) - CODE 1	(53)	
b)	Do you have a paid job of 8 or more hours a week? Yes No	1 2	 e)
	IF YES AT b) - CODE 1	(54)	
c)	Do you use <u>all day</u> day-care facilities such as a day nursery, a creche or playgroup? Yes No	1 2	Q.64
	IF NO AT c) - CODE 2	(55)	
d)	Is this because you don't need <u>all day</u> day-care for your children or because you can't get it? Don't need Can't get	1 2	Q.64 Q.64
	IF NO AT b) - CODE 2	(56)	

e)	If all day day-care facilities were available, for (all) your child/children, how likely is it you would take a paid job? Would it be...READ OUT
	    ...very likely
	    fairly likely
	    not very likely
	    or, not at all likely?
		
		1
		2
		3
		4	

64.	**ASK ALL** I would now like to ask a few questions about each person aged 16 or over normally living in this household. COMPLETE GRID FOR ALL AGED 16+. START WITH HEAD OF HOUSEHOLD	362 Card ☐5☐	(78-80) (1-4) (5-6)

HOUSEHOLD COMPOSITION: COMPLETE ONE LINE FOR EACH PERSON AGED 16+

ALL PERSONS AGED 16 +						IF CURRENTLY WORKING	
Person No.	Sex	Age last birth-day	Marital status	Relation-ship to Head of Household	Activity status	Place of work (SHOW CARDS A AND B)	
RING CODE 1	M 1 F 2	☐☐	Single 1 Married 2 Widowed 3 Divorced 4 Separated 5	Head 1	Works full(31+hrs pw)1 Works part (8-30 hrs)2 Seeking work 3 Retired 4 Sick 5 Full-time student 6 Non-working hse/wife 7 Other unemployed 8	IF CODES 01-24 ENTER ☐☐ IF CODE 25 "ELSEWHERE IN LONDON"SPECIFY _____	(7-15)
RING CODE 2	M 1 F 2	☐☐	Single 1 Married 2 Widowed 3 Divorced 4 Separated 5	Spouse 2 Child 3 Parent 4 Other relative 5 Non-rel. 6	Works full(31+hrs pw)1 Works part (8-30 hrs)2 Seeking work 3 Retired 4 Sick 5 Full-time student 6 Non-working hse/wife 7 Other unemployed 8	IF CODES 01-24 ENTER ☐☐ IF CODE 25 "ELSEWHERE IN LONDON"SPECIFY _____	(16-24)

Continued opposite

EXAMPLE OF INTERVIEW QUESTIONNAIRE (continued)

		Card [6]	(1-4) (5-6)	Col./ Code	Skip to
66a)	Apart from the Head of Household, is there anyone aged 16 or over in this household who would move out _now_ if separate accommodation was available?		Yes No	(7) 1 2	Q.67

IF YES AT a) - CODE 1 - COMPLETE A COLUMN
FOR EACH PERSON WISHING TO MOVE OUT

	(8-11)	(12-15)	(16-19)	(20-23)	(24-27)
	Persons wishing to move out				
ENTER PERSON NUMBER					
b) Has he/she actually looked for separate accommodation in the past twelve months? Yes No	1 2	1 2	1 2	1 2	1 2
c) Would he/she prefer to rent or to buy? Rent Buy	1 2	1 2	1 2	1 2	1 2
d) Which other members of the household would he/she live with? IDENTIFY MEMBERS WISHING TO LIVE TOGETHER BY GIVING THEM SAME CODE	1	1 2	1 2 3	1 2 3 4	1 2 3 4 5

RECORD FOR ALL

67a)	SUMMARY OF HEAD OF HOUSEHOLD'S ACTIVITY STATUS:		Col./Code	Skip to
		Currently working	A	b)
		Seeking work	B	b)
		Sick/retired	C	b)
		Other	D	Q.69

IF CODES A-C AT a)

b) Occupation of Head of Household:	SEG
Job Title:	(28-29)
Description of Activity:	
Qualifications for Job:	(30-31)
Supervision/Management Responsibility:	
Main Industrial Activity of Firm:	SIC
No. of People Employed at Place of Work:	
Employment Status: Self-employed A Employee B	

IF HEAD IS SEEKING WORK - CODE B AT Q.67a)

68.	How long has the head of household been out of work on this occasion?		(32)
		Under 1 month	1
		1 month but less than 3 months	2
		3 months but less than 6 months	3
		6 months but less than a year	4
		1 year or more	5

EXAMPLE OF INTERVIEW QUESTIONNAIRE (continued)

			CARD 6	Col./ Code	Skip to
73.	**ASK ALL**				
a)	SHOW CARD H I have here a card showing various categories of weekly and annual income. From this card please tell me the category into which the total income of your household comes - I mean income before tax and other deductions and from all sources? Just read out the letter in the middle that applies. ENTER CODE LETTER ☐			(46-47)	
b)	CONTINUE TO SHOW CARD H And in which category is the head of household's income on its own, again before tax and other deductions? Again, just read out the letter in the middle that applies. ENTER CODE LETTER ☐			(48-49)	
74.	INTERVIEWER CLASSIFICATION OF HOUSEHOLD'S ACCOMMODATION:			(50)	
	Lives in obvious self-contained one household unit and does not share			1	
	Lives in obvious self-contained one household unit but shares with other household(s)			2	
	Lives in other sort of accommodation			3	
75.	SHOPPING QUESTIONNAIRE: Interview Type (as on S.I.S.):			(51)	
	Head of Household - questionnaire not left			1	
	Housewife - questionnaire accepted			2	
	- questionnaire refused			3	
	Number of calls made to obtain this interview			(52)	
	N.B. A VISIT TO A RESPONDENT'S HOME COUNTS AS A 'CALL' ONLY IF IT IS MADE ON A DIFFERENT DAY AND AT A DIFFERENT TIME TO ANY EARLIER CALL.	Interview obtained at first call		1	
		Interview obtained at second call		2	
		Interview obtained at third call		3	
		Interview obtained at fourth call		4	
		Five or more calls made to obtain interview		5	
	Interview number IN THESE BOXES WRITE IN THE NUMBER OF INTERVIEWS YOU HAVE ALREADY CARRIED OUT ON THIS SURVEY (INCLUDING THIS ONE) ⟶			(53)(54)	
	Time interview completed (WRITE IN)_____				
	Date of interview / /	Length of interview (IN MINUTES)		(55) (56)(57)	
	Signature of interviewer_____	INTERVIEWER NUMBER		(58) (59)(60)	
				362 (78-80)	

EXAMPLE OF POSTAL QUESTIONNAIRE

Ref. ⬚⬚⬚⬚⬚⬚   1–6

London School of Economics
HIGHER EDUCATION RESEARCH UNIT

in association with SOCIAL & COMMUNITY PLANNING RESEARCH

SURVEY OF SOCIAL SCIENTISTS

Questionnaire

P.225

November 1971

EXAMPLE OF POSTAL QUESTIONNAIRE (continued)

Note about the questionnaire:

This questionnaire is part of a larger study, the results of which will be published.

As with nearly all questionnaires, there may be some questions which seem superfluous or irrelevant; however, we have made the questionnaire as short as possible, and each item has been inserted with a particular research objective in view. We ask you to appreciate that it is impossible to cater in advance for all the diverse facts and viewpoints we are likely to encounter, but we have tried to make the questionnaire as straightforward as possible for everyone to fill in.

We should very much welcome your comments on any aspect of the questionnaire, or any other points you may wish to make to us. Space has been provided at the end for this purpose.

We hope that all questions will be completed by all respondents. If, however, you are unable or unwilling to answer any questions, we are anxious that your replies to the others should remain unaffected. If there are some details you cannot remember precisely — for example, in Question 11, about your past career — please give estimates where you can do so with reasonable confidence, but otherwise leave a blank.

Remember that your answers will remain absolutely confidential and will not be associated with your identity at any stage.

Off. use
2   7

The first four questions ask for some details of your education.

Q1   (a)   What type of school did you last
attend before entering university?

Independent school	1
Direct grant or grant-aided school	2
Please tick the appropriate box Grammer school (or Scottish equivalent)	3
Other state school	4
Technical college	5
Overseas school	6
(Please specify) Other	7

8

(b)   Did you go directly from the above school to university,
or was there a time lag of over four months?

Please tick the appropriate box Within four months of leaving school	1
Over four months after leaving school	2

9

EXAMPLE OF POSTAL QUESTIONNAIRE (continued)

Q2   (a)   Please would you indicate which of the following
examinations you took before going to university?

Off. use

G.C.E. Advanced level	1
Higher School Certificate (before 1951)	2
Please tick the appropriate box Scottish Certificate of Education (Higher Grade)	3
Scottish Leaving Certificate (Higher Grade)	4
University intermediate, preliminary or matriculation examination	5
*(Please specify)_____*Other equivalent examination	6
NO EXAMINATION AT THIS LEVEL	7 10

(b)   Did you pass any of the following subjects at the
above examination?

Subject		Off. use
Pure mathematics	1	11
Applied mathematics	1	12
Please tick the appropriate box Mathematics, Pure & Applied	1	13
Chemistry	1	14
Physics	1	15
Economics	1	16
Economic history	1	17
History	1	18
English	1	19
British constitution	1	20
Geography	1	21
NONE OF THE ABOVE SUBJECTS	1	22

Q3   Referring now to your "social science degree" mentioned
in the letter, would you please indicate (or confirm) the
main subject area of that degree?

Please specify:

Q4   Have you obtained or started to study for any **other** qualifications or degrees, either
before or **after** the award of the degree referred to in the letter (i.e. **including** first
degrees, post-graduate degrees, certificates or diplomas and other professional or
vocational qualifications, but **excluding** the degree referred to in the letter)?

Please tick the appropriate box

Yes   1

GO TO Q6 ◄——— No   2   23

p. 5 ——►

EXAMPLE OF POSTAL QUESTIONNAIRE (continued)

Q5   This question asks for details of the post-school qualification(s) you have obtained (**EXCLUDING** the degree referred to in the letter). For each **type** of other qualification obtained or started, please place a tick in column a), and then complete the details sought in each of the four succeeding columns (b, c, d, e).

Off. use

1-6

3 | 7

Type of qualification	a) Have you (yet) obtained this qualification? *(Please tick)* Yes / No	FOR EACH QUALIFICATION TICKED IN COLUMN a)				Off. use
		b) Please specify the main subject area of this qualification, e.g. "physics", "chartered accountancy", "sociology", etc.	c) Please specify the year in which you first enrolled for this qualification	d) Were you enrolled full-time or part-time? *(Please tick)* Full Time / Part Time	e) Please specify the duration of your study for this qualification (to date)	
DOCTORATE	Yes [1] No [2] 8	Main Subject 9-10	Year 19 11-12	F.T. [1] P.T. [2] 13	Months 14-15	8-15
OTHER POST-GRADUATE DEGREE	Yes [1] No [2] 16	Main Subject 17-18	Year 19 19-20	F.T. [1] F.T. [2] 21	Months 22-23	16-23
FIRST DEGREE	Yes [1] No [2] 24	Main Subject 25-26	Year 19 27-28	F.T. [1] P.T. [2] 29	Months 30-31	24-31
POST-GRADUATE CERTIFICATE(S) OR DIPLOMA(S) 1.	Yes [1] No [2] 32	Main Subject 33-34	Year 19 35-36	F.T. [1] P.T. [2] 37	Months 38-39	32-39
2.	Yes [1] No [2] 40	Main Subject 41-42	Year 19 43-44	F.T. [1] P.T. [2] 45	Months 46-47	40-47
OTHER CERTIFICATE(S) OR DIPLOM. 1.	Yes [1] No [2] 48	Main Subject 49-50	Year 19 51-52	F.T. [1] P.T. [2] 53	Months 54-55	48-55
2.	Yes [1] No [2] 56	Main Subject 57-58	Year 19 59-60	F.T. [1] P.T. [2] 61	Months 62-63	56-63
OTHER PROFESSIONAL OR VOCATIONAL QUALIFICATION(S) 1.	Yes [1] No [2] 64	Main Subject 65-66	Year 19 67-68	F.T. [1] P.T. [2] 69	Months 70-71	64-71
2.	Yes [1] No [2] 72	Main Subject 73-74	Year 19 75-76	F.T. [1] P.T. [2] 77	Months 78-79	72-79

5 | 80

EXAMPLE OF POSTAL QUESTIONNAIRE (continued)

Questions 6-9 ask for demographic information in order to throw light on
patterns of job and occupational mobility.

			Off. Use
Q6	Please indicate the year in which you were born: ————————▶	19	24-25
Q7	Are you, or have you been married? Yes [ ] ——▶ Year of (first) marriage 19		26-27
	No [00]		
Q8	Have you any children? Yes [ ] ——▶ Year first child born (or adopted) 19		28-29
	No [00]		

Q9   Which of the following broad regions comes closest
to the region in which you work?

*Please tick the
appropriate box*

Greater London Area	1
South East, including Home Counties	2
South or South West	3
East Anglia	4
East or West Midlands	5
Wales	6
Lancs, Yorks and North (England)	7
Scotland	8
Outside Great Britain	9
NOT WORKING	0

30

Q10   At which of the following ages did your **father**
finish his full-time education?

*Please tick the
appropriate box*

14 or younger	1
15	2
16	3
17 or 18	4
19 or 20	5
21	6
22 or older	7

31

EXAMPLE OF POSTAL QUESTIONNAIRE (continued)

Q11 This question asks for particulars of your paid full-time employment (i.e. 30 hours per week or more) **since 1st January 1960.** These details are needed since an assessment of the present and future employment situation of social scientists requires a knowledge of the ways in which they have been employed in the past. Please, therefore, can you enter details of all **full-time** jobs lasting six months or more (including periods of self-employment) you have held since 1st January 1960. If you are unable to remember all particulars, please enter those that you can remember.
If you have had no full-time job since 1st January 1960, please tick the appropriate box below and go to **Question 13.**
Please enter your jobs chronologically with your current job (if any) as the last of your entries.
Please make a separate entry whenever there was either: a change of employer OR a change in job title.

			JOB 1	JOB 2
	NO FULL-TIME JOB SINCE 1-1-1960 *(Please tick)*			
(a)	In what year did the job start?	*(PLEASE ENTER)*	19	19
	And in what year did it finish?	*(PLEASE ENTER)*	19	19
	If you are still in that job, please tick the appropriate box in this line		Still in job 00	Still in job 00
(b)	Was the job based in .... the United Kingdom		1	1
	Please tick one box U.S.A. or Canada		2	2
	for each job. Western Europe		3	3
	Elsewhere		4	4
(c)	What was the business or industry of the employing organisation? (e.g. engineering company; firm of solicitors; local government; university) If self-employed, please write SELF-EMPLOYED	*(PLEASE ENTER)*		
(d)	What position did you hold? (Please describe in detail, e.g. solicitor's articled clerk; mental health social worker; senior lecturer; deputy sales manager; freelance journalist).	*(PLEASE ENTER)*		
(e)	What was your function in the job? (please give a full description, e.g. assistant to senior partner, especially on conveyancing; casework with mentally subnormal children; teaching and administration in university economics department).	*(PLEASE ENTER)*		
(f)	What were your approximate gross annual earnings from the job, before tax (including all bonuses etc., but excluding fringe benefits and outside earnings).	STARTING INCOME (or at 1-1-1960 if job started earlier) *(PLEASE ENTER)*	£	£
		FINISHING INCOME (or present, if still in the job) *(PLEASE ENTER)*	£	£

(g)			JOB 1 (i) Carrying Out	JOB 1 (ii) Obtaining	JOB 2 (i) Carrying Out	JOB 2 (ii) Obtaining
To what extent did you find that the **content** of the particular social science degree (referred to in the letter) was useful in:		Essential	5	5	5	5
i) Carrying out the job?		Very useful	4	4	4	4
ii) Obtaining the job?		Useful	3	3	3	3
(Please tick the appropriate box		Of little use	2	2	2	2
for i) and ii) in each column)		Not useful	1	1	1	1

EXAMPLE OF POSTAL QUESTIONNAIRE (continued)

						Off. use
				No.		32
				p. 8 →		
						1-6
					4	7

JOB 3 [3]	JOB 4 [4]	JOB 5 [5]	JOB 6 [6]	JOB 7 [7]	JOB 8 [8]	8
19 / 19 / Still in job ⎕ oo	19 / 19 / Still in job ⎕ oo	19 / 19 / Still in job ⎕ oo	19 / 19 / Still in job ⎕ oo	19 / 19 / Still in job ⎕ oo	19 / 19 / Still in job ⎕ oo	9-10 / 11-12
1 2 3 4	1 2 3 4	1 2 3 4	1 2 3 4	1 2 3 4	1 2 3 4	13
						14-15
						16-20
£	£	£	£	£	£	21-25
£	£	£	£	£	£	26-30

	(i) Carrying Out	(ii) Obtaining	(i) Carrying Out	(ii) Obtaining	(i) Carrying Out	(ii) Obtaining	(i) Carrying Out	(ii) Obtaining	(i) Carrying Out	(ii) Obtaining	(i) Carrying Out	(ii) Obtaining	
	5	5	5	5	5	5	5	5	5	5	5	5	
	4	4	4	4	4	4	4	4	4	4	4	4	
	3	3	3	3	3	3	3	3	3	3	3	3	
	2	2	2	2	2	2	2	2	2	2	2	2	
	1	1	1	1	1	1	1	1	1	1	1	1	31-32

Skip	33-77
225	77-80

EXAMPLE OF POSTAL QUESTIONNAIRE (continued)

Off.
use

Q12   The previous question asked for the starting and finishing income from
the jobs you have held since 1960. However, in order to obtain a basis
for comparisons over time, it would be helpful if you could give us your
best estimate of your gross annual income from your full-time job at two
particular points in time: the calendar years 1964 and 1968.
If there was any part of either of these years during which you were not
in full-time employment, please enter N/A in the appropriate box.

i)   GROSS ANNUAL INCOME FROM JOB (as defined previously) £
FOR THE CALENDAR YEAR 1964   33-37

Please enter

ii) GROSS ANNUAL INCOME FROM JOB £
FOR THE CALENDAR YEAR 1968   38-42

Q13   This question, and those on the remainder of this page, refer to your main
current job. If you are not currently in paid regular employment, either
FULL-TIME OR PART-TIME, please tick the box below and go to Q16.

NO CURRENT FULL OR PART-TIME JOB *(please tick)*   0

(a)   Is your current main employment........................ full-time (30 hrs. a week or over)   1

Please tick the appropriate box   or part-time (under 30 hrs. a week)   2   43

IF 'PART-TIME'
(b)   Please describe your current work in terms of what you do, the type
of business or industry it is in, your position, function and annual income.

Please specify	Type of business or industry	Position	Job function	
				44-45
				46-50
			Gross Annual Income £	51-54

FULL-TIME OR PART-TIME JOBS
Q14   (a)   On average, approximately how many hours per week would you estimate that you spend,
either paid or unpaid, on your main current job?
Please enter   hrs. per week   55-56

(b)   And, again on average, approximately how many weeks (or parts of weeks) per year
would you estimate that you actually work on your main current job?

Please enter   weeks per year   57-58

Q15   Do you personally have any earned income from sources other than your
main current employment?

Please tick the appropriate box   Yes   → Please enter the additional gross   £
amount earned per year

No   0   59-62

EXAMPLE OF POSTAL QUESTIONNAIRE (continued)

Questions 16 & 17 ask about your retrospective view of your choice of subject at university.

Off.
use

Q16   Can you remember the reasons which prompted you to choose
the main subject or subject combination in the "social science"
degree referred to in the letter?

Please specify:

Q17   (a)   Do you have any regrets now about that choice?   Yes

Please tick one box   GO TO Q18 ◄──── No   2   63

IF 'YES'
(b)   Which alternative subject(s) would you prefer to have chosen
or have you seriously thought about subsequently as being preferable?

Please specify:

(c)   What would have been the main advantages of that subject
over the one referred to in the letter?

Please specify:

(d)   And the main disadvantages?

Please specify:

64-65

EXAMPLE OF POSTAL QUESTIONNAIRE (continued)

Q18   Many people report that they have had - informally - to develop skills or acquire knowledge related to the social sciences for the purposes of their employment. We list below some of the most frequently mentioned of these. Can you please indicate those which you have had to acquire informally and specify any others not included in the list. Exclude those which you have studied formally and mentioned previously in the questionnaire.

		Off. use
Please tick all those which you have had to acquire.	Computing techniques 1	66
	Sample survey methods 1	67
	Interviewing techniques 1	68
	Forecasting techniques 1	69
	Systems Analysis 1	70
	Accounting methods 1	71
	Investment appraisal 1	72
	Statistical methods 1	73
(Please specify):	Others	74-75
		76-77
	225	78-80

Q19   Looking back now on **all** the academic social science training that you have had, are there any changes to the courses which you would would like to see, e.g. gaps to be filled, changes of emphasis, etc.?

N.B. Please make it clear which course(s) your comments refer to.

Please specify changes: (If none, write NONE)

EXAMPLE OF POSTAL QUESTIONNAIRE (continued)

Q20 If you have any other comments you wish to add, on the questionnaire or on other topics, we shall welcome them. Please write them in the space provided below.

We are very grateful indeed for your help. Please return the completed questionnaire, together with the completed "snowball list" in the stamped addressed envelope provided to:

Survey of Social Scientists,
Higher Education Research Unit,
London School of Economics,
c/o Social & Community Planning Research,
16 Duncan Terrace,
LONDON N1 8BZ

Index

self-completion, 128-9
tape recording, 21, 23, 52, 112, 122
Refusals, *see* Non response
Register of Electors, *see* Sampling frames
Repertory grid, 14
Respondent identification numbers, 51, 135, 139, 141, 152, 154, 161-2, 180, 186
Respondent payment, *see* Incentive payments
Response errors, 6, 12, 32, 99-101, 124, 126-7, 151, 154; *see also* Errors, Bias
Response listing, 145, 158-9; *see also* Open-ended questions
Response rates
   interview surveys, 6, 65, 71-3, 93, 111, 118, 122, 144
   postal surveys, 6, 124-5, 127-8, 130-36, 144
   see also Non response
Re-weighting, *see* Weighting

Sample size, 16-18, 51, 57, 60-61, 65, 71, 83
Samples of:
   addresses, 70, 77-8
   constituencies, 66, 74
   electors/individuals, 66, 79-82
   flows, 85-6
   households, 70, 77-9
   minorities, 81, 83-6, 125
   non-electors, 79-81
   wards/polling districts, 64, 66, 74-5
Sampling
   by firsting, 78
   design effects (deff), 68-9
   distributions, 57-60
   error, 5, 57-62, 64-5, 67-9
   fractions, 60, 64
   interval, 61-2, 67, 78
   see also Probability sampling, Quota sampling, Random route sampling
Sampling frames
   area, 74-5
   clustering, 64-5
   construction, 4-5, 62, 69-71, 84-5
   deadwood and non response, 5, 70-72, 78, 81, 92-3, 118
   electoral register, 63, 70, 72, 74-81, 83-4
   employers' registers, 71
   rating lists, 71-2, 82-3
   stratification, 63, 70

Screening surveys, 83, 125
Self completion questionnaires, 3, 125-30, 145; *see also* Postal surveys
Semantic differential scale, 34; *see also* Rating scales
Semi structured questionnaires, 9, 16
Show cards, 41-2, 52, 98
Simple random sampling, 61, 65, 67-9
Social grade classification, 172-4; *see also* Occupation coding
Socio-economic group classification, 10, 156, 172-5; *see also* Occupation coding
Standard deviation, 59
Standard error, 59, 69
Standard regions, 74, 178-9
Stratification
   area, 63, 74-5
   disproportionate, 63-4, 86
   proportionate, 62-3
   sampling error calculations, 68-9
Summary codes, 156-7
Supervision, *see* Interviewer, Coder, Quality control
Survey population, 55-6, 69-71
Systematic sampling, 61-3, 67, 74-5

Tape recorded interviews, 21, 23, 52, 112, 122
Telephone contacts, 94, 134-5; *see also* Advance notification of respondents
Thurstone scales, 37; *see also* Rating scales
Time budget surveys, 31
Timetable, 4-7, 18, 132
Trade-off questions
   see Question types
Training
   see Interviewer, Coder, Quality control

Units of enquiry, 45, 56
Universe, *see* Population
Unstructured design work
   alternative approaches, 9, 15-16
   analysis and reporting, 24-5
   communication methods, 12-13
   recording and transcribing, 23-4
   sampling and recruitment, 16-20
   use and role, 6, 10-12, 36, 40, 42, 51

Valuation lists, *see* Sampling frames
Variable sampling fractions, 64
Verification of punched cards, 147
Visual aids, 14, 41-2

Weighting, 64, 70, 73, 78-9, 81, 85, 138